PEN(

THE RETURN ON KINDNESS

Bonnie Hayden Cheng is passionate about corporate wellness—the 'S' of ESG. She holds a unique position designing and implementing cutting-edge, research-backed solutions to help companies deliver impact on real-world challenges and create awesome corporate cultures where people thrive.

She is an Associate Professor of Management and MBA Program Director of HKU Business School, University of Hong Kong, having received her PhD from the Rotman School of Management, University of Toronto. She is the Chief Resilience Officer at Human at Work, Scientific Advisor of One Mind at Work, Ex-Officio member of the Male Allies Leadership Council, an initiative of The Women's Foundation Hong Kong, and Academy of Management Scholar and Subject Matter Expert.

As a wellbeing advocate, she works closely with leading organizations to champion mental health in the workplace. Her work transforming companies to make positive change has received numerous awards across various sectors. Her research has been published in prestigious journals such as the *Academy of Management Journal* and *Journal of Applied Psychology*, and featured in outlets such as *Harvard Business Review* and *The New York Times*.

Book Endorsements for *The Return on Kindness* by Bonnie Hayden Cheng

'Kind leadership is effective leadership. Bonnie Hayden Cheng masterfully makes the case that kindness isn't a nice-to-have but a must-have for today's managers and executives. She includes fascinating research and first-person accounts from leaders that detail the surprising and unexpected benefits of kindness. This book should be required reading for anyone who is responsible for leading people, teams, and organizations, and will be especially transformative for those who are eager to drive positive change.'

—Amy Gallo, author of *Getting Along:*
How to Work with Anyone (Even Difficult People)

'One word, "wow". This book is incredibly interesting, grounded, and well-written. More than that, this book is highly important. It can truly make a huge difference in taking leadership and organizations to the next level—great success, with great kindness.'

—Steven Rogelberg, best-selling author of
The Surprising Science of Meetings: How You Can Lead
Your Team to Peak Performance

'Bonnie Cheng walks us through why kind leadership is the most sustainable way to achieve better business results. If you are a leader or future leader who wants to prove that kind leadership always wins, then this is the playbook you have been looking for.'

—Gordon Watson, CEO, AXA Asia & Africa

'If you are a leader of any kind, this needs to be at the top of your reading list. Through her research and insight, Bonnie Hayden Cheng debunks the myth that kindness is a weaker form of leadership, shows us once and for all that people perform better when led with kindness, and that employee wellbeing is intrinsically linked with corporate wellness. Valuing and caring for people can transform an organization, and quite possibly the world. Thank you, Bonnie, for putting this important research at the forefront so that all leaders can learn and grow from it.'

—David Long, Chairman and CEO,
Liberty Mutual Insurance

'Your work culture matters deeply to your health and well-being. Bonnie Hayden Cheng gives you a roadmap to a better future where work is human-centred, heartfelt, and healthier. The greatest innovation in our modern workplaces is a surprisingly ancient art—Kindness. This book will empower you to be a kind and effective leader, regardless of your title or position.'

—Kelli Harding, MD, MPH, author of
The Rabbit Effect and psychiatrist at
Columbia University Irving Medical Center

'Many hear the word kindness in relationship to leadership and think, 'soft,' 'weak,' or 'irrelevant'. And if you did, you'd be painfully mistaken. These days, in a workplace characterized by mass attrition, leadership mistrust, and competitive impossibilities, kindness is a superpower and leaders and organizations who have it win big. In this wonderful and inspirited book, Bonnie Hayden Cheng offers us all a carefully curated blueprint for how to put kindness to work and unleash the best performance from our people. Read it twice.'

—Ron Carucci, Managing Partner, Navalent,
and best-selling, award-winning author of
To Be Honest and *Rising to Power*

'This book is right on time! As the world becomes more divided, this book dares leaders to revolutionize their leadership through kindness. A deceivingly simple concept, being a kind leader takes courage and tenacity. Compelling, riveting, and will make you strive to be a better leader!'

—Celia Lao, CEO, AirAsia Hong Kong & Macao

'Insightful, intriguing and delightful to follow Bonnie on her quest of building a case for kindness in leadership through research and exploration with leaders from various industries. A good dosage of kindness will take leaders, from middle to top management, down the serving lane benefiting everyone including leaders and corporations themselves, creating a truly win-win environment for all.'

—Michelle Leung, Ex-CEO,
Fung Omni Services Limited (Li & Fung Group)

'This book is incredibly timely and important. It is wonderfully written, bridging data, storytelling, and accounts from global leaders on why kind leadership is the only sustainable way forward. It will make you rethink the meaning of kind leadership, its critical role in business strategy and provides actionable advice for all leaders on how to make needed change to their leadership.'

—Fiona Nott, CEO, The Women's Foundation

'This is a significant revelation of the fundamental qualities for successful leadership in modern organizations. Humanity has developed well in modern societies where democracy prevails. Businesses with enlightened leaders having servant leadership in mind flourish. I recommend reading this treatise to management practitioners.'

—Dr Kam-fong Leung, Chief Executive,
Tung Wah Group of Hospitals (1995-2006)

The Return on Kindness

How Kind Leadership Wins Talent, Earns Loyalty, and Builds Successful Companies

Bonnie Hayden Cheng

BUSINESS
An imprint of Penguin Random House

PENGUIN BUSINESS

USA | Canada | UK | Ireland | Australia
New Zealand | India | South Africa | China | Singapore

Penguin Business is part of the Penguin Random House group of companies
whose addresses can be found at global.penguinrandomhouse.com

Published by Penguin Random House SEA Pvt. Ltd
9, Changi South Street 3, Level 08-01,
Singapore 486361

First published in Penguin Business by Penguin Random House SEA 2023
Copyright © Bonnie Hayden Cheng 2023

ISBN 9789815017984

Typeset in Chaparral Pro by MAP Systems, Bangalore, India
Printed at Markono Print Media Pte Ltd, Singapore

www.penguin.sg

Contents

Part I

The Surprising Science of Kindness

Chapter 1

The Case for Kindness

Kindness. Such a simple concept. So rare in business.

Why kindness, and why now?

We are living in uncertain times. War. Recession. Terrorism. Pandemic. Global warming. All of which have radically changed the way we live and work. The reach is global. No one is immune.

In the past few years, we have been on the collective receiving end of a massive wake-up call on a scale never seen before. We are more interconnected than ever, yet we remain disconnected. As Hubert Joly, former Best Buy CEO, said, 'Business needs to be a force for good. Do good things in the world. Otherwise, you don't have a license to operate.'[1] We must confront the challenges of the world together.

The pandemic has raised the stakes. Gone are the days when organizations, and the leaders who run them, can separate the mental health and wellbeing of their people from the core of their business. Corporate wellness is the most crucial competitive advantage for organizations today, to future-proof themselves against relentless change and crisis. People are not the problem. They're the solution.

In a world facing change on such a catastrophic scale, the small things—the human things—become the big things.

The world needs more kindness. The world of *work* needs more kind leaders.

If corporate wellness is the *why*, kindness is the *how*. During times of crisis, history has proven, time and again, that those who adapt are those who survive and thrive. Those who refuse to change struggle to compete, get left behind, and die.

Leaders, take your pick. Play on the pitch or watch from the sidelines. Change the lives of your people, your stakeholders, your company, and yourself, for the better, or do nothing. Far from being a state of bliss, ignorance causes irreparable damage to you, and those around you.

Kindness. Simple concept. Surprisingly big returns.

The choice is yours.

* * *

Strange, isn't it, that kind workplaces, with kind leaders, are the exception, not the rule. I mean, as a species, we are hardwired to be kind. Kindness goes back to the innate 'goodness' of human nature.[2] Kindness even provided us with an evolutionary advantage, as living in social groups for millions of years has rewarded kind acts including forging alliances, shouldering the burden of cooperation, sacrificing, and general reliance on our tribe for survival. Growing up, the proverbial grandma taught us to be kind to one another. Religious teachings, in some form or another, expound the axiom to do unto others as you would have them do unto you. How did it all go so wrong in the workplace?

Formative studies of management and leadership starting from the 1930s make it plain that the focus has never been about the wellbeing of the labour force. The thrust of management placed people as cost-effective labourers at best: subordinates who were easily replaceable, even expendable, who were to do as they were told. If that sounds grim, try economists; they paint a dismal picture of the workplace, describing a principal-agent dynamic, where the principal (employer) enters into a transactional work contract with the agent (employee). Money for labour. No more, no less. Unless it was getting *more* out of workers for less.

This is what we recognize today as antiquated organizational design, fixated on systems of management styles that were top-down, authoritative, and directive. Those who climbed the ranks were presumably rewarded for being egomaniacs, competitive and uncompromising. Sadly, despite modern-day sensibilities that *this ain't it*, the prevalence of bad bosses tells us we haven't come very far. Sporadic expressions of kindness in the workplace, so obscure a phenomenon, go viral as something to be marveled at.

The Case against Kindness

Over the course of my research, I surveyed hundreds of leaders and managers on a global scale, representing a wide range of industries. I sought to understand from their perspective, what it means to lead with kindness. I collected concrete examples to determine if there were threads that would help me frame kindness in practice.

I also engaged business leaders and C-suites from diverse industries around the world in ongoing dialogue covering all things kindness, such as what being a kind leader means to them personally and how kindness manifests in their leadership. These leaders kindly, pun intended, recounted colourful stories of leadership across myriad leadership situations. I conferred with academics, authors, consultants, medical professionals, and researchers, in this space to round out the research. Voices across the spectrum, their accounts and anecdotes, are incorporated throughout this book.

I first unmasked three widely held beliefs elucidating why kindness has not figured into the proclivity of leadership:

1. **Kindness is weak:** By far the biggest misconception on leading with kindness is that it is perceived as being weak, soft, or fluffy. If that's the case, how can a leader lead with both strength and kindness? The fallacy here is that kindness doesn't drive results. 'This soft stuff isn't relevant—I have a business to run, who cares how people feel?' I explored this paradox with Dr Kathleen Pike, who heads the Columbia University-World Health Organization (WHO) Center for Global Mental Health. She conjectured that leaders dismiss kindness as a virtue because, 'They think it's easy. They imagine that anyone can do it, so it's not how they want or choose to distinguish themselves as a leader because if I am kind, I won't get the complicated, challenging work done that I need to get done.' She goes on to say that, 'Of course, in reality, kindness is a practice that is anything but easy. And when truly embraced, it is the magic that makes all the difference in successfully getting difficult things accomplished.'

2. **Kindness doesn't get me to the top:** In most organizations, kindness in a leader isn't perceived as necessary to the corporate climb. The average manager lacks the motivation, skill, or both, to put people first. Take the promotion cycle. Those who successfully climb the ladder are usually high performers or those who displayed Machiavellian leadership traits. They may manipulate their way to the top through political savviness or by developing a thick outer shell on the way. The rise of toxic bosses we see around us is prompted, in part, by these people being promoted to positions of authority, without having any idea about how to lead. And why would they? They've only ever been trained to do the job their people now hold. Cue

the micromanaging. Insecure in their abilities, they are fearful of being challenged. So, they lead like dictators, with organizational discipline as their weapon of choice. In such a workplace environment, demonstrations of kindness can be discordant with promotion. If a company is risk averse, these behaviours get passed around. New managers don't think about growing their emotional quotient, and surely not their *kindness quotient*, because they aren't measured or incentivized. That's why we get managers and not leaders. Some even vouch for putting their people through the same rite of passage to earn their stripes, perpetuating a toxic cycle.

3. **Kindness doesn't Get Sh*t Done (GSD):** In the midst of increasing volatility, uncertainty, complexity, and ambiguity, kindness is not conducive to achieving organizational goals. Kindness is not befitting in industries relying on a business lens over a humanitarian lens where profitability is the focal point, where every minute you're not producing, you make less money for yourself. Kindness is a diversion that takes resources away from delivering results. There is so much pressure to drive short-term results, which Pierre Battah, Leadership, HR and Workplace Specialist, and author of *Humanity at Work*,[3] describes as the 'fallacy of immediacy,' that positive attributes such as kindness are overcome by petulance, impatience, and even rage. Cathryn Gunther, Global Head of Associate Health and Wellbeing, Mars, Incorporated, observes, 'If we focus only on the numbers, it's easy to forget there's a human being driving those results. In reality, it's the opposite. Kindness in the workplace helps employees feel included, engaged, cared for, and valued. It is essential for a healthy

and productive culture where everyone can bring their best self to work.'

The Case for Kindness

Given these three pervasive beliefs against kindness, is the case for kindness closed? Why should leaders change at all, let alone tilt towards kindness?

In early 2020, Covid-19 threw an unprepared and ill-equipped world into social and economic turmoil. Millions of lives were lost. Our idea of work changed irrevocably. People became and continue to be despondent, dissatisfied, and disgruntled, and are no longer accepting a life working a job that is too stressful or unfulfilling. People are now re-thinking their interests and shifting the balance of priorities from work to life. Driven by the desire to do meaningful work they are passionate about has induced the 'Great Reshuffle,' where people are switching careers—investment bankers opening up coffee shops, lawyers becoming entrepreneurs—or re-crafting their professions by adopting gig work or attempting a side hustle. If people aren't re-shuffling, re-assessing, or re-inventing, they're resigning altogether, leaving the workforce in droves in the 'Great Resignation.' New generations are internalizing the motto popularized by rapper Drake, YOLO—*You Only Live Once*—using it as a catalyst for existential change. McKinsey reports that of those who voluntarily left their jobs, 44 per cent have no interest in returning to current roles, at least for the next little while.[4] Another 40 per cent[5] who have not yet made the leap are planning on making a move in the 'Great Realization.'[6] To the 'Great Escape.'[7] *Great Big Moves. Great Big Pain in the Ass.*

Setting aside the fact that a percentage of those leaving the workforce is due to baby boomers' retirement, employers' response to workplace desertion has been inadequate, to say the least. Flavour-of-the-month quick fixes—some configuration of temporary work-from-home arrangements, small bonuses—rather than halting the exodus, demonstrate a failure to understand the root cause. Don't get me wrong, money and work-life balance are important, but they are hygiene factors—what behavioural scientist Frederick Herzberg described as necessary, but not sufficient, in positively impacting motivation or satisfaction at work.[8]

People see through the ruse and unsurprisingly conclude that their company does not have their interests at heart. McKinsey's findings back this up; the top three reasons cited by people who voted with their feet are not feeling valued (54 per cent), a bad boss (52 per cent), and not feeling a sense of belonging (51 per cent).[9] In other words, people are leaving, not due to transactional elements relevant to pay and benefits, but due to a deficit of *relational elements*. People crave workplaces—leaders—that invest in them.

As people re-consider their priorities, companies must re-evaluate their retention strategies. Workplace cultures are being put under the microscope. Leadership has reached an inflection point. Leaders who approach this new reality as an opportunity will have an edge on attracting and retaining talent. The challenge—and opportunity—is that the playbook has yet to be written. Regardless of how leaders view it, the research is clear: 75 per cent of employees a) consider their boss to be the most stressful part of their daily work, and b) feel that their boss causes them more stress than happiness.[10] When we add to this the fact that people don't leave bad companies—they leave bad bosses—companies are putting themselves at risk if they ignore the obvious. So, let me ask, what is going on in your organization? Are you a company that people are escaping from? Or a company that people are escaping to?[11]

The Bad Boss Epidemic

Just how bad is a bad boss? Research links bad bosses with poor health outcomes. People who toil under a boss they deem inconsiderate, disrespectful, unfair, or critical put themselves at higher risk of death—yes, death—due to heart-related causes. The longer people remain in stressful surroundings, the riskier it gets.[12] Having a bad boss is playing Russian roulette with your life. Before that heart attack comes, bad bosses destroy morale, provoke high performers to leave, and create toxic environments that diminish wellbeing. Regrettably, bad bosses appear to be the norm rather than the exception. A US survey by global employment website Monster found that a majority (76 per cent) are working for a bad boss—someone who is power hungry, incompetent, micromanages, or completely unavailable.[13] A bad boss can literally kill you. If you don't want your epitaph to read 'Our beloved Dan, cause of death: bad boss,' get out, and fast.

In fairness to leaders, Covid-19 has completely upended work as we know it, making their job that much more difficult. As companies experimented with hybrid or remote work, the cruel irony is that some adjusted to these new work modes by finding insidious ways to track people and their productivity. Managers implemented 'clock-in-clock-out' systems. Scheduled more meetings. They must have missed the memo. Long working hours can kill you prematurely. The WHO and the International Labour Organization (ILO) reported that, since 2000, working fifty-five hours or more per week led to a 29 per cent increase in death due to stroke and heart disease, compared with working thirty-five to forty hours per week.[14] Considering that government directives recommend a maximum work week of forty-eight hours,[15] people are constantly being put at risk. Long working hours is effectively a health hazard—a serious occupational risk factor, at least for 9 per cent of the global population who are pulling these hours.

People are asking, as they should be, whether their job is worth their life.

The American Institute of Stress shows that high-pressure companies—defined as stressful work cultures that are fast-paced, demanding, with frequent time-sensitive deadlines—have health care spending that is almost 50 per cent higher compared to more humane work cultures. Stress—much of which stems from bad bosses—leads to disengagement and is detrimental to productivity, profitability, and company performance.[16] Stress is also a major factor in burnout and mental health decline. Unaddressed, a workforce suffering from burnout contributes to a persistent fear of work. Termed ergophobia—a phobia recognized in the standard classification of mental disorders, the Diagnostic and Statistical Manual of Mental Disorders, Fifth Edition (DSM-5)—a workforce that is afraid of work is the ultimate horror movie for people who must confront their fear of work each day, and for their manager should they be unsuccessful. Throw in a bad boss and you've got a prescription for post-traumatic stress disorder (PTSD). Research shows that the PTSD suffered at the hands of a toxic boss can linger even after escaping to a new job.[17] While a vaccine for Covid-19 was developed at record speed, the bad boss epidemic remains untreated. Go figure.

Turns out, leaders are operating with blinders on, grossly underestimating the fact that their people are struggling. Deloitte, in collaboration with Workplace Intelligence, recently exposed a chasm between employee and executives' perceptions, based on a survey of over 1,000 employees and 1,000 C-suite executives across the United States, United Kingdom, Canada, and Australia. While 56 per cent of employees think their company's leaders care about their wellbeing, 90 per cent of C-suites believe employees feel leaders care for them. While 53 per cent of employees think their company's leaders made decisions in their best interests during the pandemic, 88 per cent of C-suites believe they did so.[18] Not only are leaders oblivious to their people's hardship, but leaders are also on record claiming that the mental health and wellbeing efforts in their workplace are adequate. These divergent views aren't entirely startling. Tucked away in their cozy corner office, how would leaders know what's going on with their people? The research weighs up too. Not to defend C-suites, but overestimation is a common heuristic. People often consider themselves to be superior to others,[19] for example, rating their driving skills to be well above average.[20]

Plot twist. Your boss is escaping too. The Deloitte survey also found that it's not just employees who are besieged with concerns about workplace wellbeing. About 70 per cent of C-suites surveyed want to join the Great Escape, with approximately one in three C-suites reporting high levels of stress, exhaustion, loneliness, and depression. Leaders are trying to lead while running on empty. No one is impervious to mental health issues.

Joint research by Mind Share Partners, Qualtrics, and ServiceNow shows 68 per cent of millennials and 81 per cent of Gen Zs citing mental health as their primary reason to quit a job. What's more, 91 per cent of those surveyed expect companies to support their mental health.[21]

There we have it. A bad boss + toxic workplace culture + lack of mental health and wellbeing support = a foolproof, infallible formula for disaster. Thing is, why are we still having this decades-long conversation?

The case for kindness is directly in front of you. At the core of the company are humans selling products or services, making it a human company, not a finance company, not a tech company. So long as we are dealing with humans, kindness is the requisite leadership approach.

Management Is Not Leadership

Despite being used interchangeably, in the words of Harvard Business School's John Kotter, management is not leadership.[22] Both are concerned with effective goal accomplishment, but management is task-focused. Managers are operational conduits executing on a leaders' vision. Managers create structure, plan work activities, and monitor performance. Behaviours that facilitate the smooth operation of the business. In any organization, regardless of size and complexity, this is an exceedingly arduous task.

Leadership sets the tone, establishing the 'why' of the company, its purpose, its vision. But leadership is really about—drumroll please—the people. For goals to be met, relationships must be built, and people must be developed, mentored, coached.

Management and leadership serve distinct, yet essential, and complementary, functions. We need capable managers to elicit order. We rely on effective leaders to create thriving cultures for their people. Given these two functions, it is no wonder that we are never truly prepared for the enormity of this task, to the delight of management consultants. Leadership and training development programs are estimated to cost the US economy alone USD 166 billion each year.[23] Leadership was, and still is, an exercise in trial and error.

Kindness, and leadership, is needed from everyone, no matter where you fall in the formal structure or hierarchy, however vertical, flat, or matrixed your organization is. In the face of post-pandemic challenges, building trust is pivotal for getting people to commit to a future they can't see and collectively moving the organization forward to bring this future into fruition. People trust that their leader's vision of tomorrow is one where they are better off. This requires effective communication, engagement, empowerment, and providing opportunities for challenging work and advancement. It also requires nurturing a healthy workplace. This starts with kindness. Kind leaders—at all levels of the organization—create kind companies.

Kindness Is Human

Google set out to examine, in a project that started in 2008-2009, how to build better bosses.[24] Dated, I know. Bear with me. Years of data led Google researchers to come up with a list of eight behaviours and competencies that distinguished the best managers:

- good coach
- empowers
- cares for people's wellbeing and success
- productive and results-oriented
- communicates well
- supports career development
- technical skills

The interesting part of this rather obvious list was the finding that technical expertise ranked as the least important factor in being a good boss. This was surprising to Google, a company that had, for the most part, fixated on technical capabilities in selecting managers. While important, what employees value more are bosses who take an interest in them and who help them through difficult times.

This maps on to research in the 1970s from leadership theorist Robert Katz,[25] who was among the first thought leaders to identify categories of leadership skills:

- **Technical skills:** Proficiency (competence and knowledge) in your area of work
- **Conceptual skills:** Capacity to work with abstract ideas and make them concrete
- **Human skills:** Ability to connect with and motivate a diverse mix of people

Katz found that technical skills were important only at lower levels of management. This was counter to what companies such as Google at the time believed. As a manager progresses into more senior roles, technical skills become less important, aligned with Google's findings. Conceptual skills become gradually more important at senior levels of management. Human skills—the people factor—were important at *all* levels of management, a finding that Google later confirmed. Human skills, of which kindness is key, separates effective leaders from bad bosses. The case for kindness is data backed.

Leading in the New Reality

The pandemic has had some surprising benefits. Recent findings of the *World Happiness Report* reveal that, on a global scale, acts of kindness—helping strangers, donating to charity, volunteering—increased by almost 25 per cent as compared with pre-pandemic assessments. In our communities, there is ample evidence that people react compassionately during times of distress. Such evidence is lacking when it comes to the workplace.[26]

People are realizing the power of kindness in business. A survey by the World Economic Forum and Coursera found that working adults are demanding to learn skills related to personal development and self-management.[27] As compared with 2019, when the top 10 most sought-after skills were hard-lined on technical skills, such as Python, AI, and cloud computing, I find it fascinating—telling—that in 2020 the top ten skills most in demand related to kindness, mindfulness, gratitude, and listening.

The gravity of the bad boss epidemic has reached new highs—or lows. Loyalty is coming at a high cost for bad bosses. Replacing a single employee costs approximately 20 per cent of that employee's salary, and more so if they were one of your top performers.[28] That's not all. There are additional costs incurred, in terms of hiring and onboarding a replacement, development and training, lost productivity and engagement, and costs to workplace culture, all of which add up real quick.[29]

Let's rephrase: It costs more to replace your people than it costs to keep them. Meanwhile, leaders are lamenting talent retention issues while stubbornly crossing their arms, citing 'budget constraints' or 'cutbacks' as justification for denying adjustments to remuneration. This is the time people need it most, and a squandered opportunity for leaders to demonstrate loyalty and earn their people's trust. Play stupid games, win stupid prizes.

The silver lining of the pandemic is that decades and even centuries of conventional thinking on leadership are being re-written. Enlightened leaders are aspiring towards new models of leadership, recognizing that pre-pandemic management styles are unsustainable. Consequently, we are seeing rapid changes that are transforming our thinking on traditional leadership styles and the demise of doctrines that have been held with iron fists.

With the torrent of technology upending long-established models of work, what makes us human becomes paramount. Humans are, and will remain, the most critical feature of all organizations. Leaders have a responsibility to lead their people out of the pandemic that has so badly impacted mental health and wellbeing. Leaders have ordinarily approached engagement and productivity from the perspective of adopting complex systems and designs that inadvertently add to the demands of their people. What leaders are finding is that, when they show up for their people, their people discern that they are a better cut of leader. The humanity of leadership rests on the way leaders contribute to the growth, fulfillment, and success of their people. It is about *how to connect to the hearts and minds of your people.* Very different to orthodox management models that were devoid of emotion, and especially devoid of kindness.

In the midst of the Great Re-calibration, candidates now have many options available to them. If people aren't being rewarded for their loyalty, they only stand to gain by leaving. Paying them generously is basic kindness. Beyond this, what will determine whether leaders succeed in traversing the inflection point in attracting, recruiting, and retaining the best talent—creative and engaged people who drive the company forward—comes down to the premium placed on helping them manage human challenges. Leading in new realities places kindness as the point of departure. The rocket fuel. The new generation of talent wants to be challenged and productive, but their line in the sand is a kind and caring workplace, setting new bars for wellbeing and respectful treatment. They are no longer accepting the 'this is how we've always done things around here' excuse. The rules of engagement are different, and the marketplace is driving it. Companies bear a mandate beyond providing a return to their shareholders.

In the new world of work, kindness will make or break leadership. Leaders who continue to lead from a defunct playbook will witness their people joining the Great Exit. The new playbook requires a *kindness imperative,* with people at the center.

Chapter Insights

- The pandemic has sparked a revelation. People are re-calibrating their priorities in favour of meaningful pursuits that fulfil them and are no longer accepting a workplace that disregards their mental health and wellbeing. The marketplace is demanding a leadership refresh, towards a human-centred approach.

- The cost of a bad boss, for their people, is their health, their life. For the company, the cost is a loss of, and inability to attract and win new talent. As companies re-evaluate their retention strategies, leaders have no choice but to make corporate wellness a strategic imperative. Be kind, or be left behind. People first, or people flee.

Chapter 2

The Anatomy of Kindness

One of my staff had Type 2 diabetes, and it was causing issues for them. They were regularly coming down with issues and ending up in hospital with complications. This caused numerous sick days. Had I followed our policy, we would have dismissed that employee after their fourth absence, but this was in no way their fault and [they] should not be penalized for something out of their control. I was able to reassure that employee that I would be fighting for them and that they would be able to remain with us, which I was able to do.'

44-year-old Client Manager, financial services industry

The stories I collected of kind leadership from managers and leaders, like those above, ranged from helping people through trying times to downright difficult choices that came at some cost to oneself. But it was the small gestures, not the grand acts of kindness, which stood out to me. Mindful behaviour we can all do on a daily basis are impactful because together, the pendulum swings, towards a culture of kindness.

To further understand perceptions surrounding leading with kindness, I surveyed hundreds of leaders from around the world. The results were striking:

- 92 per cent strongly disagree that kindness = weakness
- 82 per cent agree or strongly agree that a kind leader is decisive
- 79 per cent agree or strongly agree that a kind leader is one that gets results
- 92 per cent agree or strongly agree that a kind leader is an effective leader
- 71 per cent agree or strongly agree that a kind leader is a strong leader
- 60 per cent agree or strongly agree that a kind leader is in demand

Let's explore the patterns emerging from the data.

Common (Mis)Perceptions about Kindness

Kindness Is Niceness

'Some of the hardest times I have had to demonstrate kindness in [a] leadership role have been when I have had to let a team member know they are not performing up to scratch. I had given them feedback they did not like to hear, but that gave them an opportunity to grow as a professional, an opportunity they would not have had without that feedback. That is hard, because we often think of kindness as treating others in a way that never takes them outside their comfort zone. That's not what kind leadership is.'

33-year-old Manager, education industry

Let's start with what kindness is *not*: an indisputable fact stemming from my research is that leading with kindness is not synonymous with being 'nice'. In fact, the word 'nice' only surfaced once or twice, none of which was related to kindness. One of these instances was in conversation with Jacqueline Carter, partner at Potential Project and co-author of *Compassionate Leadership: How to Do Hard Things in a Human Way*[1] who noted that companies with 'nice cultures' often don't have the hard conversations that help people learn and grow. The motivation behind being nice is to keep the peace, which means agreeing with majority views, saying what others want to hear, or staying quiet altogether. One symptom of leading from nice is being a people-pleaser—trying a little too hard to please the masses, craving acceptance by all. It comes from good intentions: *I just want others to be happy.* But it leads to being accommodating to others in lieu of their own needs. People-pleasing often stems from insecurity, low self-esteem, or perfectionistic tendencies.

Along with Oonagh Harpur, former CEO of law firm Berwin Leighton Paisner and a TEDx speaker, we attempted to untangle the web of kindness and niceness in the context of leadership, and how leading from nice does no favours to anyone. Says Oonagh, 'People see kindness as being nice, which can be very damaging. Nice is complacent. Nice is keeping someone who's not right for the job for twenty years because she has kids. That does more harm to people.' Under a nice leader, people become frustrated at the lack of clarity or delays in decision making due to perpetual flip-flopping, derailing organizational goals because, counter to genuine intentions of creating a 'nice' work culture, the unintentional work culture that arises is one that supports low performers. People are unmotivated to go above and beyond because no real feedback is forthcoming. All stemming from a culture of nice, led by a nice leader.

Being nice is not inherently a bad thing. Be friends with nice people. If you can't find one, be one. *Leading* from nice is ineffective. Leading from nice does not move the organization forward. Nice people shouldn't be leaders.

Kind Leaders Don't Need a Payday

'I was stuck at work for an audit that went beyond my level of accounting knowledge and with very little cooperation from a client that should have been [more] involved . . . The auditors arrived in the office at 6 a.m. and left at 10 p.m. for 2 weeks in a row, with me being there at all times too. When my director realized the amount of pressure I was under, he started to arrive at 6 and leave at 10 with me every day. He couldn't help too much with the workload as he didn't know the client, but he even took part in a few night calls with the main client in Singapore to show his support.'

27-year-old Client Accounts Manager,
financial services industry

Because people generally perceive themselves to be good, kind people, I was curious about blurred lines, situations in which kindness is faked or used strategically to collect favours. This notion of mutual backscratching—*I do something for you with the expectation that you do something for me later*—for all intents and purposes could be authentic, but there is an added element of 'What's in it for me?', an assumption of reciprocity, whether made explicit or not.

Calculated or performative kindness is incongruous with what leading with kindness is about, which is the pure-of-heart and genuine goodness induced by the humanity of leadership, amply displayed by the manager's own supervisor in the example above. Takers, as outlined by organizational psychologist and Wharton professor Adam Grant [2] may stand to gain in the short term, but are likely to be found out in the long term.

Ultimately, manipulative kindness is not the intentional kindness we want of our leaders. Sure, if your kindness leads to reciprocated benefits down the road, that's great. In fact, it probably will, because people tend to respond in kind. But acts of kindness should be done without a presupposition of selfish gain. Kindness is not transactional.

The Ego Hangup

'It's a shame most people only know they've done a good job only because no one yelled at them today. And it's that ego thing of the leader that's causing that to happen.'

Garry Ridge, CEO and Chairman, WD-40 Company

While kindness is often used interchangeably with niceness, one clear incompatibility of leading with kindness is leading from ego.[3] I had an exhilarating conversation with the energetic Garry Ridge, CEO and Chairman, WD-40 Company, maker of the fluid in the tell-tale blue and yellow cans with the little red top that magically cures squeaky doors. Garry expressed that ego prevents leaders from leading with kindness: 'We all have reasonably good intent. But why aren't we doing it? Number one—ego. I have to be successful, I have to be the best, and I have to win. Their ego eats their empathy rather than empathy eating their ego. You have to go through that 'aha' moment, that you can't do it on your own. Until you come to the realization that it's all about the people you lead, that it's not about you, you can't do it. You think you can, but you can't.'

This is the ego that needs to be kept in check. Leaders need to balance the power that comes with the title, with the needs of the people in their care. This starts with getting unstuck, breaking out of the leadership bubble surrounded by yes people that cater to their every whim, completely out of touch with the reality of their workforce. The toxic bad bosses described in Chapter 1 have failed in this endeavour, which largely contributed to the Great Resignation. Can't do it? Don't be a leader. Operating out of ego is easy because it satisfies the self. But leading from ego is completely devoid of kindness. To the detriment of the people.

Kindness Is a Worldview

With a better understanding of what kindness is not, I turned my attention to what it means to lead with kindness. Are there certain people that are more prone to kindness? A large-scale kindness test launched in September 2021 from Dr Robin Banerjee of the University of Sussex, based on over 60,000 people from 144 countries found that the personality traits most connected with kindness—giving, receiving, and observing kindness—are extroversion, openness to experience, and agreeableness.[4] This makes sense. Extroverted individuals are sociable and acquire energy being around people, creating and furthering connections, lending itself to kindness. Not to say that all extroverted people are kind, or that introverted people are unkind, these types of generalizations are unproductive. In fact (*shout out to my introverts!*), Susan Cain, author of *Quiet*, points out that introverts build an emotional repertoire that allow them to effectively understand and manage their own and others' emotions.[5] Introverts and extroverts socialize differently, making kindness likely to manifest differently. For example, while extroverts deftly navigate new social situations, introverts are more comfortable forming deep connections with a close-knit group. People who are open to new experiences are readily accepting of opinions, viewpoints, and perspectives different to their own. This tolerance accommodates kindness towards dissimilar others. Agreeable people are more prone to kindness, because they value friendships and are altruistic, prosocial, and benevolent in nature.

Markings of emotional intelligence can be detected when it comes to kindness. While emotional intelligence is a personality trait, such that people have varying degrees of EQ, the behaviours that make up EQ can be learned. This is also true with kindness. While people vary in their baseline levels of kindness, kindness can be developed and amplified in one's character.

In my exchange with Cathryn Gunther of Mars, Incorporated, she noted that calling kindness a competency isn't quite right—kindness is a way of treating others that goes beyond a skill and is part of overall emotional intelligence that is often given short shrift in hardcore business textbooks. This idea of kindness being reflected in behaviour is echoed by Lâle Kesebi, CEO of Human at Work: 'Kindness isn't a thought, it's an action. The first step of kindness is empathy. Shifting your perspective to understand, what would I want someone to say to me in this moment? Then the kindness follows as the second step. Empathy is the starter, kindness is the action. Third is, as a leader, we need to action, role model, and develop cultures that outwardly demonstrate kindness. You are the designer of a culture that reinforces kindness. The leadership standard of kindness is in service of groups of people far bigger than just your team.'

I further examined this perspective with Dr Kathleen Pike. We shared how kind leadership is a real truth-seeking of what matters, taking the time to connect to the values we hold most dear for ourselves and others, and at the heart of it, being gentle, generous, and honest. Kindness is the behavioural expression of one's core values, where kindness guides one's words and actions. As a leader who holds responsibility for decision-making, kindness means considering the dignity and impact of your actions on your people in the spirit of generosity. From that lens, Dr Pike says that leaders can let go of people or make the tough decisions with kindness, because kindness leaves intact one's own dignity, and the dignity of others: 'Leading with kindness will translate into teachable skills, but the veneer of teachable skills will not translate into leading with kindness unless you do the hard work of understanding and prioritizing the values of dignity, generosity, patience, and respect. If you just put on the Halloween costume, you don't become Superman, except to get a few pieces of candy. That's one of the opportunities and risks around any of these texts on the 'how-to.' People want the three-point checklist. But leading with kindness requires deep roots and integrity. It is about how to engage with the world.'

The Empathy Dilemma

Aside from 'nice,' kindness is often folded into the empathy and compassion mix. Dr Pike shared a humorous anecdote of her young son being adamant that there is no such thing as a synonym—there's a reason why so many different words exist. We have kindness because it captures something empathy and compassion don't. Rather than trying to put a box around kindness, Dr Pike and I mused about watercolours, an image which aptly channels the ethos of kindness. When you 'paint' the values of empathy and compassion as part of the mosaic, a portrait of kindness begins to emerge. When you get a bit of each of them, you can act in a way that is kind. Or, less artistic an image is overlapping circles in a Venn diagram, where the values of empathy and compassion overlap with kindness, yet a non-trivial portion of kindness remains uncorrelated.

I turned back to Jacqueline Carter of Potential Project to further explore the grades of variation between kindness and its watercolour cousins who, in her book, puts compassion, not empathy, front and centre on the leadership stage. For Jacqueline, there is a distinctive risk in leading from empathy. Empathy is about feeling another person's emotions and a notable wellspring of connection. Leaders, especially those with large teams, may find themselves getting stuck in the emotions of people. Paul Polman, former CEO of Unilever, has said that leading with empathy would make it impossible for him to make decisions because feeling others' emotions would prevent him from acting for the greater good. Jacqueline notes that there are also downsides to leading from empathy because we as human beings have biases that may affect judgment and decision-making as leaders, such as tending to empathize with people who look like us or who are similar to us to a higher degree. Sure enough, research has shown this similar-to-me bias to affect the outcomes of processes such as recruitment, promotion, and retention.

For contrast, Satya Nadella, as only the third CEO in Microsoft's history, has been vocal in promoting how empathy informs his leadership, which he acknowledges isn't typically seen in CEOs. In Satya's view, it is his highest priority to ground the entire Microsoft culture around empathy. He believes, in addition to confidence and experience, a CEO must have empathy. Having the kindness to understand another person's perspective, allows him to appreciate others' opinions, even if he (respectfully) disagrees.[6] In this light, leading with kindness is driven by empathy, where understanding challenges faced by your people moves you to do something about it. It is no wonder, then, that empathy tops the list of what leaders must get right to be effective,[7] so much so that the acronym CEO should be relabelled Chief Empathy Officer.[8] Encouragingly, a study by Businesssolver revealed that 91 per cent of CEOs believe that empathy is directly linked to a company's financial performance, and 82 per cent of employees are more likely to stay with an empathetic boss.[9] A far cry from the bad bosses described in Chapter 1!

In terms of compassion, for Jacqueline, compassion demonstrates an intention to be kind, moving beyond simply feeling another's pain or struggle, and getting more bang for the empathy buck. It is here, in the intention and the action, where kindness lives. Meaning, leading with kindness requires intentional action to be taken. Motivated compassion drives this action, which only appears when leaders empathize with their people. You may empathize with a direct report who had to miss her son's game due to a pressing deadline, but she has no idea you're empathizing with her. You can feel compassion for a colleague who is in bereavement, but that doesn't mean you'll do something to express it. There is no dilemma in action.

When I spoke with Jeffery Tan, board director and CEO of Jardine MINDSET Singapore,[10] he explained that kindness helps leaders relate to their people, that it adds a human factor to leadership that may not always be easy to measure but, when missing, becomes obvious: 'If you don't have the kindness factor, what you have is a very transactional organization. Without the expression of kindness, it completely dehumanizes relationships with individuals in the organization.' This notion of intentionality lays the groundwork for leaders to be kind and to do kind acts without the expectation of payback. Kindness can be dispersed without people on the receiving end ever seeing it or needing to know an act of kindness happened. That is kind leadership in its true and unadulterated form.

I find it comforting to know that most people in most circumstances will choose to do the right thing.[11] It is reassuring that kindness is a language that cuts across gender, age, and culture, and is a common language that is universally understood by people around the world.[12] If kindness is the default, it takes effort to be unkind. While I don't believe that people wake up in the morning and think to themselves: *I choose to be unkind today*, it shows up in our workplaces every day. Leading with kindness is a choice.

The Kindness Imperative

Took the long way home. Let's circle back. I define leading with kindness as *taking intentional action in service to, and for the betterment of, the people in your care*. Kindness, as a human experience, is about connecting with people on a human level. More than that, kindness is a way of engaging with the world. A way of being that is kind, embodying one's core values of, and the capacity for, being empathic, compassionate, generous, and humble.

The workplace is no different. To *lead* with kindness is to lead with humanity. Kindness is a verb—a process in action. Without action, kindness is static and therefore ineffective. Leading with kindness necessitates that it is unveiled through deliberate behaviours and practices that you take ownership of and are accountable for. The intimation is that leading with kindness can be cultivated and reinforced.

Leading with kindness is a substantial responsibility of meaningful consequence, linked to the crux of leadership, which, by definition, is about helping others succeed. This is driven by the genuine desire to champion, support, and advocate for your people. Integral to leading with kindness is a level of toughness that goes hand in hand to drive impact by achieving corporate objectives while prioritizing the people.

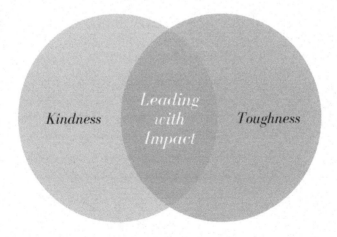

The kindness imperative is this: kindness is not just the right thing to do, it's good for business. Kindness is not an ancillary behaviour for leaders—a nice to have—it is a *need to have* to stay competitive. To enable the organization to anticipate, confront, and adapt to the varied and constant challenges in a global world requires leaders who amplify kindness to an overarching, core business strategy guiding every aspect of the company.

Chapter Insights

- Leading with kindness is defined as taking intentional action in service to, and for the betterment of, the people in your care.
- Leading with kindness is driven by the innate goodness of humanity—empathy, compassion, generosity, and humility—that manifest as taking responsible action of the mental health, wellbeing, and growth of your people.
- There is no compromise between kindness and toughness. Kind leaders are tough, effectively addressing complex organizational challenges by leveraging a collaborative approach that creates shared value.

Chapter 3

Leading with Impact = Kindness + Toughness

Despite the misconception that leading with kindness is a weakness, in almost every conversation I had with senior executives and from the experiences shared by the people they led, I uncovered stories to the contrary. The duality of kindness *and* toughness came through in their leadership. I kept digging deeper into this seeming paradox.

I first looked into the literature with the inquisitiveness of whether tough love might be an appropriate representation of kind and effective leadership. What's love got to do with it? Let's count the ways. Harvard Business School professor Frances Frei, along with executive founder of The Leadership Consortium, Anne Morriss, define tough love as a combination of holding high standards while being highly devoted.[1] Toughness and love are not in opposition. Leaders challenge and support. Success for leaders is found in embracing both kindness and toughness. But it requires intention to reveal both.

This idea is supplemented by the work of management theorists Robert R. Blake and Jane Mouton. In their Managerial Grid, the Team Management leadership style is a leader with high concern for people *and* task.[2] Leaders must be able to use various tools at their disposal to make their people's lives better and to create conditions for healthy relationships. In a highly engaged workplace, people know they are held to high standards but also know they will receive the support they need to achieve results.

Kindness and toughness can live harmoniously together without conflict as co-habitable opposites. This brought to mind the 'genius of the AND', a concept developed by Jim Collins.[3] It stems from Chinese philosophy embracing the duality of yin and yang, with leaders who accept contradictory ideas, not merely as a 50-50 balancing act but finding ways to be consistently both. These are the leaders that take their companies, as Collins has shown us, from good to great. Being kind and tough is representative of the complexities of paradoxical leadership, in which seemingly antithetical behaviours are interrelated in bringing out the best in people and companies. Dialectical thinking balances a worldview that accepts contrasting ideas, shifting from a stubborn either/or mindset to a both/and paradox mindset.[4] Kindness does not negate toughness, discipline, and the ability to be all the things a leader needs to be effective. Any perception to the contrary is narrow-minded and misguided. Love and kindness coincide with toughness and holding high standards. And they are not, second-hand emotions.

The Kind Leadership Matrix

Leadership is exhibited through the demonstration of behaviours. The duality of leadership can be represented by two dimensions, one representing a leader's degree of kindness, the other representing a leader's degree of toughness. Bisecting them creates four quadrants and produces four leadership personas you are likely familiar with.

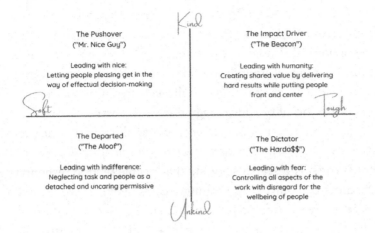

The Pushover
("Mr. Nice Guy")

Leading with nice:
Letting people pleasing get in the
way of effectual decision-making

The Impact Driver
("The Beacon")

Leading with humanity:
Creating shared value by delivering
hard results while putting people
front and center

The Departed
("The Aloof")

Leading with indifference:
Neglecting task and people as a
detached and uncaring permissive

The Dictator
("The Harda$$")

Leading with fear:
Controlling all aspects of the
work with disregard for the
wellbeing of people

Unkind + Tough = The Dictator

Hello, old friend. We meet again. Leaders who are unkind and tough live in the southeast quadrant. The archaic toxic bosses described in Chapter 1. The Dictator is representative of the 'my way or the highway' bosses. They rule with fear. They prioritize task, not people. Well, not all people, just themselves, because they are selfish leaders who lead from ego. To everyone else, they are inflexible. Unforgiving. Callous. Cruel.

Relationships are purely short-term and transactional—do x, get y reward. Dangles carrot. Don't do x, get z punishment. Cracks whip. Wellbeing is for the weak. Forget wellness, these leaders demand workaholics. The Dictator is unable or unwilling to communicate except by yelling at people, like the schoolyard bully we tried hard to avoid. They love to name blame and shame, they are never in the wrong. They are uninterested in any input, suggestions, or feedback from you. With a negative and cynical outlook, they discourage and frustrate, shooting people down because they know it all. They know it best. And they say nothing at all (to help you develop).

The destructive effects of abusive Dictators are well-documented. We saw in Chapter 1 that Dictators contribute to ergophobia, PTSD, and are even capable of killing you prematurely. They score an F all around, in terms of trust-building, motivation, and contributing to people's overall wellbeing.[5] Even more subtle forms of incivility—microaggressions or ostracism—from a Dictator can have negative effects on morale, performance, and stress. You might be thinking, *I would never put up with a Dictator!* But surprising research suggests that people tend to respond to Dictators by doing, well, nothing. People avoid confronting the Dictator, even attempting to convince themselves that *it's not a big deal.* Only 1 per cent to 6 per cent of people experiencing incivility ever filed a formal complaint.[6] If you work for a Dictator, don't walk. Run.

Kind + Soft = The Pushover

Leaders who are kind and soft live in the northwest quadrant. These are the Pushovers. The ones who over-prioritize maintaining friendships (or pseudo-friendships) at the expense of a productive, challenging, and fulfilling work context that raises people up. The Pushover says words that are nice to hear but contribute nothing to growing people by way of tangible direction. The Pushover may provide basic support and resources, but not much else.

The Pushover might not sound all that bad. *At least my boss is nice!* Unlike the Dictator that people will (eventually) willfully abandon, or the Departed where people know what to expect (not much), the Pushover gives people false hope. Hope that their boss will take an active role in their career growth, hope that their boss will initiate meaningful dialogue. *Maybe today's the day!* Yet, they soon realize that the Pushover is too nice to take decisive action to push initiatives through, too soft to provide needed guidance to deliver results. They avoid supplying honest feedback, perhaps even doling out false positive feedback to protect people's feelings. They avoid confronting bad behaviour by turning a blind eye or making illogical rationalizations of 'good intentions.' Lacking conviction to make authoritative decisions that drive change, and without structure and a transparent process in place, minimal progress is made on organizational objectives. The morale of an already exasperated team further declines. In an effort to satisfy all, all become dissatisfied. It does not help your people to be everyone's friend.

Unkind + Soft = The Departed

Combining the Jekyll of the Dictator with the Hyde of the Pushover produces a corporate monster—a ghost—called the Departed. Working for a boss who stays out of people's way and who lets them do as they please may seem appealing to some. This is misinformed. We're not talking about Casper. This is not the hands-off leader that empowers through autonomy. This is the do-nothing leader that disregards the people and the work, with an anything goes, unconcerned permissive attitude. You're unlikely to have a conversation with them about your interests outside of work, because they just don't care. Workwise, they give perfunctory effort, with no strategic direction or resources for daily operations. You barely see them, especially when you need them. The Departed is simply passing time, skating by until retirement. The less actual work needs to be done, the better. Stuck in the project planning phase? Not my problem. Having a conflict? Sort it out yourself. Or not. So long as you get your work done and don't bother them.

Research shows that doing the bare minimum as a mediocre manager can restrict people's career advancement and future opportunities. This leader may be tolerable for a short while if you work well independently and don't need frequent check-ins. But people end up scratching their heads, confused about their roles and responsibilities, lacking support, contributing to stress and even conflict.[7] Growth and progression are not in the cards, unless you proactively network around these leaders.

Kind + Tough = The Impact Driver

The kindness compass points this way. The energizing space in the northeast is where leaders lead with impact, with kindness and proportioned toughness. Kind is not weak. Tough is not unkind. You do not—should not—have to choose between being an effective leader and being a good person. This is a human-centred leadership approach that prioritizes people without lowering standards for the work or sacrificing business objectives. This means two things. First, Impact Drivers espouse a coaching or mentorship role in service of their people, facilitators who work collaboratively with their people, providing clarity, context, and resources. They then get out of the way to allow their people to shine. These leaders wholeheartedly champion and advocate for their people, investing in their personal growth and career progression. These leaders identify and create stretch assignments for their people, steadily expanding their capability. Under an Impact Driver, people and organizations are set up for success.

Second, leading with kindness is not about being nice. It's about being inclusive. Impact Drivers adopt a leadership approach that creates shared value. It goes beyond old-world leadership approaches and reflects a model that is structurally aligned with value creation. This takes on heightened relevance when we consider the global challenges faced today around mental health, wellbeing, diversity, equity, and inclusion (DEI), and an increasingly (dis)connected society. Impact Drivers fold mental health and wellbeing into the core of their business strategy, recognizing that it is the most competitive strategy for building resilient and agile companies. They build cultures that are positive and uplifting, that support the wellbeing of their people because they understand that people who are happy, in mind, body, and spirit, drive change, innovate, and produce. With people as the foundation, this care and consideration extends to an investment in the mental health and wellbeing of families, which supports communities, so that society benefits.

Leading with Kindness is Tough

Kindness and toughness, two ingredients seemingly diametrically opposed that blend to make a formidable combination, is what gets leaders to impact. But it takes resolve. I spoke with Dr Kelli Harding, board certified psychiatrist, assistant clinical professor at Columbia University, public health expert, and author of *The Rabbit Effect*,[8] about this presumed tension between kindness and toughness. She described a misunderstanding about kindness, because 'true kindness takes a lot of courage, to bring up opinions that contrast others while still respecting them.' To Dr Harding, leaders need to sow the seeds of human connection. Once sown, difficult conversations become easier. With courage, candour, and a spirit of generosity, delivering honest feedback and holding tough conversations are welcomed, appreciated even, because people understand your motives and trust that tough conversations are coming from a good place. If bad news is to be had, it is preferable to hold an uncomfortable conversation with someone who you feel cares about you.

The roadmap for leaders to reach the land of the Impact Driver will be different depending on the starting point. Too far to the west on the Kindness Matrix means that leaders must amp up on toughness. Being nice and soft does more harm than good, as top performers become dejected as people learn that doing the bare minimum is tolerated. Without clear direction, people flounder. It does not make you a 'bad boss' to set expectations and create boundaries. In fact, these actions are a kindness you give to your people. It provides role clarity and builds trust, allowing people to do their work with purpose. Leaders who are starting from the south side, rise up. You were likely working for a Dictator on your way up and are modelling your own leadership after the only perspective you've known. There is another way. A better way.

Impact Drivers in Action

I delved into impact creation with NiQ Lai, Co-owner and Group CEO of Hong Kong Broadband Network (HKBN), a publicly-listed telecommunications company that went from a start-up funded by family and friends in 1992 to a publicly-listed company with a market cap of HKD 11 billion. The HKBN culture is not unlike what you would see in Silicon Valley-based tech companies such as Google, or start-ups with a free-spirited approach to leadership, due in large part to the way NiQ leads. NiQ likened the juxtaposition of kindness and toughness with the parenting principle. In his view, being kind to your children might mean allowing them to eat junk food and go online 24/7 (however foolish). But that wouldn't benefit them. So, a parent leads by setting examples and setting boundaries. Sure, his kids protest. But to NiQ, as a parent, connecting over dinner is sacrosanct as it forms quality family bonds.

Likewise, it is the job of a leader to make decisions grounded in kindness and fairness, for the good of the people. There is nothing soft about that. Despite comparisons to parenting, NiQ rejects the idea that a company is a type of family. A family offers unconditional love, and that love often forgives bad behaviour. Rather, HKBN operates more like an elite sports team with clearly mapped high-performance objectives. They take a tough stance by exiting the bottom 5 per cent of performers every year. Is that kindness? NiQ argues that this allows HKBN to anchor limited resources on the top 95 per cent, which, to NiQ, represents the dualism of kindness and toughness. HKBN made a conscious choice to help B Talents (they have no employees, only Talents) rise to the level of A+ performers, rather than helping D players get to C level. Alongside the toughness is the kindness of offering all necessary resources and support for their Talents to succeed.

With Alain Li, Regional Chief Executive, Richemont Asia Pacific, a publicly-listed leading luxury goods groups with a portfolio of businesses including jewellery (e.g., Cartier, Van Cleef & Arpels) and specialist watchmakers (e.g., IWC, Piaget, Vacheron Constantin), with a market cap of over EUR 62 billion, I had a thought-provoking conversation on the bifurcation of being kind and tough. Alain says, 'Being a kind and tough leader means you can set a standard and demand this of your people, but you can also help them reach these objectives. In a professional sports team, the players are given all the necessary resources and conditions to allow each individual player to excel, but there are also demands that the team is required to follow through on. And each team is ultra-competitive. Not only are they demanding of themselves, but they hold each of their teammates to that same standard. But they can also do this in a kind and empathetic caring environment. So, kindness and toughness are not mutually exclusive. Though, it requires an environment where people are self-motivated, driven, and have tenacity.'

Leading with kindness is not for the weak. Weak bosses lead from nice. Nice leaders shy away from providing challenging feedback. But tough conversations can be delivered with kindness. When I spoke with Dawn Frazier-Bohnert, EVP, Global DEI Officer of Liberty Mutual Insurance (the first to hold this role in the company), a Fortune 100 company and the sixth-largest property and casualty insurer in the United States, about the interplay between kindness and toughness, Dawn recounts an experience when she was tough with one of her direct reports. Tears were shed, says Dawn. But at the end of that conversation this individual wanted to hug Dawn, saying, 'I've never received such tough and challenging feedback said in such a kind way before. You've allowed me to hear it and now I think I'll be able to do something about it.'

Sigal Atzmon, President and CEO of Medix Global, a global provider of innovative and quality health management solutions, is unswerving in her view that providing direct feedback *is* an act of kindness. As a leader, it is a kind action to take the time to sit someone down to have a frank and honest conversation about what's working, what's not, and why. Making the effort to understand what's happening from their perspective is time that could otherwise be spent on other, arguably more important things for a leader, such as growing the business.

From a leader's perspective, it takes deep strength to marry the fact that the response you get from this individual may fall into the realm of ingratitude, even indignation, but in the long run kindness makes you as a leader happier, more fulfilled, and more successful. Sigal says, 'Being a leader, being a CEO, is difficult. It's a very lonely, solitary position, even if you're working in a team. Because at the end of day, it's a CEO's responsibility. It's the CEO who leads and who drives, for good or for bad. Being kind makes it more fulfilling, and makes it a healthier environment, and it lives together with being demanding, critical, and passionate. It's not one or the either. You can be both blonde and tall.'

On leading with kindness, Sigal emphasizes, 'There is no other option other than being kind. Being kind is a strength. Acknowledging feelings, of yourself as a leader or of others, is a strength. Showing emotions makes you a better leader and a stronger person.' She considers kindness in lock step with being demanding and critical. This is particularly true during difficult times: 'In times of crisis, leaders need to make decisions. I have a responsibility not just to make my people happy at the moment so I get good scores. I also have a social responsibility to the company.' For Sigal, kindness doesn't come at the expense of success. Sigal describes how, as a healthcare company, they have a relationship with their customers, who are dealing with major illnesses. While it is important to be empathetic, sometimes, she says, being an Impact Driver means 'not being nice—telling people things they might not want to hear. For some companies, they do whatever it takes to get high customer ratings, but we don't do that. We are here to save lives, so if that means speaking up for what's right, we have to be okay with that. It's a kind act to fight for someone's life.'

Kindness Converts

One of my favourite stories emerging from my conversations on kindness came from my interactions with Frank Wong, President of Scholastic Asia, based in Hong Kong. Over lunch one day, he emphatically told me, 'I'm not the right person to talk to about leading with kindness—I'm not a kind leader!'

Fast forward to a few months later when Frank and I were catching up. He was visibly distressed. He told me about how New York headquarters saw the business in Southeast Asia, having been severely affected by the pandemic, to be an unnecessary risk. To reduce volatility, head office decided to shut them down.

When Frank caught wind of this decision, he was upset. Frank has known these salespeople for over twenty years. Many were second generation in this business, making it the only business they've ever known. As their livelihood was based solely on commission, they would not receive severance if HQ shut them down. Frank knew he had to come up with a solution to address New York's concerns but also preserve jobs.

Over the course of four weeks, Frank spent his days helping the local business manager, who has been with the company for over thirty years, build a viable financial model to take over the business as a separate entity, while spending his nights negotiating with New York. In the end a deal was finalized, and he was able to create a win for all. Most precious for Frank, was that the salespeople were able to stay on. I listened to Frank with a big smile on my face. When he finished relaying the story, I said to him, 'Frank, you do realize that you've just presented an example of how you led with kindness, don't you? And you said you weren't kind!' The actions Frank took for his people, being tough on the problem and soft on the people, not shying away from tough conversations, were prime examples of kind leadership in action. An unkind leader would have put their hands up, shrugged their shoulders, and said this was a corporate decision. It wasn't in Frank to do that. Frank has been leading with kindness all along; he just didn't see kindness as a business principle that was driving the action. Frank had assumed that kindness and toughness were incompatible, as he has always been vocal about being a tough leader that delivers results.

Frank is not alone. A global survey of 300 senior leaders across a broad range of industries found that 61 per cent of leaders struggle to balance their demand for high performance with providing support to their people, as if this was a binary conversation.[9] In reality, kind does not undercut tough.

A few weeks later, I met with Frank on a rainy day over coffee. Frank noted that he'd come to the realization that the two are interwoven: 'Being tough and being kind are not, and should not be, mutually exclusive. If you have one without the other, your business cannot be well-run. I've realized that, the fact that you care about someone gives you license to be tough on their performance.'

I was thrilled with this new Frank—a kindness convert! When leaders set a context of kindness, people are willing to accept the high standards expected of them. If you don't have kindness as the backdrop, if people don't feel you care about them or their personal growth, the company culture becomes more like what Frank calls a 'mercenary—people are only here for the money. But, you can't keep people that way.'

I tested the waters with Frank, and asked him whether he's seen the impact of kindness. Frank was resolute: 'There is a very tangible cost to talent management. You can put a dollar value to replacing talent, recruitment fees, and all the hidden costs of losing a talent. Think about how you keep top talent. The talent you want to keep have a lot of options. Money is not a motivator for them, because these people walk around with two offers in their back pocket. So, if it's not about the money, what's it about? People want to feel they can grow here. That their boss really cares about them—which includes having their boss be tough on them because they want to see you grow.' Frank's story accentuates the importance of understanding what kindness is, what it is not, and redefining the narrative of kind leadership.

Putting Kind Leadership to the Test

Encouraged by a kindness convert, I wanted to test the bounds of this idea with leaders in the financial services industry. The litmus test of kindness is presumably an industry primarily consumed by the hard stuff.

I first discussed this with Caryl Athanasiu, independent board director, Varo Bank and former EVP and Chief Operational Risk Officer of Wells Fargo & Company, of which she was a twenty-eight-year veteran. Caryl shared that her personal experience at Wells Fargo contributed to her belief that leaders who cared about their team members' wellbeing were repaid by having high-performing teams: 'Fear and loathing doesn't—cannot—create anything good.'

Caryl confessed that her journey to kindness was more of a pilgrimage. In her early years, working as a young woman trying to prove herself in finance, she thought she needed to be aggressive to succeed, insensitive to all the collateral damage along the way. She recounts the good fortune of having senior leaders care enough to teach her a life lesson. 'One senior leader took me to dinner one night and told me that when I come into the office in the morning I am already so much in my head that I walk right past people who say good morning to me. That was a wake-up call for me. I started paying attention to the little things, because when you're in a leadership role, little things weigh more heavily. I then saw a key part of my job as making things better for my people. I became the person to say good morning to everyone. I made it my purpose to make every person who worked for me the best person they could be.'

Caryl's code became that of bona fide commitment to the success of every single person on her team. Not just business success, but personal best. Caryl developed a reputation for making everyone around her better. Sometimes, that even meant encouraging her high performers to take up another opportunity elsewhere, a decision that was best for the individual, not Caryl or the organization.

Looking back at her time as a senior leader at Wells Fargo, Caryl wonders what her people would say if they were asked if she was kind. Not because she *wasn't* kind, but because of the intricacies of what kindness is by definition: 'If you ask me if I were *nice*, probably not. Kindness is not telling people what they want to hear. I was all about tough love, I was known for having incredibly high expectations. Some would have called me a ballbuster! But I was genuinely 100 per cent committed to each person on my team and supporting them on their personal path as they evolved.'

Caryl shares an example from 2008, when Wells Fargo acquired Wachovia Corporation. The deal was finalized just before Christmas. She learned that she would inherit members from their risk management group. Caryl got on a plane, flew to Charlotte, and sat in a conference room for two solid days, meeting with every single person—managers, those one-level down, administrative assistants. She committed to each of them that they would not be returning post-holidays to a pink slip, that they could go home and enjoy the time with their families. She also wanted to understand what each person excelled at and what they enjoyed doing, so she could create opportunities for them. She listened and learned from her team—what issues they had, and suggestions for making things better. The outcome? 'They were some of the most amazing team members I've ever had.' Had she not met with each person face to face, Caryl maintains that whatever message would have come from the top would not have cut it. They would have worried for weeks over the holiday. 'But these are human beings! That's just not how I operate.'

I rebutted, 'Of course, high-performing teams are always going to produce better results. But, is it the case that if you have that personal commitment to each person, to lead with kindness, you are going to produce a *better* result?' Without hesitation, Caryl responded: 'Every. Single. Time.' I asked her how she could be so sure. 'Because people who want to be better come to work in those environments, and everybody becomes better over time.'

Caryl recalls one instance when she had to let a senior leader go, in what could only be described as a delicate situation. She again chose to get on plane to deliver the message personally. Not a fly-in fly-out situation, as depicted by travelling corporate downsizer played by George Clooney in the movie *Up in the Air*. Rather, she blocked hours in her schedule before the meeting to make sure she was calm, clear, and would deliver the message the right way. A humane way. She booked out the conference room for a long time afterwards, compassionately explaining to this individual that she would stay until all questions were answered, and would also let this individual be alone, as long as they needed, if they preferred time to themselves. 'It was thinking about how to do it in a respectful way but also in a way that was committed to this individual. The kernel of the kindness bit is the commitment to the other person. Because as soon as the commitment is to the result, or to your own personal gain, or to your own personal status, or whatever that is, the kindness is gone. But if the person you're speaking with really believes your commitment is to *them*, that's when it passes into kindness.'

To add a complementary perspective that crosses culture, I talked to Christine Ip, CEO, Greater China, United Overseas Bank (UOB), based in Hong Kong. Christine was deeply passionate about our conversation on kindness and leadership, given the rarity of female CEOs particularly in Asia, and the many connotations and expectations tied to such a role: 'People think you have to be cruel to be successful in business, and in finance.' What she has found, instead, is that it takes guts to be kind. Being kind and tough means not side-stepping the essential responsibility of a leader to give direct and honest feedback. She says that while the financial industry is generally all about the numbers, UOB believes in a balanced scorecard, where 50 per cent is about finance and a full 50 per cent is made up of values and attributes, including honour, enterprise, unity and commitment. Christine admits that a focus on values and attributes to a tune of 50 per cent is a lot compared to other financial institutions. However, in her view, 'You cannot do well in finance but be a nasty person. But you also cannot be a 'nice' person and not perform. Happy organizations should have a balanced approach.'

For Christine, kindness is not about giving people an easy ride. Pushovers are nice, but ineffective. In fact, she believes leaders still need carrot and stick. But the stick—whether verbal feedback, warnings, even punishments—can only be justified if the leader has done her part to provide clear guidelines through proper dialogue. It also needs to be transparent and fair, so that people know what exactly is expected of them. Otherwise, you end up in Dictator territory. Kindness for leaders comes from understanding that people make mistakes and that they need to take chances on people.

These leaders are unequivocal in their shared perspective that leading with impact is the joint demonstration of kindness and toughness. It's time we reconcile the irreconcilable.

Chapter Insights

- A leader's degree of kindness and toughness produces four personas:
  - o *The Dictator:* Unkind and tough, Dictators lead from fear. Fear of losing control and of exposing insecurities, prompting a tighter grip on authority. Dictators hold unreasonable expectations and spread cultures of stress and distrust.
  - o *The Pushover:* Kind and soft, Pushovers are the nice leaders. Initially a pleasant environment, this quickly falls apart due to the desire to please and lacking the decisiveness needed to take calculated risks in pushing objectives through with clear and explicit direction.
  - o *The Departed:* Unkind and soft, the Departed lead with indifference. Uncaring, permissive, unconcerned with

project goals and broader purpose, and completely uninvolved in their people's lives.

o   *The Impact Driver:* Kind and tough, Impact Drivers lead with humanity. Impact Drivers are committed to elevating their people through collaboration, partnership, and mentorship, which sees the application of toughness to building cultures around their people's wellbeing that creates shared value for stakeholders.

Chapter 4

Kind Leadership Is Genderless

According to the ILO, women currently make up approximately 47 per cent of the global workforce.[1] Despite these figures, women remain underrepresented in managerial positions, and women of color even less so. McKinsey reports that, in 2021, white women represented 20 per cent of the C-suite and women of colour 4 per cent, while white men represented 62 per cent of the C-suite and men of colour 13 per cent. For every 100 men promoted to first-level manager, only 86 women are promoted.[2] What conclusions can we draw from these statistics?

Gender biases in leadership have been present for as long as women have been in the workforce. The BEM Sex Role Inventory ascribes kindness, compassion, tenderness, and warmth as feminine traits, while assertiveness, aggressiveness, dominance, and even a characteristic labeled 'leadership ability' are ascribed as masculine traits. Feminine traits were considered de facto weaknesses and in opposition to conventional masculine leadership practices. Male leaders dismissed kindness as a tool in their leadership inventory, as did female leaders who felt that kindness was detrimental to getting ahead.

You can see how this gets complicated. If you're a woman, or someone who identifies as a woman, in a leadership role, not only are you managing intricate gendered issues already, never mind race, but let's add kindness to the mix as a brain tease. If you're *too* kind, you're not going to project the leadership type that others will respect. Hillary Clinton was pilloried for expressing emotion during an interview, considered incompatible to the job description of a political leader, as seen when *The Atlantic* ran a headline 'Fear of a Female President' in 2016.[3] Women in politics were, and still are to a degree, expected to adopt masculine behavioural traits. Hence Margaret Thatcher was trained to lower the pitch of her voice to suggest communicating with more authority. Clinton altered her pitch and the pundits at the *Washington Post* wrote 'Hillary Clinton talks more like a man than she used to.'[4] Damned if you do, damned if you don't. Women have always faced this double bind. As a result, women in leadership positions feel the need to tread a fine line between being kind while being 'just assertive enough' to be taken seriously.

Despite the press, or maybe to spite the myopia of the press, more women are being elected to political roles. UN Women reported that as of January 1, 2023, thirty-one women were serving as heads of state and/or government in thirty-one countries.[5] Role models such as Jacinda Ardern are shattering the myths of what it means to be a kind leader.

While most management positions were, and still are, held by men, women play a critical role in shaping the evolution of workplace culture. One of the most significant and enduring aspects of their legacy is that they paved the way for the next generations to lead with kindness. Dr Kathleen Pike sees models of leadership based in kindness as an appreciable way of offering new possibilities of what leadership will look like, in terms of greater gender equality based on expanded models of leadership. For women to experience kindness from leaders as a form of empowerment would be long overdue validation for what has been labelled a feminine leadership trait. For men to experience kindness from leaders would open up possibilities for role modelling kind leadership behaviours that become the norms of leadership. Barack Obama, Bob Iger, and Satya Nadella are examples of male leaders demonstrating kindness, openly expressing emotions, and setting positive examples of kind leadership to turn the tide of the patriarchy.

Breaking through a Culture of Alienation

Kindness doesn't pay. Literally. At least, for men. Research shows that kind male leaders are punished in that they earn significantly lower income as compared with disagreeable men.[6] Disagreeable males *do* seem to value earning money over building relationships, and that may explain, in part, these findings. Are disagreeable male leaders more competent? Well, not necessarily, although research suggests that people are more likely to perceive them to be. Behaviours aligned with being disagreeable—expressing anger, being critical, lacking warmth—are considered to reflect status and competence, which affects reward recommendations. Kind male leaders violate conventional gender norms in terms of what is expected of them as male leaders and are being penalized for it. Now, this research was published in 2011. Purely rhetorical question: Would we expect these same findings over a decade later? It's no wonder we don't see many kind (male) leaders out there. Nice guys finish last in terms of bringing home the bacon.

To explore the gendered perspective of kindness and leadership from a male frame of reference, I consulted with Patrick Kennedy, former member of the US House of Representatives, founder of The Kennedy Forum, and the US's leading political voice on mental illness, addiction, and other brain diseases.

Patrick and I discussed the manifestation of kindness at the highest level of leadership, in government, where most seats are held by men. Patrick was immediate in his openness to be vulnerable about the inner work he has done over the years in battling addiction, with the aid of 12 Step support groups.

Patrick spoke of the transformative power of participating in a men's group made up of high-status individuals—generals, admirals, cabinet officers, senators—and contributing to a communal sense of vulnerability. Within the confines of the four walls where they hold their group meetings, there is no such thing as titles or hierarchy. All participants drop their guard and openly disclose their fears and irrationalities with respect to the way they approach their lives. Patrick found real power emanating in shared vulnerability: 'Everyone in the group came away stronger than when they went in. The release is in the connection.' Rather than being perceived as 'weak' for baring their souls, they became superhuman. On the gendered story of kind leadership, Patrick notes the strength of men coming together to chronicle accounts of their mental health. What it does, according to Patrick, is 'break down the alienation in a culture where we're filling whatever your predestined role is in society, either as a female, male, or whatever. Roles that we feel we're stuck playing because we're acculturated.' The key to breaking down alienation in the workplace is, as evidenced by Patrick's men's group, ensuring there is a safe place for people to be vulnerable, and that commands a culture of kindness.

I experienced this recently when I was invited by the American Chamber of Commerce in Hong Kong, in partnership with City Mental Health Alliance Hong Kong, to participate in a Men and Mental Health session, zeroing in on the power of vulnerability. It was a transcendent experience to serve as an ally and engage in dialogue on workplace mental health issues in a culture where men should not share their emotions. That's the impact a leader carries today—relating to each other based not upon societal titles but based on how willing one is to be vulnerable.

The president of the University of British Columbia, Santa Ono, courageously opened up about his own mental health journey, one that saw him spiraling into depression, with attempts on his own life due to feelings of inadequacy and hopelessness growing up. His personal experience allowed him to understand the immense pressures students are under and commit to those who are struggling.[7] A leader who understands, supports, and normalizes mental health by embedding wellbeing into every facet of campus culture is providing assurance to students, faculty, and staff that *we are in this together*.

I held a conversation with Professor Wisdom J. Tettey, VP, University of Toronto and Principal, University of Toronto Scarborough (UTSC), my own alma mater, in which he referenced Santa Ono's candour as an enabler of shattering gendered notions of kindness and leadership. Vulnerability breaks ground for connection and trust. It does a disservice, as a leader, to only air your strengths or to maintain a façade in an attempt to impress: 'Hiding your vulnerabilities may be a sign of weakness. Being tough when it's not necessary to be tough is a sign of weakness. The fact you're fighting very hard to keep that out of the public glare is itself a sign of weakness. It's not a question of male or female. It's gendered in the sense that sometimes women who occupy these roles take on the characteristic of being the stoic strong leader because, if they don't, they're seen as weak. But we're at a point where that approach to leadership can only take you so far. You'll look behind you and see no followers, because people won't want to work for that type of person.'

To break this pattern, requires that we each understand our own role in society as differentiated by a role that is imposed on us by the culture we grow up in. The transformation comes when we appreciate our strength as a community and as a collective, because we're operating on a human level, completely apart from our roles in society. Kindness is a superpower. Kindness is for everyone.

A Leadership Catch-22 for Women

If you've ever felt like a fraud at work—doubting your own abilities, unable to accept your own accomplishments and denying the merit you deserve, you've experienced *imposter syndrome*. Seminal research by Clance and Imes followed high-achieving women who, despite exceptional academic and professional accomplishments, felt they were not as intelligent as others perceived them to be, and were simply successful in fooling those around them.[8]

Beyond *feeling* like a phony, people with imposter syndrome have persistent fears of being exposed as such. Although research suggests that those experiencing imposter syndrome are actually perceived more favourably and are more likeable, not surprisingly imposter syndrome is associated with negative outcomes for the person experiencing it—lower self-esteem, wellbeing, and even self-handicapping.

A contributing factor to imposter syndrome comes from societal conversation that places an unfair burden on female leaders to be 'perfect.'[9] Perfectionism, the BFF of imposter syndrome and a sizeable source of anxiety, in combination with feeling like an underachiever, becomes a toxic cycle that holds women back. Since women report more frequent and extensive experiences with imposter syndrome as compared with men, this results in one of two reactions. One is that women rebel against or defy established feminine traits to prove themselves in the workplace. The other is that women are kinder to others because they empathize and relate to struggles faced themselves.

Sigal Atzmon of Medix Global told me that to succeed as a leader she was expected to be tougher than men. The research says that women are at risk of being disliked for adopting masculine leadership traits (not to mention being called out for lack of authenticity). On the flip side, adopting a feminine leadership style may lead to less respect, but a higher degree of likability. Gender (in)congruence in leaders affects perceptions of favourability.[10] This double-bind puts women in a catch-22 situation. To succeed, women leaders are expected to act more masculine, but women are also more likely to be punished for doing so. What's worse, these are unconscious biases that are ingrained in society. To manage this double-bind, women simultaneously portray masculine and feminine leadership traits. Competence and warmth. Kindness and toughness.

In talking to Christine Ip from UOB, Christine noted that she, in contrast to convention, holds kindness as a leadership capacity that gives her an advantage in a culture where men struggle to expand their leadership capabilities. In a zero-sum game, leaders, particularly men, feel the pressure to be tough, and specifically in Asian cultures, kindness in business is unconventional, even disrespected.

Christine details growing up in Hong Kong, where the school system distributes and rank-orders students' standing. The impact of this labelling takes a toll on young people's self-esteem and confidence. Similar settings, such as sports, rely on a pecking order and pits competitors against each other, promoting a backdrop that is ruthless and win-at-all-costs. Let's be honest—people love watching the drama and conflict unfold on reality TV. People tune in to watch Gordon Ramsay belittle competitors on an expletive-filled cooking show (*full disclosure: guilty pleasure!*). No one ever tuned into a kindness competition.

Christine describes the additional challenge of growing up in Chinese culture—a collectivistic society where people do not openly express themselves, let alone nuanced emotions (beyond 'good or bad') that would unearth your dismay, envy, grief, or amusement. She recounts being instructed not to cry in front of her staff because emotions make you weak. That impacted her. But it also made her stronger. Kinder. Christine pointedly bucks tradition and expresses her emotions without restraint, embodying authentic leadership. Christine considers smiling to be an important part of her daily leadership behaviour. A simple manifestation of kindness. I have observed that Christine is always smiling, unwittingly ascribing it to her positive attitude and sunny disposition. That she categorically zeros in on smiling during a discussion on leadership was riveting. Why smiling, I asked? With an even bigger smile, Christine explains that smiling relaxes her, and it relaxes the people around her, by breaking boundaries and building trust. Christine depicts smiling as a critical behaviour for leaders during virtual meetings: 'Everyone looks so stern on Zoom. But on a video call, you're blocked by one level. When you smile, it breaks barriers and engages people.' A genuine Duchenne smile that reaches the eyes is even detectable behind a mask, so no excuses there. For Christine, such a cardinal yet unadorned act represents an expression of who she is and how she relates to her people. A warm smile connects leaders to each of her people on a human level and communicates approachability and kind intention.

Too often, we encounter grumpy colleagues, unamused bosses, and angry customers. In a world with so much darkness, be a light for your people. Smiling makes you happier. Smiling is contagious. It is difficult not to return a smile unless social awkwardness is your thing. What a wonderful way to energize and uplift your people from down the hall or through a screen. And the clincher. Smiling faces, as compared with neutral or non-smiling expressions, are perceived to be more attractive, sincere, sociable, and competent.[11] Like kindness, smiling is a rudimentary action with big impact.

Perception aside, there is hard evidence that kindness, for women, is effective for their leadership. During the onset of the pandemic, researchers from the University of Liverpool and University of Reading, found that countries led by women experienced fewer Covid-19 cases and deaths as compared to similar countries run by men.[12] Kind leadership, historically classified as feminine leadership, embodying empathy, compassion, and decisiveness, is influential. Lifesaving, even.

Kindness Is Progressive

As the great equalizer, leading with kindness in the future world of work departs from a gendered story. Where do we start? We start with language. Leaders are often unaware, or don't contemplate, how they build norms of acceptance around what is tolerated through discourse. Equating kindness with a 'soft skill' perpetuates stereotypes of feminine and masculine leadership traits. Vernacular associated with perfectionism appropriates impossible standards. This is a heavy burden for women to carry.[13] We need to fix the system that upholds harmful ideals by tossing these terminologies—*imposter syndrome, perfectionism, soft skills*—out the vocabulary window.

This includes gendered language in leader assessments. In a large-scale military dataset of 80,000 performance reviews, researchers discovered that managers tended to use more positive words to describe male leaders—*competent, articulate, confident,* and *dependable,* but more negative words to describe female

leaders—*inept, selfish, frivolous, passive,* and *scattered.* In fact, the
most positive word used to describe male leaders was *analytical,*
whereas for women leaders, it was *compassionate.*[14] Being called
compassionate is hardly a knock, but from a business standpoint,
analytical is work relevant and reflects ability, competency,
strategy, while compassion is constrained to the interpersonal
domain, crucial for building networks and establishing positive
cultures, disconnected from work performance.

Skills required to bulletproof against the ever-changing
world of work are related to interpersonal dexterity—kindness,
empathy, inspiring trust, humility, as well as skills unique to
self-leadership and understanding and managing emotions—
foundational skills that have been framed as feminine traits.[15]
Given this, it would only benefit companies to propel women to
leadership positions. Research shows having even one woman on
a team, does far more for the team than allowing companies to
simply check diversity off the list. These teams outperform all-
male teams working on complex tasks, so long as team members
act on her suggestions.[16] Female CFOs are also 2.6 per cent less
likely to misreport corporate finances than male CFOs.[17] Elevate
women, make their voices heard, and give them the platform
to drive change with kindness. This demands concerted effort
to dismantle systemic power structures in organizations that
thwart the advancement of women, in policy and practice.[18]
Women supporting women. Male allies actively advocating for,
sponsoring, advancing, and promoting women. Allyship is a verb,
not a noun. Allyship is *with,* not *for.* Allyship is decentering away
from *me* and towards *you.* Allyship is not performative, boastful,
or self-interested.[19]

This is an opportunity to rebalance. Rather than ascribing
leadership traits to certain genders, it is more productive to hold
a dialogue on the many ways kindness can be exemplified in

an organization, in line with the values of the company. In this sense, gender becomes irrelevant in that it dilutes our shared responsibility in how we treat each other. Leaders set the tone for holding everyone accountable to the same set of values, rooted in being kind to each other. The kindness may come through differently, simply by way of our unique upbringing and diverse experiences, yet, if we all own our part in kind leadership, we become active contributors in creating, shaping, and driving positive work cultures.

Chapter Insights

- The question that must be asked is whether the growing presence of women in the workplace is advancing a more progressive, *kinder*, form of leadership. When leading with kindness unequivocally emerges as the most effective leadership approach in driving innovation and creating a competitive advantage for organizations, biases must be targeted and eliminated. Gender roles are restrictive and confining for everyone.
- Call to action: Kindness takes all of us. As a progressive leadership approach, re-write the leadership playbook with kindness as the gold standard.

Part II

The Shared Value of Kind Leadership

Chapter 5

The Return on Kindness

The case for kindness offers infinite possibilities for creating impact as a leader. Larry Fink, CEO, Blackrock, admonished in his 2022 open letter to CEOs: 'In today's globally interconnected world, a company must create value for and be valued by its full range of stakeholders in order to deliver long-term value for its shareholders,'[1] echoing Hubert Joly's plea for business to *do good*.

Fink continued: 'The pandemic shone a light on issues like racial equity, childcare, and mental health. These themes are now center stage for CEOs, who must be thoughtful about how they use their voice and connect on social issues important to their employees.' He concluded with a call for leaders to step up.

It starts with kindness as a foundation. Kind leadership that engages people and gives people a sense that there is genuine care about them as human beings, opens opportunities for them to fulfil their potential. This goes beyond the job people are hired to do, beyond financial results and KPIs. It creates a sense of purpose that brings people together to explore meaningful pursuits that contribute to a better society, a better world. It allows people to be themselves, while rallying as a tribe to realize their ambitions.

When leaders model kindness, people adopt kindness as the default course of action. As kindness spreads, it extends beyond the people and the culture. The shared value of kindness is far-reaching, impacting people, company, community, and society. The whole ecosystem working collectively to benefit each other. Companies that create shared value recognize the interdependence of business and community. Kind leaders expand the scope of shared value beyond the interdependence of profit and purpose, to the integration of mental health and wellbeing. It's the genius of the *and*, where economic value and societal value are not in opposition but are co-created through caring for the mental health and wellbeing of the people. When people are happy and healthy, the company thrives. A successful business creates opportunities for the community and contributes to a thriving economy and society. A successful community feeds back into the business in the utilization of its products and services. Communities and society flourish because families are happier and healthier. Shared value is created when companies blend purpose and profits in a cohesive system, making an impact on social progress through mutually reinforcing pursuits.[2] Make no mistake. Kind companies do not sacrifice economic impact. Kind leaders drive impact by creating value for their stakeholders.

Kindness Creates Value

Companies, in minimizing short-term costs to remain viable, are not treating critical issues around mental health and wellbeing as a strategic imperative that can deliver a return on investment over the long term. Yet organizations are under increasing pressure to create socially responsible environments, of which building a healthy work culture is table stakes. Seeing as making improvements in mental health is not easily converted to performance metrics and KPIs, a paradigm shift is needed. From Key Performance Indicators, to Keeping People Inspired.[3] Informed. Integrated. Involved. One that connects mental health to the personal nature of the wellbeing experience, while aligning with broader workplace culture as a component of community, society, and cultural wellbeing.

Universities, as institutions that nurture and grow new generations of leaders, seemed like a sensible juncture for exploring the shared value of kindness. I consulted Professor Tettey, University of Toronto, about how kindness shows up in academic leadership. For Professor Tettey, kindness encapsulates the heart of leadership. Kindness is the guiding premise behind strategic decision-making that drives daily actions to create alignment: 'The idea is to be able to connect with people . . . Looking at colleagues, not just as cogs in a machine, but as individuals, who bring particular assets to the organization. In order for the organization to be well, they have to be well. You must tie the health of the organization to the people.'

We dug into how kindness and leadership intersect with the wellbeing of the people, and what this means for the success of an organization. We shared the view that universities, perhaps more so than other organizations, have a responsibility to be kind and to inculcate kindness, because a university's very purpose is to cultivate new talent that will become leaders of companies. Countries. He emphasizes wraparound support: 'The motivation should not be 'how do we support students so that they can continue to pay tuition.' It's 'how do we support them so they can thrive, and be successful, because if they're successful, we're meeting our social compact with broader society in terms of turning out future leaders who are able to sustain our democracy, our institution, our society, and our economy.' It's important that we take care of those people so they can take care of broader society.'

From this view, there is an integrated 'skin in the game' approach to leadership, kindness, and wellbeing. To meet the organization's social mandate, leaders must be responsible for caring for all, individually and collectively, which dovetails caring for the organization's needs and those in broader society. An organization that is responsive to the needs of its community is the stronger organization over the long term. And this goes for academic or corporate institutions, public or private, for profit or not-for-profit. Professor Tettey puts it this way: 'If you're an excellent institution but don't care about the people who are here, then what is your value?' It is the kindness of leadership that seizes this responsiveness derived from a sense of mutual obligation and commitment to one another's wellbeing.

Intentionally building a diverse workforce helps to reflect the community you serve, which creates value for stakeholders. Kindness is the connective tissue, and drives actions geared towards inclusion and making people feel a part of the whole collective. On intentionality, Professor Tettey noted: 'If that's what drives you, you're going to be challenging existing structures that don't allow that. But, if your motivation is superficial, then you're going to go with existing structures and processes. Because when push comes to shove, you default to that way of doing things. But if, in fact, your true motivation is to embrace and be kind and caring, then if an existing structure or policy is in the way, you will effect change to make way for people to be a part of the organization.'

When companies adopt kindness as the core value, kindness becomes the engine driving the company's strategy. All strategic decision-making is made with kindness as the guiding principle. This touches everything, from strategy to culture to operations, affecting all realms of influence, internal and external.

Social and environmental considerations are approached with the same degree of rigour as any hardcore business initiative, because it is not philanthropy; rather, it is a cardinal responsibility to develop sustainable solutions to complex challenges. Ensuring that the company's environmental footprint not only meets regulatory requirements, but that the company is a leader in this space, reconceiving products and their development as necessary. Impact Drivers follow-through on the principle of kindness with decisions on sustainable and responsible investments.

With kindness as the base, hiring, firing, and promotion processes are situated in kind values, from the front lines to the boardroom in equal measure, because kindness cannot be compromised. It means mental health and wellbeing are integrated holistically and are at the heart of all tactical decisions, not delegated to a department. With wellbeing as the overarching frame, responsible employers move beyond isolated inputs to provide a comprehensive wellness solution concentrated on whole person health, which is data-driven with a long-term orientation.

Kind leaders encourage people to share in the human experience and to be part of the change, by being responsible to the community. Kind cultures give back as a social responsibility, whether through fundraising, donations, sponsorship, volunteering, or supporting additional environmental, social, and governance (ESG) and DEI efforts and turning this into competitive advantage. As a shared value initiative, there is a coordinated effort with government bodies, NGOs, businesses, and community members, each leveraging their strengths and pooling resources, funding, clout, and technical expertise.

From Professor Tettey's perspective: 'If you're a financial organization operating in an underserved community and you're not willing to be inclusive and find ways to serve and uplift that community, then you're operating in an environment that's not conducive to your own work. This is because people will not want to come in and do business with you when you're located in a place that is considered dangerous or unsafe. In a way, you should see yourself as an anchor in that community, helping it to be uplifted.'

This is the collective impact of kindness. There is no trade-off. Value creation expands the pie of revenue and profits that benefits a greater number of shareholders.

Kindness Is a Responsibility

Impact Drivers create thriving workplaces that build value and generate return for stakeholders in a tightknit ecosystem of kindness. I raised this with Dr Gary Gottlieb, professor of psychiatry at Harvard Medical School and former CEO of Partners in Health, a global NGO providing preferential healthcare options for millions of the poorest people in the world. Gary sees kind organizations as ones that are steeped in social justice. Being in healthcare, Gary views the shared mission of healthcare as improving the human condition, of which kindness is one ingredient. Says Gary: 'The question is how well connected is leadership to every person in the organization and to the critical issues of those relationships. The way a leader interacts with her direct reports or the large leadership team is most direct but the policies that she and they as a collective develop and implement across the entire workforce affects each person. This is not limited to wages, working conditions, job expectations, or measures of performance. Leaders must be deeply sensitive to the demands of each job and the life circumstances of their people.' The pronouncement is unmistakeable. There is no other way to view kindness for a leader but as a responsibility.

I broached this topic with a publicly-listed company in Hong Kong, HKBN. When I spoke with NiQ Lai, in his distinctive no-nonsense manner, NiQ stated: 'Leading with kindness is doing the right thing. If you get the people right, the company will do great.' This pragmatic view of kindness leaves no room for ifs, ands, or buts. At HKBN, leaders are guided by a 3-step 'sunshine test' when making decisions. They first envision a public decision-making process. Would the decisions make the team feel proud or ashamed? A second test is whether the decision at hand is one they would advise their children to make, as typically, parents set a higher ethical standard for their children. A final test flips the script: Would they accept the same terms from others? This sunshine test was in line with my discussion with Ron Carucci, Managing Partner at Navalent and author of *To Be Honest*,[4] who asks: 'If a video camera captured your leadership team in action for a full day, how would you feel about that video being used as training for the rest of the organization? Serving on a leadership team should be viewed as a privilege. And along with that privilege comes a responsibility to behave in ways you would be proud to have the rest of the organization emulate.'

If kindness is a leader's responsibility that creates shared value, the sunshine test shows great promise for bringing kindness forward. Leaders on display in a fishbowl or under the glare of a smartphone lens, where someone is always watching and nothing escapes notice, have no excuse to treat those around them poorly.

This new era that blurs boundaries between work and wellbeing is attracting investors who are socially motivated and demanding companies produce value beyond maximizing profits. There is also a snowballing expectation for companies to report on ESG metrics. This global movement towards ESG advocacy, with a capital S, can be seen in statistics indicating that the global corporate wellness market is projected to reach USD 90 billion by 2026.[5] Leaders, with an imperative for kindness, must ensure they are a part of the change, and on the right side of history.

ROK the Boat with Kindness

Leaders often ask, 'What is the ROI for investing in kindness?' What they're really asking is *Can kindness be measured?* and a post-script, *Why be kind if it doesn't bring any returns?*

The business world understands Return on Investment (ROI), a metric used to evaluate the amount of return on a particular investment, relative to the cost of investment. To calculate ROI, the benefit (or return) of an investment is divided by the cost of the investment. The result is expressed as a percentage or a ratio.

Kindness, as a philosophical worldview guiding your interactions with the world, should be measured using the Return on Kindness (ROK), where the benefit to an organization (or return) is divided by the kindness investment. Here's the catch. Unlike its ROI cousin, the ROK is a non-linear equation, because kindness multiplies, results of which are sweeping and multi-layered. Kindness seeps into every aspect of the company, guiding business decisions and affecting interpersonal dealings with every stakeholder, internal and external. Viewed this way, the measurement of kind leadership is not 1:1. In the ROI world, 1+1 = 2. In ROK terms, 1+1 may well exceed 100. Kindness is made up of innumerable unquantifiable, even invisible pieces that, over time, create kind cultures.

The effects of kind leadership, though, are real. There is a visceral demonstration of kindness that you will see as behaviours change and shape the culture. How will you know if kindness is making an impact? You will see it and feel it in the spirit of the culture. Kindness creates a positive electric energy that jump starts organizations. People speak highly of a company that does kindness well and that reverberates through the industry, the community, and broader society.

To be sure, there are quantifiable pieces. All the intangibles of kindness, in combination, lift the bottom line. Just look at the metrics of cousin ROI! There is a clear positive ROI in kind companies with kind cultures and kind leaders.

- Fact: Kind leaders create happy and engaged people
- Fact: Kind leaders earn trust, loyalty, and commitment
- Fact: Kind leaders produce productive teams that move the organization forward

People who feel happy, safe, and empowered in an organization are more innovative, engaged, and committed, and that translates to the amount of time spent solving team and company challenges. It translates to individual, team, and company performance. Incorporating kindness into leadership practices undoubtedly bolsters the stuff of hard metrics.

The tangibles of kindness are evidenced when kind leaders care about their people's mental health and wellbeing. While there is a wide range in potential returns, a Deloitte study reported an average ROI of 5:1. These returns range from the reduction in medical claims to attracting and retaining talent.[6] Companies adopting wellbeing initiatives geared towards prevention and building resilience, experience the largest returns. PwC has reported an average ROI of USD $2.30 such that, every dollar invested into mental health, ranging from preventative measures, to work-related measures such as resilience training, mental health education, and wellbeing checks, translated to a 33 per cent reduction in health-related costs.[7] Similarly, a separate Deloitte study showed that companies that invested in mental health initiatives enjoyed stock appreciation over a six-year period based on the S&P 500 Index. Those with high health and wellness scores experienced a 235 per cent stock appreciation, in comparison with the 159 per cent overall S&P 500 appreciation.[8] Kind leaders build kind companies. Kind companies enjoy huge ROK.

War and Peas

The ROK in Action

During my conversation with the animated Garry Ridge, Chairman and CEO of WD-40 Company, there was no mistaking his fervour for creating a kind culture there. We discussed everything from leadership, to kindness, to culture, topics we are both passionate about, the joy of two kids in a candy store.

I asked him whether leading with kindness can have direct impacts on the bottom line. More specifically, I asked him whether he has *witnessed* the impact of kind leadership on hard business metrics. Garry practically jumped out of his seat: 'You can measure it!' He showed me his algorithm:

Success = The Will of Our People × Strategy

He explained that two components are vitally important for business success. First is strategy—a company needs to have a solid, sound, and viable business strategy. Can't argue with that. Second is the execution of that strategy: 'Let's say we wrote a strategic plan, took it to one of the best business schools anywhere. Ask them to give us a mark out of 100. Let's say we get a score of seventy on that strategy. But the engagement of the people was at a ten, meaning that only ten people out of the 100 in the organization were absolutely dedicated and passionate about getting behind the execution of that strategy.

$$\text{Low Will of the People} \times \text{Good Strategy: } 10 \times 70 = 700$$

'Now, let's say 80 per cent of the people were passionate, dedicated, and excited about executing that strategy. This translates to:

$$\text{High Will of the People} \times \text{Good Strategy: } 80 \times 70 = 5600$$

'What gets you to the 5600 or higher?' Garry shows me another formula, this time, for culture:

$$\text{Culture} = (\text{Values} + \text{Behaviour}) \times \text{Consistency}$$

'Culture is what happens when your company has a clear set of values and behaviours, a culture in which leaders care about people enough to applaud them and reward them for doing good work, and are brave enough to redirect them when they need to be redirected, and do this consistently. Magic. When you build a strong culture, a strong culture builds a high will of the people.'

Well, that's great, Garry, I thought to myself, but does any of this work? Do you have any quantifiable pieces to support the ROK?

WD-40 Company has collected employee engagement data from their people for twenty years in seven different languages. High-level results from 2022 paint a picture of WD-40 Company's culture globally:

- 93 per cent are engaged
- 98 per cent say they love working for WD-40
- 96 per cent know what results are expected of them
- 97 per cent feel their opinions and values are a good fit with company culture
- 97 per cent say they respect their coach (WD-40 doesn't have leaders, only coaches)
- 94 per cent say they are excited about the company's future direction
- 94 per cent say their coach cares about their wellbeing
- 92 per cent say they are given the opportunity to participate in decision making
- 93 per cent say they feel they are a valued member

These numbers, I exclaimed to Garry, were mind-blowing! The scores are so high that WD-40 Company now conducts engagement surveys every other year, so hard it is to move the needle once it comes down to micro, rather than macro, changes. For context, according to Gallup, just 21 per cent of employees globally are engaged at work.[9] The engaged person is easy to spot, and the benefits of having engaged employees are clear. That's why companies distribute annual engagement surveys like clockwork. When people are engaged, they work harder, they get more done. They are enthusiastic and have a sense of ownership over their work. They're less likely to call in sick when they're not (*absenteeism*), less likely to show up when they're *not* well due to the pressure of working for bad bosses (*presenteeism*), and less likely to leave the organization altogether. Engaged people drive performance and innovation, leading to higher customer metrics, higher sales, and increased profitability. Contrast that with the 19 per cent globally who are *actively disengaged*. They're not just unhappy at work—they are miserable, resentful of the misery, and act out by, among other things, withholding their best work. Covert rebellion is seen in *quiet quitting*, or the refusal to do more than what is expected, a direct result of bad bosses.[10] Low engagement costs the global economy USD 7.8 trillion.

Gallup conducted an employee engagement meta-analysis, which statistically combines results of previously conducted independent research to calculate an overall effect, incorporating decades of engagement data of over 100,000 teams and over 2 million employees across 54 industries. They found that employee engagement had a strong impact on employee wellbeing.[11] The evidence is clear: Happy employees = happy workplace = happy financial returns.

The WD-40 Company tribe are living proof. Gary wasn't done. He was thrilled to see the astonishment on my face. 'Let's talk about financial results!' Over the past twenty years, WD-40 Company has taken market cap as a public company from about USD 250 million to nearly 3 billion. 'But we just sell oil in a can! No, we don't, we create positive lasting memories.' Purpose driven, passionate people, guided by their values, create amazing outcomes. WD-40 Company has proven it. Since my conversation with Garry, he announced that he will step down as CEO. As an Impact Driver, it came as no surprise that he was honored with a Lifetime Achievement Award at the 2022 CEO of the Year Awards.

The Intangibles of ROK

Although the ROK can be evidenced in hard ROIs, kindness also brings intangibles. I was inquisitive during my discussion with Melanie Foley, EVP and Chief Administrative Officer, Liberty Mutual Insurance, a Fortune 100 company ranked no. 35 on *Fortune*'s 2021 Best Place to Work in financial services and insurance list, and asked her whether she has seen the impact of kind leadership.

In the last decade, Melanie has observed a dramatic improvement in engagement, productivity, and retention due to the care and compassion of the leadership team. During this period, the company adopted values of 'put people first' and 'act responsibly' and completely leaned into these values. Far beyond writing on the wall, values are exhibited in its influence on decision-making at all levels, starting top down. Melanie stresses: 'If there is a business situation where acting responsibly or putting people first was in conflict with profit, our CEO, David Long, would never make the trade-off in favour of profit.'

It is this culture of inclusion that gave people this feeling of security, the effect of which is an increase in trust in senior leadership, because people feel listened to and feel a sense of belonging. Trust can be measured in some sense. But there are indiscernible elements at play. Referencing Maya Angelou, Melanie says: 'People will remember that you treated them with kindness. They will also remember when you made them feel uninspired, unmotivated, shamed, or insecure. I would much rather be working with or for someone who leads with kindness than leads with a fearful approach.' Me too.

Some time back, I got to know Gordon Watson, CEO, AXA Asia and Africa, which is a part of AXA Group; a worldwide leader in insurance and asset management, with 149,000 employees serving 95 million clients in 50 countries. During one of our conversations, he opened up to me about a specific example of how kindness elicited the desire to win the hearts and minds of a new team:

> I was in my thirties and had been appointed as the CEO of a very large, and formerly bankrupt, life insurance company in Japan. When I walked into my first meeting with the leadership team, I realised most were more than twenty years older than me and did not speak English. The company was also a mess and needed a total transformation. It was all a bit daunting.

Without speaking the same language and having grown up in two completely different cultures, how would I earn their trust? Without their trust, how could I convince them to make transformative changes to fix the company? It was obvious they were shocked that a young *gaijin* had been made the CEO, not an older Japanese man.

I figured I had two options in front of me. I could stay the course and do nothing, or I could try something new. The first is easy. The second is harder, riskier. I took a bit of a gamble. I walked into my second leadership meeting and advised my executive committee that I was going to take them for an offsite for five days to teach them how to draw. Not exactly what they were expecting.

Before we started, I asked them to draw a self-portrait of themselves. They reluctantly agreed. Next, I asked them to copy a famous Picasso drawing, to which they protested that I haven't taught them anything yet. I asked them to turn the Picasso drawing upside down: 'Now draw it.' After an hour, I asked them to turn their drawing back right side up. They were shocked to see how good their drawing was. They were drawing what was there and not what they thought was there. Had it been the correct way up, they would have tried too hard to make it look like a Picasso. Upside down, they just drew what was in front of them. They drew the lines. Similar to business, you need to address the facts as they are and not what you perceive them to be. This was a large learning for them.

On the last day of the workshop, everyone drew their self-portrait, again. They were truly amazing, and everyone was proud of their work. Over the course of those five days, we bonded. We struggled in a difficult task together as a team, and I earned their trust. I put the before and after self-portraits together and displayed them in the lobby of the building so every employee could see the transformation of the leadership team. The impact was huge. The employees were surprised and impressed that we managed such a large and positive change in their leaders in such a short time. While this was only art, it was symbolic that we could work together, transform quickly for the better, and that the leader has strong influence to change and lead. Together, we went on to achieve great things with high employee engagement scores.

Was the transformation successful because of Gordon's kind leadership? Hard to say. I would wager a bet, however, that, had he approached the team from a position of authority and immediately started firing orders, the results would be very different. This is the intangibility of the ROK.

Back to academia. Professor Tettey and I discussed the immeasurable effect of kind leadership. He shares how he wrote to the community recently after they lost a colleague, an action he considers critical: 'In moments of grief, knowing a family member worked for an organization that cared enough about them, having a shared sense of bereavement, connects people. An organization should make people feel that *my organization cares about me*. People ask, *is this place worth sacrificing for*? The way we measure this is in terms of employee satisfaction, a sense of loyalty to the organization. But it comes from this other piece, kindness.' The unfortunate reality in many organizations is that an untimely passing of an employee gets swept under the rug, and hiring their replacement is floated around the next day. The employer you're 'killing' yourself for will not hesitate to replace you. The intangibility of kindness is showing the human side of an otherwise faceless organization. This is the ROK in action. Kindness, while difficult to quantify, has infinite incalculable returns.

The Cost of Being Unkind is 5:1

Let's flip it in reverse for a minute. What do the numbers tell us about the cost of being *un*kind? What's the extent of the damage done by the Dictators? Seminal research published in 2001 by social psychologist Roy Baumeister and colleagues, subsequently cited almost a whopping 10,000x, reveals that, well, *bad* is stronger than *good*.[12] Bad events carry disproportionately greater weight than good events. We know this to be true with traumatic events. But researchers found this to be the case with everyday events we experience as well, such as a brief but unpleasant interaction we had with our boss, or that passive-aggressive remark we heard our colleague make of our work. These negatives tend to stick with us much longer than positive events. There is also neurological evidence to support this fact; our brain reacts more strongly to bad events than good.[13]

Kindness is in the eye of the beholder. The next time you think about saying something to your team that might criticize, find fault, or accuse (*You did this wrong. I told you to do it my way!*), think again. Every word or tone the receiver perceives to be unkind, undoes five kind things you've said previously to them.[14]

It is only natural to fault others when something goes wrong. It is such a common bias, there is a term for this—*fundamental attribution error*—we are quick to attribute other people's mistakes to a flaw in their personality, but when we're in the hot seat, *it wasn't me, it was [insert any number of excuses]*. A co-worker arriving late to the meeting is unprofessional and unreliable, our tardiness is due to traffic.

Instead, practice the 3Rs:

- **Rest:** *Deep breaths—on the count of 'I am a rock star' x3*
- **Reflect:** *Assume positive intent*
- **Reframe:** *Move from negative (unkind) to positive (kind): I notice you took a different approach here. Can you walk me through it?*

The second R in this 3R framework—to reflect inwards—combats a blame culture, according to Alain Li of Richemont Asia Pacific:

'It is easy to say *this person didn't pull their weight*. But I also need to reflect inwards. The first person you should challenge is not the other person, but yourself, as a leader.' Leaders need to ask themselves if sufficient resources were provided, if communication was clear. Continues Alain: 'Being honest with yourself and being the first to step up and say *I could have done this better*, and *collectively, we could have done better* is how I cultivate a culture of kindness.' To be human means that human error is a constant in anything we do. And that's okay.

Management research corroborates this 5:1 ratio.[15] For example, employees from various industries were tracked across two to three weeks. At random points throughout the workday, these employees were asked to report their mood. The researchers found that people tended to go through their workday in relatively neutral, albeit slightly positive, moods. But when a negative event occurred, it impacted their mood 5x more than if a positive event occurred. This principle has also been applied to studying happy vs. unhappy marriages, led by the Gottman Institute. Negative interactions between partners were categorized into behaviours that were critical, defensive, or emotionally dismissive. To undo the damage? Requires new positive interactions, such as showing genuine interest, expressing appreciation, demonstrating empathy, apologizing, and using humour—behaviours stemming from kindness.

If there's a cost of being *un*kind, what about being *too* kind? For leaders, it can be a difficult balancing act. Being perceived as *too* kind as a leader can potentially lead to being taken advantage of. Not only do you land in Pushover territory, but a territory where kindness is taken advantage of, the learning becomes to refrain from kindness. In such a situation, the foundations for kindness are likely shaky. The culture has not been adequately set. There are those who are still free-riding off of the generosity of kind people. Takers who are benefitting from the kindness of their peers. The balance requires shifting from leading from 'nice', to leading with kindness, of which toughness is a key component driving impact.

Given the limitless potential of a ROK, Professor Tettey and I discussed what's needed from leaders to move towards the value creation kindness brings. Leaders need to re-think risk calculations. Currently, the risk calculus is so steeped in terms of financial implications. Risk matrices are tethered to pecuniary outcomes as opposed to things that are relational and supportive of people. But the lack of kindness poses a reputational risk and comes at a cost. Organizations that are not seen as kind or inclusive, particularly in a globalized, multicultural world, carry risks, and even add negative value. A company that is seen as unforgiving, punitive, and unkind is not going to be well-served. Companies need to weigh the downsides of not being kind. If you have a risk register, the leadership team needs to address the following questions:

- What does it mean to be a company that nobody wants to work for?
- What does it mean to be a company that people feel is not supportive of them?
- What does it mean when people are leaving organizations because they don't feel a sense of safety?

The workaround is to lead with kindness. The ROK is guided by the principle that enhancing your people's mental health and wellbeing creates shared value. Care for your people, and your people will care for the company. The boomerang effect of kindness is a healthy, engaged, and productive workforce. And a healthy economic return.

The Kindness Quotient

I'll end this chapter with promising new research on measures of kindness. Signature Consultants, in collaboration with research and data firm Dynata, developed the Humankindex (HKI) to assess companies' adoption and practice of kind leadership on a scale of 1 to 100. The HKI is based on a Kindness Quotient (KQ), indicative of the degree to which a company exemplifies a kind culture and the extent to which employees feel the substantive effects of kind leadership.

The 2022 findings[16] detected that US companies scored an HKI of 60.6 and on average scored 34.1 (out of 100) on the KQ. Companies scoring higher on kind leadership are 5x more likely to be considered innovative by employees. Discouragingly, 34 per cent report that leaders in their company have put profits before people since the pandemic. Demonstrating the desire for kind leadership, six out of ten report preferring a leader that helps them find meaning in their work over receiving a 5 per cent pay increase. There is a clear connection between leading with kindness and creating competitive advantage for organizations.

While Signature Consultants produces a KQ at the company level, Kindness.org, in conjunction with psychologists from Harvard, measures kindness at the individual level. Kindness.org conducts scientific research that measurably helps build a kinder world. Kindbase is a database of approximately 1,000 actions, based on reports of over 16,000 survey respondents who were asked to rate various acts of kindness on how costly or beneficial they are. These acts were progressively more demanding, such as whether, given the opportunity, they would make their colleague a cup of coffee, donate their vacation time to a colleague, or donate a kidney to a colleague. Kindbase takes stock of the costs and benefits of kind acts to produce a KQ score, such that kindness acts can have: low-cost high-benefit; high-cost low-benefit; high-cost high-benefit; or low-cost low-benefit. Costlier acts are considered kinder, as, for example, holding a door open for the person behind you is low-cost low-benefit, while donating a kidney is a high-cost, high-benefit act of kindness. When I spoke with Dr Oliver Scott Curry, Chief Science Officer at Kindness.org, research affiliate at University of Oxford, and research associate at London School of Economics, he elaborated that because kindness comes at some cost to the actor, it is important to identify people's capacity for kindness. To the extent to which the costs of kind acts are reduced, more acts of kindness may result. In its initial research, Dr Curry notes that people's KQ is about 60 per cent to strangers, meaning that people care about strangers about 60 per cent as much as they care about themselves. It is also possible to have a KQ beyond 100 per cent, for example, towards your kids, and no upper limit has yet been identified. As a leader, what is your KQ?

Chapter Insights

- Kindness is a responsibility, the foundation by which companies create positive value for their shareholders, inclusive of people, community, and society.
- The ROK is a non-linear equation with tangible and intangible impact that is sweeping and multi-layered. Kindness brings compound returns on quantifiable and unquantifiable pieces related to mental health, wellbeing, engagement, trust, cohesiveness, collaboration, creativity, innovation, performance, productivity, and thriving communities.
- The cost of being unkind is 5:1. For every unkind behaviour you push on your people, intentionally or not, it will take five positive interactions with them to undo it. And, because bad is stronger than good, it never really feels the same.

Chapter 6

Kindness as the Basis for Corporate Wellness

'An employee suffered from mental health issues. We had a lengthy chat and I told him that he's a person first and an employee second and that he is a valuable person. I let him know he can take as much time as he wanted to get himself right again and to not worry about work. I also had a chat with the entire team, and without revealing his issues spoke generally about mental health and that we're here to support everyone.'

40-year-old Team Lead, healthcare industry

In 2022, Gallup's global emotions report[1] announced record-shattering statistics. The world is more sad, more worried, and more restless than ever. The pandemic has increased anxiety and depression by 25 per cent worldwide. So severe is the experience of work stress and anxiety, that the WHO has been said to describe it as the global health epidemic of the 21st century.[2] Leaders dismissive of these statistics, impatient for a return 'back to normal,' are delusional and grossly mistaken. On the surface, there may be a superficial sense of normalcy, but the stress has persisted, unresolved.

If that doesn't spark a code red for leaders, the financial damage of mental health, depression, and anxiety in workers should, as it is costing the global economy over USD 1 trillion annually in lost productivity.[3] Even more terrifying, the World Economic Forum predicts that the global price tag of poor mental health will rise to USD 16.3 trillion by the year 2030.[4] That's not too far away. These unnerving figures are indicative that current strategies are insufficient in addressing corporate wellness. No matter how you slice it, the data is compelling. People are crying out for help, and saying enough is enough.

In this day and age, companies cannot separate work from the wellbeing of their people. The workforce is demanding leaders who advocate for their wellbeing. US-based results of a 2022 McKinsey study of nurses indicate that a critical factor determining whether people remain with their company is the availability of support (45 per cent) and mental health resources (16 per cent). So indispensable is wellbeing to the health of an organization that 37 per cent of those surveyed even desire employers who monitor for signs of employee distress.[5]

When people feel that their mental health is being tended to at work, as demonstrated in the example above, they are 26 per cent less likely to experience mental health symptoms, to call in sick, and to have their performance negatively affected.[6] Mental health support contributes to job motivation, satisfaction, and positive relationships with supervisors. When companies prioritize people's wellbeing, 89 per cent are more likely to recommend their company as a good place to work.[7]

Wellness, as a broad umbrella term, bridges the health of the whole person, inclusive of mind, body, and spirit. Wellness also converges with the S of ESG, as Social has a human element that, enlarged, makes the organization richer. It also crosses DEI, with research demonstrating that 54 per cent of respondents perceive that mental health is a DEI issue.[8]

The Oneness of Mental Wellness and Illness

Wellness is multi-dimensional. While our physical health tends to receive the most focus, wellness is a delicate tapestry of our mental, spiritual, emotional, and social health. As our comprehension of mental illness and wellness continues to unfold, current understanding of mental wellness is that of a dynamic, internal renewable resource that helps us think, feel, relate, and function. It is an active process requiring our utmost attention, investment, and care.[9] When we are well mentally, we feel like we have purpose and a sense of direction in life. We have energy to accomplish what we want to do. We can cope with life's ups and downs. We can fully contribute to the relationships in our lives, at home, at work, and in the community, which builds resilience that reinforces our mental health. Our mental health usually takes a backseat to our physical health, like a neglected middle child. Yet, there are synergies between our physical and mental health, and when we accentuate one area, the imbalance contributes to a lopsided equilibrium that can eventually diminish our overall health.

Contrast this with mental illness, which can be a diagnosed or undiagnosed medical condition that disrupts our thinking, feeling, mood, ability to relate to others, and even daily functioning. When we are ill mentally, we don't feel like we can cope with the daily demands of life. The intricacies of mental health are such that it is not always apparent when someone is coping with a mental health issue, unlike the obvious symptoms of influenza or a broken bone. Poor mental health has countless symptoms, many of which are invisible, further exacerbating feelings of loneliness and isolation. Depression or anxiety can present as a happy face. Mental health professionals call it *smiling depression*, suffering silently on the inside while powering through the day with a smile planted on your face. And because people 'seem fine,' organizations are less likely or willing to invest if *it ain't broke.*

When we think of mental wellness and illness, we think of extreme ends of a continuum where clinical depression looms on one end and happiness and flourishing resides on the other, an elusive pot of gold we all strive towards. But the messy truth is that, as a deeply personal journey, mental health is constantly fluctuating. The absence of one is not indicative of the presence of the other. Just because someone is not mentally ill does not automatically imply mental wellness. We all go through times when we feel down or anxious. These experiences vary by degree and can change day by day, along with our coping mechanisms. You have likely experienced those days when you are not your usual energetic self, but not terribly down, either—hovering in the 'meh' zone.[10] The 'in between,' reminiscent of *Stranger Things*, although perhaps less (or just as) scary. There is a term for this co-existence of mental illness and wellness. You are *languishing*, my friend.[11]

The symptoms of languishing: Trouble concentrating? Brain fog? Unable to function at full capacity? Or just, feeling stuck? Check. Check. Check. What's depressing (*pun count = 2*), about floating in this languishing state is that people who are most likely to develop depression and anxiety disorders are the ones who are currently in the languishing zone. Great. We're being sucked deeper and deeper into the in-between by the demogorgon. To crawl out of this state of meh-ness, slow and steady wins the race. It may seem impossible, given that we wake up to a steady stream of distressing news—gun violence, hate crimes, a new virus of the day, USD $10 bread. Rather than crawling into a dark hole with a Costco-size bag of Cheetos and wallowing in thoughts of *What's the point* . . . find small things in your day that spark joy. Something as simple as having a few minutes to yourself in the morning enjoying a hot cup of coffee. Connecting with an old friend. Snuggles with your pets. The comfort of a solid routine. Kondo-fy your life in the same manner as you would your closet, because letting go is at times more important than adding. Take a cold hard look at your daily routine. What isn't serving you? Say thank you for your service. Goodbye.

Apart from finding small sparks of joy, is the recognition that mental health is a lifelong journey. It is *pro*active about developing healthy practices that support all facets of wellbeing. That starts with speaking up, speaking out, and voicing what you're going through. Put a name to what you're feeling. Naming it means taming it. The sooner we realize that absolutely everyone is struggling with something, the sooner we can make space for shared experiences. Self-kindness opens us up for kindness towards others. Open expressions and shared mental health experiences validate feelings and normalizes their occurrence. A common vocabulary around mental health creates mutual understanding, connects us to each other, and takes the power away from stigma and mental illness. We climb out of it together. But it is much easier said than done.

We Have to Talk about Mental Health

People are reluctant to discuss mental health, and mental illness in particular. No fewer than eight out of ten people with a mental health condition say shame and stigma prevented them from seeking mental health care.[12] Never mind seeking mental health care, stigma prevents people from even *talking* about mental health in the first place! Awareness of mental health is growing, but people struggling with mental health issues still face discrimination and an uphill battle getting needed help. As a result, many conceal their suffering due to fear of judgment, ostracism, not to mention potential repercussions to career advancement. People are feeling increasingly disenfranchised.

When people show up to work physically, but are mentally, emotionally, or psychologically unable to be at their best, this presenteeism is damaging, and is costing businesses more than absenteeism in lost productivity.[13]

The cost of staying silent is alarming. The mental health of your people and your company's bottom line are linked. What might have started as a 'meh' day, endured in silence, turns into a series of 'meh' days that, over time, intensifies into languishing. Unaddressed, this develops into new or worsened symptoms that approach burnout or depression. Eventually, it manifests in physical symptoms that can no longer be ignored due to its visibility, and only then, are acknowledged. But it's too late. People now need to take sick or disability leave. This adds up pretty quickly. The Centers for Disease Control and Prevention estimate workdays lost due to depression in the US at 200 million per year, at an annual cost of USD 17 to 44 billion.[14] All because wellbeing was not prioritized and care was not taken in creating kind spaces where people feel safe speaking up about their struggles.

I get it. Shifting a company's culture to prioritize the mental health and wellbeing of its people may take some time. Start today. Kind leaders drive impact by being transparent about their own struggles. Hold small group discussions. Fireside chats. Townhalls. Shout it from the rooftops. Opening up allows people to do the same. Give your people a symbolic permission slip to bring mental health to the surface. The stigma of mental health is eliminated through consistent and frequent dialogue. Simply ignoring the issue doesn't make it go away. It is impossible to compartmentalize different facets of wellbeing. Emotions aren't simply checked at the workplace door. It simmers under the surface until it explodes, the cost of which is much greater to everyone involved. If you think you're already being vocal, think again. A recent Deloitte report declared that a meagre 22 per cent of employees believed the leadership team in their companies were transparent about their wellbeing, while 73 per cent of the C-suite insists they are.[15] That one ambiguous conversation that imperceptibly touched on mental health doesn't count.

I consulted with Jeffery Tan of Jardine MINDSET Singapore, about how he championed mental health at the company level: 'When you want to see people in your organization do well in general, there is no distinction between physical and mental health. Champion health generally, rather than trying to separate or distinguish mental health from wellness—it's easier to get people connected to this issue. If we think physical health is important, why would we not treat mental health on the same level? You also need leaders to be willing to talk about it. Everyone is affected by mental health challenges. Being able to talk about it normalizes it.'

I asked Jeffery about the challenges of addressing mental health in countries such as Singapore and Hong Kong, known for their high-stress 'pressure cooker' surroundings: 'If you have a hectic environment, you need to take care of your mental health even more so, just as you would your physical health. We are not built like machines. Even machines need to be treated well or they will go haywire!' There is no magic formula. Everyone is different, and what works for one person may not work for another. One simple metric for gauging whether you've got it right? 'When your people tell you they're comfortable.'

Mental health and wellbeing belong to all of us. Kind leaders foster collective ownership of suffering.[16] For kindness to make an impact, leaders have the responsibility of shattering the stigma of mental health, of creating cultures imbued with safety and trust.

Kindness as the Missing Piece

How is leading with kindness the basis for corporate wellness? In all possible ways. Research across diverse domains has found a robust relationship between kindness and wellbeing. Kindness has been found to:

- increase happiness[17, 18, 19]
- improve positive mood and flourishing[20]
- improve cardiovascular health[21]
- lower blood pressure[22]
- lower depressive symptoms and loneliness[23]
- improve optimism and purpose in life[24]
- prevent disease[25]
- improve stress coping and emotional wellbeing[26]
- reduce social anxiety[27]
- improve wellbeing of the kindness giver and receiver[28]
- increase life satisfaction of the general population[29]
- and the coup de grâce—lower mortality![30, 31]

Imagine that! Kind leaders have the potential of prolonging their people's lives by lowering their experienced stress, which enhances their cardiovascular health.[32] If bad bosses can literally kill you, leading with kindness is the antidote.

One of my favourite pieces of data-backed science demonstrating the effect of kindness was published by Dr Kelli Harding in her book *The Rabbit Effect*. She titled her book after a science lab experiment in the 1970s. Researchers were studying the effects of cholesterol on cardiovascular illness in rabbits that were fed a high-fat diet. The researchers discovered that rabbits in one particular pen that were fed the same high-fat diet as other rabbits did not show any cardiovascular impact. In other words, this group of rabbits remained healthy while the other rabbits developed symptoms that degraded their health. The researchers couldn't figure out why. Genetically, these were the same rabbits! A series of tests were conducted to figure out why this group of rabbits remained healthy. What they came to find instead, was a much simpler explanation. A research assistant had been playing with the rabbits from this pen—singing to them, petting them, and caring for them. Kindness was proving to be the cure for ill health.

I spoke with Dr Harding at length about how this finding transcends beyond rabbits. She explained: 'In the US, we think about health as healthcare, yet so much of health lies outside a clinic. It's in how we're treated in the workplace. When we are kind leaders at work, our people are more likely to show up for us through difficult times. This finding even goes so far as re-defining leadership, as kindness empowers everyone to be a leader, regardless of whether you have the corner office.'

Dr Harding and I discussed the futility of companies offering one-off approaches such as a morning mindfulness session. These are band-aid solutions to a larger structural problem. Nothing against mindfulness sessions, but any approach to wellbeing cannot be superficial or isolated offerings as a means of checking 'wellness' off the list. The wellbeing of your people rests on the development of a comprehensive, holistic, multi-pronged strategy that is built directly into the business and embedded into the culture. On the surface, gym memberships, massage sessions, and a shiny FitBit might seem like attractive perks, but these benefits are restricted to physical health and those who already practice self-care. Those who are suffering from mental ill health or are in a certain life stage that is vulnerable to risk— when illness strikes or upon death of a family member—and need the company to support them, will not find any solace in being shown the way to the gym. The issue is that an unkind workplace culture that's stressing people out will cancel out any beneficial effects of fragmented approaches.

The practice of kindness includes being able to call out a workplace that falls short in caring for people, for not emphasizing and tackling wellbeing on a larger and broader scale. There are leaders who are making this their mission. Caryl Athanasiu, formerly of Wells Fargo & Company, is passionate about addressing the faults of current patchwork solutions to mental health. She and I had a fervent discussion about how, because we are all interconnected, leaders need to shift their worldview to that of whole systems networks. When leaders understand that work and family are inextricably tied, it opens up possibilities for leaders to create healthy contexts at work, which then supports healthy home spheres. It is short-sighted to think only of creating a happy ambience at work, because when—not if—your people have eldercare issues, or a child with an anxiety disorder, but insurance coverage has been stripped down to the point that they can't get care, the whole system breaks down. Your people will collapse from the pressure, and they won't be their best self at work anyway. There is an unaddressed ripple effect of mental illness that spreads beyond the person who is suffering to affect families, friends, support systems, and communities. These effects are seen and felt emotionally, socially, and financially, and put pressure on healthcare systems.

In Caryl's impassioned words, 'Businesses are not doing enough of the right things around mental health and often doing absolutely the wrong ones! Providing Employee Assistance Programs (EAPs) and a list of phone numbers you can call if you're having a mental health issue. No—that doesn't work. Try looking at your damn insurance coverage! You've just harmed so many people who work for you who are going to get off meds they really need because they can't afford the deductible. That is just so stupid.'

We need to go back to the fundamentals. And the fundamentals are the connection between wellbeing and performance. Accounting for good stress, how do you support your people during periods of bad stress? Mental health and wellbeing are not concessions to be made in exchange for company success. Like the pernicious falsehood of ascribing kindness and toughness to mutual exclusivity, wellbeing and performance are complementary. When your people are well, they will flourish. Personally and professionally. Kindness is integral to creating happy workplaces where people do their best work.

One company taking mental health seriously is pharmaceutical company Janssen of Johnson & Johnson, which has, since the 1950s, been leading the charge on being a responsible workplace that increases awareness of mental health, eliminating stigma, and targeting both prevention and treatment. In 2017, Janssen launched the One Mind at Work initiative, a leading mental health non-profit with a global coalition of organizations including Aon, AXA Asia and Africa, Bank of America, and Prudential, committed to transforming how mental health is approached in the workplace. The goal is to deliver a gold standard for mental health and wellbeing globally. As a scientific advisor to One Mind at Work, we meet monthly to shift the trajectory of mental health at work, including supporting their guiding council on various initiatives. One exciting development is the launch of a Mental Health at Work Index in early 2023, in which organizations can benchmark their programs and services.

Chapter Insights

- Our mental health is constantly fluctuating and made up of mental, physical, spiritual, emotional, and social elements. The absence of mental illness is not indicative of the presence of mental wellness.
- Everyone has their own personal journey with their mental health, making it an 'all of us' journey, not an 'I am alone' journey. The more we talk about *our* collective mental health, and check in on each other, the more we move the needle from stigmatized to normalized.

Chapter 7

Kindness and the Mental Health Revolution

In December 2020, during the height of the pandemic, along with Neurum Health, a digital mental wellness platform, we co-created a white paper to make a business case to senior executives that investing in workforce mental health leads to healthy business.[1] Widely distributed to corporate executives including John Swire & Sons, Bloomberg, and Swiss Re, this piece provided a mental health blueprint in guiding internal employee wellbeing strategy, accruing the buy-in from relevant stakeholders and moving the conversation from awareness to commitment and engagement, a big step towards building a sustainable wellbeing strategy. In the blueprint, we discuss the need to shift from reactive approaches to addressing wellbeing through proactive and preventative approaches. Rather than focusing on sickness (a *pathogenic* approach), let's promote wellness (a *salutogenic* approach). As our understanding of health and wellbeing evolves, so too should our solutions, ensuring wellbeing is not one-size-fits-all and resources are not a one-off.

Kindness Starts with 'How are you?'

The social context of work, fast-forwarded by the pandemic which has materially changed how and where work is being done, if nothing else, highlights leaders' responsibility to care for their people. People are overstretched and under-recovered. As a leader, how often do you ask your people 'How are you'? I don't mean a flippant 'How are you?' at the start of a meeting that leaves no room for meaningful responses once the formalized agenda commences. Not check-*ups*, where people get the sense that you're monitoring their output or productivity. I mean, making time for personalized check-*ins*, where people feel seen and heard. Asked with earnestness and intention, 'How are you?' forms a commitment to action. Without support, it is merely an empty string of pleasantries. Garry Ridge explains the potency of this simple question: 'The real servant leader or the coaching leader says, "Bonnie, I noticed you're not achieving your sales target. Are you okay? Is everything okay?"'

On checking in, how much care is put into letting people know they don't always have to respond with the default 'fine' or 'good' because it's okay to have meh days? Alternatively, how often do you, in good faith, try to cheer your people up with platitudes such as 'look on the bright side' or 'don't be sad'? *Toxic positivity*, the belief that one must be sunshine and rainbows at all times, is a thing.[2] Dismissing people of their feelings by telling them to 'cheer up' or 'don't worry, be happy' is about as helpful as telling an anxious person to 'stop worrying' or 'calm down.' Instead try, 'Take your time. I'm with you and I'm listening' or 'It's okay to feel down. How can I support you?' Your people need to know that their feelings are valid, whether they are positive, negative, or just meh, and that they don't have to put on a smiling face to please you.

The same goes for leaders. It does not serve your people to ignore, suppress, or hide your own less-than-happy moments. Research shows that the emotional labour involved in faking emotions you're not really feeling, such as positive emotions that are not truly felt—*surface acting*—is damaging, as this practice contributes to stress, impaired wellbeing and even affects performance.[3,4]

It's time for a mental health revolution, starting with kindness. Impact Drivers, in being responsible employers, support workplace cultures that are mental health forward. 'How are you' is a simple, bare minimum step one, to make kindness visible. Through dialogue, action, and building community, kindness can be scaled.

Leading through Anxiety

The pandemic took the world by storm, rudely flicking what we know and how we operate upside down. Suddenly, leaders were faced with an insurmountable challenge. *How do I take care of my people's mental health?* As if leadership alone wasn't hard enough, leaders, not immune to their own anxieties, were now expected to lead through that anxiety. *How do I comfort and motivate my people when I'm struggling myself?*[5] It should go without saying that it is completely normal to experience anxiety. Even if you aren't a generally anxious person, the pandemic may have created new anxieties about work—job security, turnover, role ambiguity. Colleagues whose anxieties were so contagious you caught it like a common cold. Maybe you're a high-functioning anxious person—not anxious to the point of diagnosis, but constantly worried about something. Your worries have worries. I get anxiety just doing captcha tests. *If I click on this sliver of fire hydrant that appears in the next frame, am I not human?* You find yourself replaying workplace scenarios, ruminating and overanalyzing unproductively. You become preoccupied over whether you made the right impression during a meeting, spoke up too often, or not enough. Just as your cup of self-doubt teeters on the brink of overflowing, the anxiety affects your appetite, mood, and sleep. The ultimate overthinker. Still, you can reasonably manage your work and personal life. Being a high-functioning anxious type, you've developed make-shift coping strategies that have served you well throughout the years. You may be so good at faking it that no one would even believe you if you were to disclose your anxiety.

Anxiety is a response to perceived stress. The thing with anxiety is that it is anticipatory. Forward-looking. FOF: *Fear of Future*. You might wake up in the morning and be plagued by insecurities over the uncertainty of the day or week ahead. *What if I bomb this client meeting? Why did Nina ask to speak to me today? She usually gives me some context ahead of time*. You can see how irrational anxiety can be. Your day unfolds just fine and you worried for nothing. It is in the anticipation, that feeling of dread, where anxiety lives, contributing to insecurity and a lack of confidence. Good ol' imposter syndrome really doesn't help in this regard either.

The reason why self-care *is* important is that we build mental fortitude by taking care of ourselves so that we can take care of our people. The mindset of a leader warrants clarity on anxiety. How you *think* about anxiety affects how you *react* to anxiety. If you perceive anxiety as a hindrance, an overwhelming barrier to personal growth and performance, your behaviours will naturally fall in line with this thinking. You will be quick to abandon or avoid challenging tasks, talking yourself out of new opportunities because of the *other* FOF: *Fear of Failure*. Conversely, perceiving anxiety as something that is there to help you grow, because growth and resilience are built in moments of discomfort, you will be quick to take on challenging tasks when you align your thinking and your behaviours with this mindset.

This is evidence-based. Research demonstrates that athletes who perform better perceive their pre-competition anxiety as facilitative to their performance, as compared with those athletes who perceive pre-competition anxiety in a negative way. They hone in on what can go wrong and talk themselves out of winning. Viewed as a challenge generates a positive mindset towards achieving their personal best.

When leading through anxiety, try mindset reframing. When I taught undergraduate students, I showed them that they could alter perceptions or the way they thought about anxiety. I engaged them in an experiential learning exercise. Unbeknownst to them, there were two different sets of instructions. Half of the class read a statement about the debilitating effects of anxiety, while the other half read the same statement with a few pivotal changes about how anxiety is beneficial (in brackets):

'Research consistently shows that feeling anxious, worried, or nervous is *bad (good)* for you. When your heart is racing, when your hands are sweaty, this is your body *telling you to stop what you are doing (preparing you for action)*. Research shows that anxiety is a signal for you to *back down (rise to the challenge)*. Most importantly, research shows that anxiety is *harmful (helpful)* to your performance.'

All students were then asked to write about a recent time where they experienced anxiety, and to describe that time in detail: what happened, what were they feeling, thinking, and doing. Those who read about 'bad anxiety' ('good anxiety') were asked to write about how that experience of anxiety *hurt (helped)* their performance. Finally, all students answered a few questions indicating their degree of agreement with statements on anxiety, such as 'Being nervous is functional.'

During the final week of class, I showed them the results. Students who were prompted to think of anxiety as a negative experience, who recounted a specific experience when they were anxious, and described how anxiety contributed to poor performance, concluded that anxiety is a negative experience to be avoided at all costs. In contrast, students prompted to think about anxiety as a positive experience, who described an experience where their anxiety facilitated their performance, ended up thinking about anxiety as a positive experience. These different perceptions were statistically significant, meaning, unlikely to be due to chance.

Being aware that perceptions can be changed can have a real impact. While we may not be able to stop our over-anxious brain, we can *brain train*—yep, train the brain to perceive anxiety as a positive. At least, enough so that it doesn't negatively impact you. The applications to organizational contexts are many. When faced with stressful situations, such as job interviews, demanding projects, or difficult clients, a simple but effective tool is reframing the way we perceive our anxiety, as something that can help us, rather than being an experience we run away from. And, because perceptions drive our behavioural response, our assessment of anxiety facilitates how we approach various situations.

One student described the impact this experiential exercise had on her:

> I took this research and applied [it] to my week before and during finals . . . I was able to study better and prepare myself for the exams. [This] was motivating not just for me but for my friends and family [. . .] My networks were really inspired to do the same thing. It truly amazes me [. . .] how anxiety can be turned around to become more successful in any task.

A fascinating feature of anxiety that makes it different to other emotions is that it functions like our personal bodyguard. The evolutionary advantage of anxiety is that of a warning signal when something wasn't right, removing us from dangerous situations. Like a sixth sense, or a gut reaction, anxiety helped us survive. In modern times, anxiety signals to us when something needs to change. It could be a sign we're not passionate about what we're doing. Or maybe we're burning out. Trouble is when this crosses into destructive territory when our anxiety bodyguard works overtime, unreasonably (mis)firing distress signals round the clock.

Anxiety can be an opportunity for growth, for development, for learning. The way our brain functions can help us with this. When we start thinking about a problem, our brains can't help but think about ways to solve it. Seen this way, anxiety elicits actions that reverse engineer our own success. Making a list of the challenges at the root of your anxiety, instigates working through how to address each obstacle. Bonus points for pegging ways to prevent those problems from happening altogether. If anxiety is about anticipating what can go wrong, and not being able to control what you don't know, this strategy helps counteract everything that can go wrong, by working through each plausible scenario.

This strategy works, because it addresses several anxiety traps:[6]

- **Catastrophizing:** Imagining worst-case scenarios and generating storylines that go straight to end-of-the-world logic. *I will be fired if this presentation doesn't go perfectly.*
- **Mind reading:** Thinking you know how situations will unfold, confident in a negative outcome. *I know she doesn't like working for me, because she thinks I'm stupid.*
- **Black and white thinking:** Considering only two possible outcomes, disregarding the fact that the world operates in shades of grey. *I'll either get a promotion or get fired.*
- **Overgeneralizing:** Making broad conclusions based on a single outcome, such as thinking that one bad outcome reflects on your competence overall. *My project didn't go well. I never get things right.*

Targeting these anxiety traps serves as a springboard for action by approaching anxiety from all angles—a cognitive perspective that reframes perceptions of anxiety and a problem-solving perspective that presents a way forward. Hold an honest check-in with yourself to identify your triggers. Any time that trigger materializes, you've trained your brain to react in a way that benefits you rather than defeats you. The trigger could be a specific individual that brings out the worst in you. It could be certain words you've associated with past traumatic experiences. In any case, you've recognized a pattern of behaviour based on past reactions that are not conducive to growth.

Mindsets oriented towards positioning anxiety as an enabler for growth, in combination with strategies that harness the best of anxiety, yield more effective leadership through anxiety. The inner work is no joke, because stress and pressure are antithetical to kindness. In my conversation with Caryl Athanasiu about leading through anxiety, she put it this way: 'Nobody is their best self under stress. Under stress, their evil twin shows up. As a leader, if you create an environment that's a breeding ground for evil twins, that's a problem.'

Kindness is easy when the house is in order and the lights are on. The trouble is the home we are in. The way society has evolved to perpetuate and fuel high levels of stress is incompatible with our ability to handle it. We were not designed to be chronically stressed, and this impedes our capacity for kindness. Neuroscience tells us that when we are constantly operating from a place of stress, our overstimulated nervous system blocks our kindness quotient because we are in sustained threat mode.[7] In the midst of threat, our bodies shift our modus operandi to fight or flight mode. Leading with kindness is not for the weak. When I spoke with Ron Carucci of Navalent, he pulled no punches: 'Of course it's harder to be kind when it's tough—that's why it's called leadership!' Fortunately, there is an answer for what helps leaders to be kind under pressure and to lead through anxiety. Double down on kindness. It is precisely when people are stretched that a leader should be kind, to help them see through all the fog.

I was eager to speak with Dr Kathleen Pike about anxiety, not only because she has been involved with global initiatives around mental health and education, but because of her work leading the Columbia University—WHO Center for Global Mental Health. Says Dr Pike: 'There's a difference between anxiety disorders and anxiety. Experiencing anxiety when the system is healthy can be a beneficial and potentially life-saving experience. It's our body and brain telling us we need to be alert. Anxiety is an important, constructive experience when it's in a context where we can respond appropriately before it overwhelms us. That cultural context depends on trust, and a culture where people engage with kindness.'

The challenge for leaders is two-fold. First, leaders must intentionally make kindness their default, especially during times of stress and anxiety, to subdue or overpower their evil twin. The real test of kindness for leaders is whether, at the hardest of moments, leaders can engage with kindness. Second, leaders must approach this from a broader, cultural level. Workplaces that willfully create stress to produce results are actively harming their people. Workplaces that unintentionally create stress are also harming their people. In acknowledging that stress and anxiety cannot completely be eliminated from this domain, the critical issue for leaders is how to ensure that people are recovering in a positive and resilient way. It takes intention. The leader who commits the means to enhance the health of their people demonstrates a responsibility for kindness.

The reality is that leaders don't receive training for this. Mental health is not a topic we cover in all our years of school, and certainly does not feature in business school. Students graduate elementary school with the proficiency to play a plastic recorder, graduate high school with basic knowledge of trigonometry. MBA students learn macroeconomics and those in Executive

MBA programs learn business strategy for managing whole enterprises, but nowhere does mental health and wellbeing feature in education. Upon entry to the workplace, wellbeing is relegated to an individual's problem, entirely independent of the corporation. This is a costly mistake, if the USD 1 trillion figure from the WHO is any indication. Leadership is about the people, and learning how to effectively care for the wellbeing of our people and how to properly build wellbeing into corporate strategy, should figure prominently in the education system.

My research on corporate wellness started with genuine intrigue about people's work lives—their motivation behind pursuing a certain line of work, their day-to-day work experience, the ambitions they had for themselves, and the impact they wanted to make. This was driven by my upbringing as a first-generation Chinese-Canadian, born and raised in Toronto, Canada. Being the only Chinese family in an all-White neighbourhood readily contributed to being an observer of people and the intricacies of social dynamics.

I took up a bachelor's degree, followed by a master's degree, in social and personality psychology, so innately curious I was about the complexity of human nature and *why people do what they do*. My dissertation examined how people gain status in social groups. Studying dormitories as the social context, along with my advisor, Dr Marc Fournier from the University of Toronto, we found that those who earned status were the ones who *made others feel good*. This perspective, that one can *get ahead by getting along*, ran counter to the predominant view at the time, which favoured dominance as the path to leadership. A precipitation for the study of kindness.

I continued my graduate studies at the doctoral level. Over the years, my conversations with people about their work inevitably touched on their anxiety at work, and I would receive half-joking offers to be a case study for my research, so ubiquitous was the experience, even before the pandemic. The prevailing view of anxiety in the literature is dark: anxiety undermines performance, lowers negotiation ability and outcomes, increases counterproductive and even unethical work behaviours. Didn't look too promising. As an organizational psychologist, should I be advising companies to screen out anxious people? I didn't accept that. Intuitively, we know that anxiety is essential at times; it lights a fire under our butts, motivating us to meet deadlines. Anecdotally, I had met many anxious people who were exceptional in their respective fields. We all have. We see this in public spheres, and recently, there has been a shift, with those at the top of their game speaking out about mental health. Lady Gaga has been transparent about her lifelong mental health struggles. In 2018, NBA basketball players Demar Derozen and Kevin Love divulged their experience with anxiety, a taboo subject in the world of professional sports. Michael Phelps, Olympic swimmer, announced his decision to take charge of his mental health battle, something he now works on daily. He describes in a Healthline article: 'Throughout my career, I had a team of people around me that were paying attention to my physical health . . . But mentally that wasn't the case.'[8] It's still a contentious issue. Naomi Osaka, one of the world's foremost professional tennis players, faced outrage when she bypassed the media trail at the French Open due to her anxiety. A headline subsequently proclaimed: 'The backlash against Naomi Osaka proves many people don't care about mental health.'[9]

This tension between the dark side of anxiety and the potential for a bright side, guided my decision to devote my doctoral research to advancing a conceptual framework on how workplace anxiety can undermine *and* enhance work performance. The genius of the *and*. Along with my PhD advisor, Professor Julie McCarthy, from the Rotman School of Management, University of Toronto, we mapped out how workplace anxiety debilitates job performance, through distraction and emotional exhaustion (a component of burnout). We also advanced how workplace anxiety can facilitate job performance. When we feel anxious, the way we self-regulate, matters. Self-regulation really boils down to self-management: how we regulate our thoughts (*how we think about anxiety*); our emotions (*how we manage our anxiety*); and our behaviours (*how we respond to anxiety*). Rather than withdrawing from work in an attempt to stop the anxiety, harnessing its energy to engage with our work, through setting clear and reasonable goals, making purposeful adjustments, and monitoring goal progress, enhances performance.

For leaders, a higher capacity for self-regulation counteracts toxicity, making this an important leadership skill.[10] There are factors that can help. Motivation, for one thing. Ability, for another. And emotional intelligence, comprising emotional awareness—being adept at managing and using your emotions, and empathy. That's the connection to kindness.

Because my research looks at the 'bright side' of anxiety at work, particularly how to harness its benefits, I often get questions about (and even misquoted on) whether the implication is for companies and leaders to promote or encourage anxiety at work. That's click bait. This research in no way condones a hall pass for making people more anxious—that's Dictator territory. It should also not conflate work anxiety within a normal range of functioning with clinically diagnosed anxiety disorders, which compels medical or therapeutic intervention.

Burning Up and Burning Out

A severe byproduct of the bad boss epidemic, and a stressful work culture, is burnout. Burnout is chronic. It doesn't just—*poof*—decide to show up one day, but is the result of an extended period—weeks, months, even years—of stress, anxiety, and overall poor mental health and wellbeing. Which means, the time to address burnout isn't at the point in which it appears, but way back, when burnout was *developing*.

Christina Maslach's seminal research revealed three components of burnout:

- **Emotional exhaustion:** Feeling a loss of energy, fatigue, and overall depletion
- **Depersonalization:** Feeling detached, withdrawn, and cynical towards work
- **Reduced professional efficacy:** Lower productivity[11]

In 2019, the WHO officially recognized burnout in the International Classification of Diseases (ICD-11). The WHO was careful to clarify that it was not categorizing burnout as a disease or medical condition, but was recognizing burnout as a workplace syndrome resulting from *chronic workplace stress that has not been successfully managed.*[12]

Recent research demonstrates that self-directed kindness can mitigate the exhaustion component of burnout, as it promotes feelings of self-control, while other-directed kindness helps with the depersonalization component due to a sense of belonging gained by helping others, and both self-directed and other-directed kindness helps with the inefficacy component of burnout as it increases self-esteem.[13] This suggests that kindness acts as a form of self-care, feasible even for targeting burnout.

Decades of research have pinpointed the external work environment as the largest culprit of burnout. The main sources of burnout have been identified to be unfair treatment, unmanageable workloads, unreasonable timelines, lack of clarity, and a lack of support and communication from management.[14] The stuff of toxic bosses and toxic workplaces, where people don't feel valued or safe. Those who experience toxic behaviour at work are 8x more likely to experience burnout.[15]

Burnout is a workplace issue, not a people issue. And when a flower doesn't bloom, you fix the environment in which it grows, not the flower. Not to say that self-care isn't important, but sorry (not sorry) to say that a single yoga session is not going to reverse the effects of a toxic workplace. In offering piecemeal wellbeing offerings geared towards self-care, organizations may erroneously send the message that employees must deal with their mental health on their own, undermining organizational efforts to provide total solutions.[16] The solution to burnout is an integrated, systems-level solution, not a self-help regime. Workplaces that circumvent burnout provide:

- a sense of purpose
- a manageable workload
- a safe and open space to discuss mental health at work
- an empathetic manager
- a strong sense of connection to family and friends[17]

The common denominator? Kind workplaces. Kind workplaces are all about responsible growth, the value proposition of which is to ensure people are mentally well so that they can move the company forward. Responsible growth is about success of the company, but doing so without sacrificing the people. It's not a toss-up.

Kind companies that are responsible in their growth are companies that are revisiting their business models to come from an employee-centric, people-forward, business lens, creating value by embedding wellbeing directly into business strategy and building competitive advantage that is sustainable in the long-term.

Resilience Is a Team Sport

A discussion on wellbeing goes hand in hand with resilience. For good reason. Resilience is the ability to bounce back, or rebound, from setback. Resilience fosters effective coping with stress and burnout. Resilience has become an essential leadership skill for leaders who are expected to lead through their own anxiety.

Resilience isn't just about bouncing back. Bouncing back implies recovery back to pre-stressor levels. Resilience is about growth. Resilience captures the capacity to surpass previous levels, *because of* what you went through. This is referred to as 'failing up,' in which people who endure traumatic events grow due to the experience.[18] Resilient people enjoy higher work engagement, satisfaction at work, and overall wellbeing.

Resilience, interestingly, starts with stress. Because it is squarely during times of adversity and change that growth happens. Positive psychology research outlines a study where participants were asked to write about three life experiences in which they experienced the most growth. Ninety per cent of the responses referenced stressful life experiences with substantial change.[19] ADP's *Global Workplace Study 2020* surveyed 25,000 working adults in twenty-five countries on the topic of resilience and found that those who faced considerable change in their work due to the pandemic, such as changes to work structure or layoffs, were 13x more likely to be resilient, as compared with those who did not face change, or who only experienced a single change.[20]

Since resilience is about growth, it is not set in stone. It is a skill that can be strengthened over time, and when crisis hits, the resilience muscle automatically flexes. It's how we face stressful life experiences—how we respond—that lays the foundation for resilience. Uncontrollable as life may be, how we react is within our control.

Leaders, with the best of intentions, sometimes try to shield their people from challenges. But the research is suggestive of not sugarcoating or downplaying the reality of a situation to protect people. By not addressing the reality of the situation, employees are left to their own devices coming up with their own version of reality, which spirals into worst case scenarios, where fear spreads and rumors abound. Kind leaders build resilience through being direct and honest about what is happening, while opening the channels of communication and encouraging courageous conversations led with compassion and understanding.

Building resilience feels like a solitary activity.[21] The difference between successful and unsuccessful people has been said to come down to resilience as the secret ingredient. Successful leaders love sharing stories of past failures to play up their awe-inspiring voyage to 'making it.' Co-founder and former executive chairman of Alibaba Group Jack Ma boasts of having been rejected from a long list of jobs, including at KFC. Spanx CEO Sara Blakely recounts hearing 'no' at least a thousand times. These stories all share a plot centered on resilience, the attribute of persistent individuals who rose above through sheer determination and grit.

But resilience is actually a team sport. Resilience connects an army of people who support you, whom you support in turn. As a social species, our individual health and wellbeing are tied to others. Your tribe of people offers different resources you can tap into as needs arise, including empathy, vision, perspective, purpose, and humour. Within your support network, there are people you naturally gravitate towards when you need to vent about work, knowing they got you. There are others you call on to share your successes, knowing they will celebrate your wins.

You might approach others to share ideas, knowing they will offer different perspectives and help you sort through your jumbled thoughts.[22]

Kind leaders help their people build a strong community and are active contributors of this community, offering varied resources to their people. Kind leaders frame adversity as belonging to the collective.[23] Even if a few members are experiencing distress or struggling in some form, giving the problem to the whole team strengthens connections and a sense of togetherness as each member shoulders a piece of the burden and work together to climb out of adversity. The result is a more resilient team and a stronger identity as a collective unit.

This point was reiterated by Dr Kelli Harding as she defines kindness from a public health lens as being inherently social: 'In medicine, the largest determinant of health is one's social world and every day social interactions from all our ecosystems, work, home, and beyond. When we look at health outcomes, the positive was always around kindness. Kindness is the glue that holds us together. From a biological standpoint, when we feel valued and supported by people at work we are more creative and better problem solvers.'

A highly integrated network needs to be deliberately and consistently developed. Resilient teams prosper during good times and are strong during hard times. The test of a resilient team is whether its members genuinely care for each other and are deeply committed to each other's success beyond their own.[24] Resilience, like in sports, can't be done alone, even if you're a star. Research on highly interdependent sports, such as basketball and soccer (*forgive my Canadian-ness*), has found that NBA and Premier League teams with more star players were associated with worse team performance (win-loss record). This 'too-much-talent' effect is due to star players competing for the spotlight within the team rather than working jointly and uniting against other teams.[25]

The caveat is that resilience alone is not enough to compensate for a toxic boss or a toxic workplace.[26] Resilience is an important component, a critical skill, but it is only one piece of an elaborate puzzle. It would be foolish for leaders to place the burden of responsibility on employees, citing growth and adaptability as just cause for a toxic culture. No. Burnout is not a personal issue. Bottom-up strategies cannot compensate for a toxic workplace. The onus falls squarely on leaders to make meaningful systems-level changes to re-design the workplace towards kindness.

Kindness and the Mental Health Revolution in Action

'Within the last 18 months I suffered some severe workplace anxiety related to a redefinition of my existing role which saw me taking on much more responsibility at the senior leadership level of the organization . . . My line manager spoke to me about taking advantage of some workplace mental health services that are on offer, and spoke candidly with me . . . we agreed to lessen some of my responsibilities for a few months while I spoke with the mental health counsellors. My manager was great about checking in with me over the coming months about my progress without making me feel awkward about anything. Gradually I shifted into my expected role fully and I am now in a better place mentally.'

44-year-old Engineer, technology industry

Establishing cultures of kindness is a reflection of caring about people's mental health and wellbeing. When leaders operate from kindness, the care for their people will be brought forward by a commitment to investing in the wellbeing of the people.

Alain Li from Richemont Asia Pacific describes a program called *We Care*, where everyone in the company, along with their family members, has direct access to a counselor so they can speak to a professional as needed. Alain sees it as the responsibility of leaders to help their people be happier in their own lives, because this impacts their work life.

WD-40 Company has built a culture of corporate wellness. Garry Ridge defines a program called the *Fortress of Health* that identifies and makes available different resources that leaders in the company are frankly not skilled at, because 'there's only so much free pizza that can make people happy.' Beyond that, it again goes back to square one. When we touched on DEI, Garry shared: 'DEI—there has to be another letter added to that, which is 'B' for belonging. At WD-40 Company, we believe that belonging is the psychological feeling of acceptance, connectedness, security, support, inclusion, and identity. If you have all those aspects, people feel like they belong. One of the greatest needs we have as human beings is the need to belong, need to be loved, need to be shown empathy, and need to be shown gratitude. In a business environment, you can do that.'

Psychological safety,[27] a term developed by Harvard Business School professor Amy Edmondson, refers to the *absence of interpersonal fear*. It is the belief that you will not be humiliated or embarrassed for speaking up with ideas, questions, concerns, or mistakes. It is the feeling that you can bring your full authentic self to work. To do this, Garry conjoins DEI-B with their company's core value, which is creating positive lasting memories. 'We don't create positive lasting memories if people don't feel like they belong. Why do people leave companies? Because they don't feel like they belong. Why don't they feel like they belong? Because people haven't been warm to them, haven't treated them with dignity.'

And, since WD-40 Company has been doing this for well over twenty years, the company didn't need a pandemic to teach them to be compassionate to their people. They've built a strong culture that protects their people and cultivates resilience in the face of drastic change, uncertainty, and turmoil. This culture of belonging at WD-40 Company is why the company has 93 per cent employee engagement, and why it has a compounded annual growth rate of total shareholder return of 15 per cent, and why it has a 96 per cent retention rate. People at WD-40 Company aren't participating in the Great Escape because they are treated with respect and dignity.

We have data linking kindness and wellbeing. Where kindness is not practiced, we have data linking bad bosses to illness and even death. Mental health covers such a wide array of illnesses that kindness cannot cure, and indeed the proviso is that kindness alone is not a cure. But I have also never seen a single leadership case where kindness didn't help.

Leading with kindness drives impact by revolutionizing corporate wellness, incorporating mental health and wellbeing as a linchpin of business strategy that goes beyond lip-service. When it comes to kindness and its manifestations in the workplace, there is an intersection around mind, body, and health. We create opportunities for our people to forge social connections that benefit their health and wellbeing, including supporting their initiative to achieve their full potential, which pays dividends for the company.

Chapter Insights

- We all, at times, experience anxiety at work. Within the normal range of anxiety, reframing perceptions of anxiety matters. Self-regulation, matters. How we build resilience, matters. Resilience is a collective effort that builds a cohesive community for people to lean on and draw strength from during anxious times.

- Toxic bosses and a stressful workplace are a recipe for burnout. While individual employees suffer the effects of burnout, the solution to burnout is company driven. Kind companies with responsible leaders prevent burnout through sustainable, people-forward cultures that support mental health and wellbeing.

Part III

The Leader's Journey to Kindness

Chapter 8

Kindness Is an Inside Job

With the foundation for kindness laid (Part I and II), leaders can now begin their journey towards kind leadership by setting an intention for kindness and committing to their own behavioural change. While kindness is the active ingredient that can transform the culture of an organization, leading with kindness starts with you. Piece of cake. Except for this: 'The hardest person you will ever have to lead is yourself,' maintains Bill George, Harvard Business School professor. So difficult is this task that he wrote a book on the topic, *Discover Your True North*.[1] The relationship you have with yourself is the most important. Delicate. Confusing. You can walk away from anyone else if they've annoyed or upset you. You don't have this luxury with yourself. You must accept every flaw, forgive every slip-up. At the end of the day, you have to look yourself in the mirror and be at peace with the decisions you make as a leader.

Which is why being a leader, even a kind one, can be lonely. You are no longer included in office talk. You become the outlier, the *subject* of office gossip. People don't speak freely in the group chat anymore. You live 24/7 with the presumption (and the anxiety that goes with it) that every decision you make will be challenged. So, how can you square leadership with kindness, which sets the expectation that a 'nice boss' will never step on anyone's toes, call anybody out, or make unpopular decisions that upset the team?

Awareness Is the Seed of Kindness

Self-awareness is an essential, yet underrated skill leaders need to master.[2] As mentioned in Chapter 1, US companies spend USD 166 billion annually on leadership training. This figure grows to USD 366 billion when accounting for global leadership development.[3] LinkedIn puts it more bluntly: *+$50 Billion Wasted Annually on Leadership Development.*[4] Despite this enormous investment, executives still identify 'leadership' among their Top 5 business challenges,[5] with 'building self-awareness' included top of list. Although leaders may perceive themselves to be self-aware, research estimates that only 10 to 15 per cent of leaders actually make the cut, for reasons that correspond with the lack of kindness in the workplace.[6] Seniority is often accompanied by overconfidence, ego, and self-absorption. Funny how self-awareness is lacking in leaders, considering all the focus on *me, myself, and I.* The small pool of self-aware leaders are those who have done the inner work to make space for kindness.

Self-awareness is the ability to assess whether your thoughts, feelings, and actions are in line with your internal standards and values. It entails answering questions surrounding *How do I want to be perceived as a leader? What do I stand for? Why should anyone be led by me?*[7] These questions are about self-identity. Having clarity and conviction around who you are as a person, as a leader, what values define you, and how that influences the way you help your people succeed, are markers of self-awareness.

Let's frame this discussion on self-awareness in terms of the Kindness Matrix. Recall that leading with impact lives at the intersection of kind and tough behaviours. The Dictator, in prioritizing task, not people, is the selfish and inflexible leader who leads from ego. Somewhere along the way, Dictators have missed the mark on self-awareness. Not only are they *not* self-aware, they don't seem to care. The Departed, as the hands-off leader that disregards the people and the work, have similarly skipped the self-awareness lesson. Their lack of care and concern indicates that they don't consider consequences of their actions on their people. Then there's the Pushover. Kind and soft leaders who aim to please. Could be a breath of fresh air for someone who was ruled by a Dictator, giving people hope. This is indicative that the Pushover has some degree of self-awareness. At least they try hard to relate to people. But something's missing. A blind spot in their awareness mirror. Worrying too much about what people think denotes a public self-awareness that is concerned with image. These externalities are superficial and result in a lack of conviction behind tough decisions grounded in doing what's right, regardless of what people think. The Impact Driver is uninterested in being the 'nice' or 'fun' boss that aims to please. Their human-centred leadership approach prioritizes their people, while creating shared value, through kindness, to multiple stakeholders, which often requires tough decisions. In terms of self-awareness, these are the 10 to 15 per cent of leaders who are all about self-improvement.

If leaders don't know who they are, they cannot reasonably expect anyone to follow them. That's the gift of self-awareness. There is a certain integrity embedded in the transparency of a self-awareness process, a structural connectivity between your personhood, your spirituality, regardless of your religion or beliefs, and your community—the people around you—that gives license for self-acceptance.

The Problem with Introspection

Self-awareness, as a reflective process, is linked to your inner voice. An inner monologue that, like a fourth wall, narrates your life at the extreme, or plays out (fictitious) scenarios and conversations in your head.[8] At times, self-talk keeps you up at night. I always assumed this was a natural part of life, so was baffled to discover that some people don't have an inner voice.[9,10] *You mean to tell me not everyone talks to themselves?* Right . . . me neither.

Some people are naturally self-reflective. And, while it would seem that introspection goes hand in hand with self-awareness, introspection doesn't always reinforce self-awareness. The problem with introspection is that we tend to ask ourselves *why* questions.[11] *Why did I respond that way at the meeting? Why was Debbie so opposed to my great idea?* Asking *why* questions, while great for entertainment value, do little by way of giving us access to objective truth. We end up fabricating stories, and back stories to support those stories, and convincing ourselves of their truth. Asking *why* can also contribute to a downward spiral if the outcome is negative. We end up ruminating about *why* it seems like Jeff is avoiding me lately, feeding the imposter monster and giving it stronger legs to propel our insecurities and make us (even) more anxious. Instead of asking why questions, shift to asking *what* questions. *What* questions encourage the search for unbiased truth-seeking and move us towards taking proactive actions. Instead of asking *Why am I anxious all the time?*, asking *What are the conditions that are making me anxious?* propels solutions-oriented problem-solving.

Leaders' Self-Awareness in Action

Many of my conversations with leaders about kindness landed on this theme of self-awareness. Setting along this path to self-awareness is a conscious commitment leaders make to themselves and to their people. A higher-order purpose to *be* better and *do* better. All in service of our people.

In my conversations with Gordon Watson of AXA Asia and Africa, he stressed that self-awareness precipitates authenticity: 'Bring your authentic self—who you really are—to work. If you're not yourself, it's hard to be effective during stretch times. When the sun is shining and you can't be yourself, how can you be your authentic self when you're stressed?' Pierre Battah, author of *Humanity at Work*, underscores the value of self-awareness during times that challenge leadership. Leaders under pressure will revert to their default leadership style. If that default falls into the Dictator category, people will experience that version of you (your evil twin, as Caryl Athanasiu puts it). Pierre offered this insight: 'The higher-order thinking around leadership is to be able to look in your drawer and recognize, okay, I have four approaches . . . Let me reflect on which is most appropriate here. Will it serve the situation here? Under the gun, I'm going to revert, because reverting is always quicker. So, the recognition that it's happening is important. Learning your triggers. To know when my defaults are serving me, and when they're not serving me. And at least consider that there may be other options.' The fix lies in a strong sense of self and discerning whether your actions are serving you or serving your people.

Self-awareness also affixes leaders to workplace mental health and wellbeing. My conversation with Patrick Kennedy was salient, as Patrick spent his 16-year career representing Rhode Island in Congress, fighting a national battle to end medical and societal discrimination against mental illness, addiction, and other brain diseases. Patrick sponsored the Mental Health Parity and Addiction Equity Act—the Federal Parity Law, which was passed with bi-partisan support and signed into law by President George W. Bush on October 3, 2008. This law provides millions of Americans who were previously denied care with access to mental health and addiction treatment. Patrick has been courageous in openly voicing and sharing his own health challenges. On self-awareness and mental health and wellbeing, he underlined: 'Stress is the asbestos of our mental wellbeing that corrodes and lays bare other pathologies that may not ever arise but in a stressful situation manifests in our lives and may take us down. To be a good leader, you really have to understand your own self. It's a sense of understanding that comes from the wisdom of the group. So you have to be plugged into your tribe.'

This begins with self-awareness. At Liberty Mutual Insurance, practicing self-focus is a guidepost for delivering kindness. Says Francis Hyatt, EVP, Chief Sustainability Officer for Liberty Mutual Insurance: 'We are raised in a world that tends to think in the binary, but it doesn't always have to be black and white. I can be angry and recognize the need to be respectful and kind. We need to look at and acknowledge multiple possible solutions. We also need to teach people how to notice their interpersonal content. The content is the work we do. What is my own baggage that I'm bringing that is influencing how I'm approaching this? Being mindful of how I show up. Being mindful of how we engage with others.'

Dawn Frazier-Bohnert, from Liberty Mutual Insurance, noted that leading with kindness starts with a profound understanding of yourself as a leader. This goes as far back as your roots—where you came from, how that contributed to your development as an individual and as a human being, and what you were taught from past generations and the community around you. This insight allows people to deal with past traumas and acknowledge any unconscious biases that may have stunted their growth as an accepting and empathetic leader. Dawn reflects: 'If people aren't kind, are they mean? Maybe not—maybe they just haven't developed the ability to be vulnerable. They're protecting themselves, which makes it hard for them to extend themselves to kindness. Maybe they were hurt or bruised early on.'

This was resonant in my conversation with Ron Carucci: 'If you're in a culture that is cutthroat, secretive, and rivalrous, the stress of sustaining your own values, your own leadership, may be too painful for you. Some people have lots of trauma that has created a shield of armour around their heart.' It all comes down to what's happening inside, in our inner world. Self-awareness is the inner homework leaders need to do that creates space for kindness.

What do leaders need to do to aspire to become an Impact Driver? Through reflection and growing self-awareness, Dictators need to give up authority and control, and acknowledge the greatness of a team. The Departed needs to contemplate on how they arrived at a place where disinterest was the go-to. At what point did the fire go out? The reflective awareness for the Pushover surrounds the source of people pleasing. A values refresh brings consistency to decision-making, as it establishes guidelines for their actions, based on the values they commit to. This soul searching can be deeply uncomfortable, but richly rewarding.

Self-awareness is the basis for DEI. To value, cherish, and celebrate each individual's uniqueness and appreciate how their disparate experiences and outlook enables a diversified approach to solving compound challenges faced by the organization. Looking inward using an unfiltered lens is the first layer of self-awareness, the self-reflective process. Reflecting inward with kindness and compassion for our past experiences promotes understanding of how our behaviours affect others and shapes the world around us. This ushers in the second layer, self-acceptance, of which can be an intensely therapeutic process that avails leaders to inclusivity, empathy, and kindness towards self and others. Sure enough, whenever people ask Dawn where to start with DEI, Dawn tells them to start within: 'Not in a blame or shame way, but in a gentle and caring way. With introspection.'

For Alain Li, self-awareness empowered him to transcend stereotypes. He is a firm believer in incorporating self-awareness training for leaders, a role he assumes in a mentorship capacity: 'It's in the way you yourself, as a leader, behave with people. People observe how leaders conduct themselves. Not just within the organization, but when they see how you treat others outside, at a business event. Kindness isn't just about what you say—it's what you do. If communication is only 20 per cent verbal but 80 per cent body language, kindness is evident through how you behave on a day-to-day basis. You have to be self-aware of how you communicate and, more than that, how it's received.'

Self-discovery starts with a solo expedition. A difficult and humbling experience with no shortcuts. A full roughing it in the woods experience. There's no 5-star hotel nearby. Only 10 to 15 per cent of leaders attempt this journey, but fortune favours the brave. The ROK is enlightened leaders who lead with impact.

Be Kind to Yourself

Self-awareness supports a capacity for self-kindness. We are often hardest on ourselves, and this is all the more true for leaders. Leaders question their own decisions, second-guess their judgments, and internalize criticism and failures. All this before others have a turn.

I spoke with Dr Srikumar Rao about self-kindness. Dr Rao is an elite executive coach, former business school professor, and creator of Creativity and Personal Mastery. His TED talk, on happiness, has over one million views. Dr Rao has dedicated his life's work to the thesis that we must live in an other-centred world (*read:* leadership is not about you). Doing this necessitates working on ourselves first, as leaders: 'From a leadership perspective, be kind to others because they're no different from you. When you're kind to others, you're being kind to yourself.' How meta. Being kind to yourself starts with a mindset shift. When leaders shift towards kindness, a waterfall of kindness follows. If everyone shifts just 1 per cent, the boat changes direction. That is the essence of starting a movement. So consequential is the inner work for a leader, Dr Rao advised: 'Your role as a senior executive is a tool for you to work on yourself. If you are kind, it is an outward expression of who you are.'

New research from Dr Klodiana Lanaj, a professor at Warrington College of Business at Florida State University, and her team, validated the practice of self-kindness and demonstrated its benefits.[12] Over the course of ten days, a group of employed adults in the US were asked to practice a *self-compassionate mindset*—a mindset that embraces being kind, gentle, and forgiving to yourself during hard times at work. On days a self-compassionate mindset was activated, their wellbeing and performance improved due to an enhanced resource capacity, which translated into gains in resilience, work engagement, and meaning in life. This work builds on Dr Lanaj's earlier work demonstrating that, when leaders operate with self-compassion, their people perceived them to be competent and caring.[13] Not only does self-kindness pay off for leaders' own wellbeing, it also strengthens people's perceptions of them.

The Kindness Equation

The new normal stipulates that leaders possess a leadership capability[14] identified by Bill Boulding, dean of Duke University's Fuqua School of Business, consisting of:

$$IQ + EQ + DQ$$

It is no longer adequate for leaders to have intellect (IQ and business competency), nor is it sufficient for leaders to have emotional intelligence (EQ). IQ and EQ do not automatically imply the presence of kindness, compassion, and integrity. IQ and EQ do not preordain that leaders will do what's best for others. For leaders to succeed now, and in the future, a decency quotient, DQ, is essential. Intellect and emotional intelligence are vital, but it is decency that ensures IQ and EQ are used to benefit society, not tear it down.

How do leaders lead with decency? Take a wild guess. Ron Carucci's fifteen-year study of over 3,000 leaders[15] found that simply being reliable and having integrity were insufficient. In addition to reliability and integrity, kindness contributed to leaders' being appraised as 16x more trustworthy. Kindness is an essential characteristic of successful and impactful leaders. Leaders who work on themselves are availed to kindness, making them a triple-threat on driving impact.

Chapter Insights

- Kindness radiates from inside out. Introspection builds awareness builds acceptance builds kindness, resulting in a leadership philosophy founded on kindness. Dig deep. A little soul searching never hurt nobody.
- The true test of leadership is in action. Simply saying the words is meaningless if people are not buying into you as a leader they would willingly follow and becomes an empty exercise in shameless self-promotion. Leading with kindness is the cumulative layering of actions, each reflecting on you as a person and as a leader which, over time, dramatically shapes culture and how your organization operates.

Chapter Exercise: Inner Work

What inner work do I need to do on:
- Awareness

- Acceptance
- Creating space for kindness

Questions to Guide Self-Reflection

1. What is my leadership philosophy?
2. What are my core guiding values?
3. What are the behavioural expressions of those values?
4. What unconscious biases may have been limiting me from kindness?
5. How can I be more mindful of my words and actions in a way that serves my people?

Chapter 9

Get Your Mind Right

The summer before my first year of undergraduate studies began, I was practicing intensely for an examination to earn an Associateship Certification with the Royal Conservatory of Music (ARCT)—a piano performer's degree. I started playing piano at the tender age of four, too short for my feet to reach the pedals, yet determined to play, even while my mother gently suggested that I find another hobby (*unheard of for an Asian mom, I know*). One of the pieces I was to perform was Bach, a composer I came to strongly dislike after many years of attempting to master his fugues. Simply hearing his music now is the equivalent of nails on a chalkboard. No matter how many hours I devoted to practicing this particular piece, it never seemed to come together. Bach and I should have just broken up. Chopin, on the other hand, sparked joy. I loved playing and listening to his music. What was obstructing any prospect of a top score, though, was my nemesis, Bach. Every day, despite wanting to play Chopin, I begrudgingly played the stupid fugue. To paraphrase John Lennon, I passed the audition, but with a performance I rated as only passable.

In reflecting on our leadership, in doing the necessary inner work, ask where there's room for improvement and you're not likely to hear 'I have a certain strength that I'd like to develop into a superpower.' That's because our mind skips to weaknesses. The availability heuristic crudely places weaknesses top of mind. Must fix the fugue. Weaknesses can (hopefully, unlike my fugue) be improved with the right training or mentorship.

It's a nice thought that with enough elbow grease we can move from weakness to strength. Malcolm Gladwell claimed that with 10,000 hours of practice we are capable of mastering a craft,[1] a thought that has been debunked[2,3] (and of which I could have discredited after my 10,001 hour playing the same fugue). But another, perhaps more productive idea is that of spending our limited and precious energy, and the collective resources of the organization, strengthening our strengths.[4] Shifting a weakness into an acceptable zone prevents companies from getting the best from their people. Considering that companies pay people to do what they are great at, leaders can redefine the way they lead by building a culture that allows people to do their best work, where collective teamwork overcomes an individual's weakness. Of course, there are fatal flaws, such as a lack of kindness, for which this does not apply. The cherry on top? Research from positive psychology suggests that investing in developing strengths increases wellbeing.[5]

We saw how HKBN puts their full backing into developing top talent, a decision endorsed by Netflix. Patty McCord, former Chief Talent Officer at Netflix, describes her stalwart defence of this approach: 'The best thing you can do for your employees—a perk better than foosball or free sushi—is hire only 'A' players to work alongside them. Excellent colleagues trump everything else.'[6]

Kindness is in the Mind

Part of the inner work leaders do through self-awareness is to establish the right mindset. Think of it as a leadership supertrait. Stanford professor Carol Dweck's research observed children who were given challenges to solve to see how they would respond. She consistently found that there was one group of kids that tended to respond to challenges in a positive way (*I love puzzles!*), and another group that lacked the confidence and initiative to overcome the obstacle (*Oh no, not another puzzle!*). Over time, this becomes a pattern of behaviour. The latter behaviour of avoiding difficult tasks because of a fear of failure or pursuing tasks with a guaranteed chance of success characterizes a fixed mindset, in contrast to the group of kids exemplifying a growth mindset. One implication stemming from this research is that people with a growth mindset devote the time, energy, and effort to improving themselves. Those who have a fixed mindset remain within self-imposed limitations.

Can you identify any fixed mindsets on your team? If so, resist playing the blame game. Is the corporate set-up encouraging fixed mindset behaviours? Consider that the standard accountability process consists of scorekeeping measures. Toxic cultures that feel like Big Brother, where every action is being monitored for red flags until you strike out. The Dictators, the Departed, the Pushovers, are operating from *scarcity*. Impact Drivers re-orient accountability measures to focus on process and minimize fixation on the outcome.[7] Process appreciates experimentation. Process values learning. Process rewards growth. Scarcity asks *what did you accomplish this week?* Growth asks *what did you learn this week?* These should be informal conversations with your people that are entirely separate from performance appraisals. Workplaces that revolve around growth enjoy cultures that are positive and generous. Growth begets growth.

Mind Over Matter

In the last chapter we talked about awareness. Exploring what might help the Dictator, the Departed, and the Pushover develop awareness, and the Impact Driver to maintain awareness, led me to mindfulness. Admittedly, I'm a bit of a sceptic. With its roots in the Eastern world, in Buddhist philosophy, and dating back about 2500 years, it seems fair to ask *what relevance does mindfulness have to organizations?*

Mindfulness is the practice of being fully present in the moment and accepting your thoughts without judgment. The goal of mindfulness isn't to stop thinking or to empty your mind of all thoughts. The point is to pay close attention to the *now*. By virtue of concentrating on the present, you see your thoughts and emotions more clearly, without making assumptions.

Okay, I can start to see how mindfulness, as an exercise in self-awareness, aids self-acceptance. During my conversation with Jacqueline Carter of Potential Project, she offered that mindfulness is about quietening the mind: 'It's being aware of how crazy your mind is and working with it in a positive way. If you're not here, you can't care as a leader.' Soothing the mind will come as a gratifying respite for those leading through anxiety, whose minds are constantly in overdrive. We all have the capacity to be mindful, though the degree to which we are mindful fluctuates. During a meeting, we might pay close attention one minute, and find ourselves distracted the next (*what's for dinner?*). Mindfulness can occur during various activities, repealing the stereotype of sitting in a meditative pose. Some channel it best while meditating; others simply take a nature walk during lunch.

The burgeoning literature that couples mindfulness and the workplace presents a long and impressive resume of benefits.[8] Mindfulness improves health and wellbeing: it lowers blood pressure and aids the immune system, reduces stress, anxiety, and depression, improves sleep, boosts positive moods, energy, and happiness.[9] Mindfulness improves cognitive functioning: it enhances cognitive flexibility, problem solving, and task focus,[10] all of which impact engagement, satisfaction, and performance at work.[11] Seems I've answered my own question of the relevance of incorporating mindful practice into the workplace.

But wait: the mindfulness CV doesn't stop there. Research demonstrates that mindfulness can literally change our brain.[12] Participants in an eight-week mindfulness-based stress reduction (MBSR) program exhibited changes in the amount of grey matter concentration within the brain (as measured pre-course and post-course), which has direct implications for learning and memory, emotion regulation, information processing, and perspective taking. And since participants were new to mindfulness, this suggests that eight weeks of mindfulness can change a newbie brain for the better.

Further bridging the mindfulness-workplace divide, recent research found that people perceive mindful leaders as more authentic leaders.[13] Checks out. Being mindful allows you to be deliberate in your approach and thoughtful in your response. That takes confidence and authenticity.

I wanted to extend investigations on the utility of mindful practice at work. In ongoing research, my doctoral student Yaxian Zhou and I examined the impact of mindfulness across a series of controlled studies, with a combined total of approximately four hundred working adults from a range of industries across the UK, US, and Hong Kong. We found that partaking in a 5-minute daily mindfulness practice, even for one day, enhances resources devoted to meta-cognition, a self-regulatory strategy in which people manage and productively shape their thoughts, which in turn improves performance and lowers work-related anxiety.

Now for the fine print. Mindfulness, for all its advantages, is not a magic cure. Experimental research has found that mind-body practices such as yoga and meditation, which stress the importance of mindfulness, directly contradict the 'ego-quieting' philosophical tenets of these practices. Rather, this research finds that these practices may contribute to self-enhancement and even narcissism, the perception of being better than others.[14]

Where does this leave us? Based on an extensive and combined pool of research, mindfulness carries weight, so long as leaders are mindful (*pun count* = 3) that the introspective process does not hover in the *me* but is channelled outwards towards the *we*. Mindfulness alone is also not enough. Just as bottom-up strategies for addressing anxiety and burnout at work are not enough. That being said, mindfulness is conducive for quelling an active mind, abating anxiety, creating space for the inner work demanded of leaders. Seen this way, a re-centring, calming technique, used wisely, is a competitive advantage. That's step one. Leading with kindness is rooted in action.

Mindfulness is steadily being integrated into corporate wellness programs. Aetna, a US-based publicly-listed health insurance company with a market cap of USD 69 billion, introduced a Mindfulness Initiative, partnering with the Integrative Medicine Program at Duke University. This initiative was steered by former Aetna CEO, Mark Bertolini, who overcame a near-death skiing accident in 2004. Experiencing the benefits of mindfulness first-hand during his recovery led to the active promotion of mindfulness at Aetna. Over the last decade, more than 20,000 employees participated.

At the time, internal studies estimated that highly stressed employees incurred an additional USD 2,000 per year in healthcare costs compared to their less-stressed peers. In a company of Aetna's size, stress-related health issues amounted to millions of dollars annually. As a result of partaking in mindfulness, the participants experienced, on average, a 28 per cent decrease in stress levels and a 20 per cent improvement in sleep quality, gaining an average of 62 minutes per week in added productivity. In 2012, as the mindfulness programs ramped up, healthcare costs fell 7 per cent. While these results cannot be fully attributed to mindfulness, it certainly plays a role. Reducing stress, directly or indirectly, can only contribute to the bottom line. Aetna estimates that the productivity gains alone were approximately USD 3,000 per employee, an 11:1 return on investment.

Thank You for Being You

Mindfulness is one vessel through which to build out a growth mindset. To shift from a mindset of scarcity to one of abundance, practice gratitude. We experience gratitude when we redirect attention from what we don't have to what we *do* have. Self-reflection and self-awareness, aided by mindfulness practice, avails us to being thankful. Over a decade of research[15] on gratitude has demonstrated that those who regularly practice gratitude are more:

- helpful, connected to others, and likely to have stronger relationships
- patient and loyal even at a cost to themselves
- resilient and more likely to build resilient teams
- inspiring to teams, who are subsequently more productive
- healthy and happy

Gratitude counters the negativity brought on by the stress of leading through anxiety.[16] Living a life of gratitude is an act of rebellion against the cynicism life brings. We all know people who, without fail, zero in on the bad. It could be a perfectly productive meeting, and someone will say it was a waste of time.

Positive reflection, stemming from positive psychology, breaks this pattern. Reflecting on positive events increases the likelihood of rehashing it with others, granting a second dose of positive emotions. It also establishes positive triggers (*why* did this positive event happen, *who* were you with, *where* were you when it happened), facilitating additional positive moments. Over time, noticing the good becomes a new habit.

This is data-backed. Researchers conducted a three-week study to put this positive reflection training to the test. The task was simple. At the end of each day, participants were asked to record three good things that happened that day. An entry could be as nondescript as 'I helped someone with a work task today.' They were also asked to explain *why* they thought these positive events happened. Maybe it's 'I saw my colleague struggling and I wanted to help.' Researchers found that on days participants completed this exercise, they experienced reduced stress and had less health complaints, as compared with the days they did not reflect positively.[17] If the cost of being unkind is 5:1, consider the exponential benefit of practicing gratitude. It may be time to incorporate positive morning affirmations into the morning routine.

A crucial aspect of gratitude is expressing appreciation towards others. Research shows that *giving* compliments and employing positive reinforcement makes people happier than *receiving* compliments themselves, because of the strong social bonds that are generated as a result.[18] Practicing gratitude by validating others and their work confers respect, builds trust, and elevates people's self-esteem.[19] Our brain releases the happy hormones, dopamine and serotonin, that make us feel positive.[20] As a leader, never underestimate the impact of 'thank you.' Make it your very purpose to express heartfelt thanks at every opportunity. Kindness contributes to a sense of meaning and fulfilment in work and life. Level up by attaching specific praise to the expression of gratitude. Instead of 'Thanks for your hard work', try 'I really appreciated the comment you gave during the meeting today. It alerted us to a potential limitation we will have to address before we move to the next phase.' This level of attention to detail is precisely what the team needs. Gratitude is overlooked and under-delivered, yet gratitude makes kindness concrete.

The 1 per cent of Greatest Leaders Are Humble

Impact Drivers are guided by kindness and toughness, and that stems from humility. Humility, central to the self-awareness process that renders self-acceptance, is what separates the best leaders from the pack. Arguably the most poignant work to link humility to leadership was research conducted in the late 1990s by Jim Collins. In analyzing over 1,400 companies over a 40-year period, Jim and his team identified only eleven companies that went from good to great. The 1 per cent. Naturally, Collins and his team tried to figure out what made these eleven companies successful. Lo and behold, they inferred five levels of leadership from their research findings, described in the book *Good to Great*[21]:

- **Level 1 leaders:** Highly capable individual performers
- **Level 2 leaders:** Team players
- **Level 3 leaders:** Competent managers
- **Level 4 leaders:** Effective leaders
- **Level 5 leaders:** Executive leaders

Being an executive does not automatically make you a Level 5 leader. The incredible part of this framework is what separates the Level 5s from the Level 4s. Level 4s are competent, but that didn't cut VIP status of the 1 per cent. Level 4 leaders are absorbed with their own self-interests and ambitions and did not set their companies up for enduring success, wanting the legacy to end with them. The eleven leaders that qualified in the top 1 per cent had two additional characteristics—the seemingly contradictory blend of humility and being strong willed. That's the genius of the *and*. A precursor of kindness and toughness. Level 5s, with much the same drive as Level 4s, wholeheartedly prioritized the people, distributing power so that company longevity was not dependent on the leader. That was their legacy.

> Humility is such an important part of being an effective leader, it separates the top 1 per cent, the best of the best. Don't get it twisted. Narcissism and arrogance are *not* what catapults leaders to the top. Kindness matters. Kindness wins.

Humility and leadership don't often go together. Same shots fired at kindness: Humble leaders lack the aggressiveness, the decisiveness, to compete in today's market. Humble leaders are too introverted, too weak, and lacking in charisma. How did we get to a place where the qualities of kindness, humility, and overall goodness, are scoffed at?

Adopting humility in leadership stems from the inner work involved in self-leadership, arising from an ongoing process of self-awareness. Humility, a prominent fixture in theology and philosophy that captures virtues relevant to morality, is more productively thought of in terms of *expressed humility* with respect to the social context of organizational leadership. There are three components of expressed humility in leadership: [22]

- A willingness to see yourself accurately
- An appreciation of others' strengths and contributions
- Teachability

Like kindness, humility is couched in action. Expressed humility implicates the role of behaviours that are externally observed by others, making humility relational. The social context affixes leaders to their people, aiding continual adaptation in a leader's self-perception. Expressed humility as a leader entails genuine valuation of others' work, efforts, and abilities, and a demonstrated openness to learn from others. It is a willingness to seek feedback from those around them for an accurate and objective self-view, to gather new and different perspectives.

Humility is a receptiveness to ask for help, recognizing, even embracing, that no one has the answer to, or knows, everything. It is absurd that, in a global market where challenges are progressively complex, problems are frequent, change is constant, and answers are few, one person would have all the answers. Humility removes all pretenses as a leader. As the saying goes, 'If you're the smartest person in the room, you're in the wrong room.' Find another room. Humble leaders evince Adam Grant's concept of *confident humility* or having the self-awareness to know what you don't know, wielding strength.[23]

Saying *I don't know* is difficult for many leaders, because leaders are expected to have the answers. Those struggling with deep-rooted insecurities may feel the need to overcompensate. Confident humility gives leaders the courage to rely on their team and raise others up: 'I'm not sure about that, so let me refer you to my fantastic colleague who can answer your question on this issue.' Kind leaders provide context, clarity, support, and resources, then have the confident humility to get out of their people's way. Contrary to leaders' belief that this behaviour projects incompetence, research shows that, when leaders solicit help and ask more questions, it conveys trustworthiness, builds strong connections, and leads to better decisions.[24]

Garry Ridge imparted that one of his biggest learnings was getting comfortable with what are now considered the three most important words in his life: *I don't know*. He said to me: 'Bonnie, you might laugh, but this is how I introduce myself to people: "G'day. I'm Garry Ridge. I'm the consciously incompetent, probably wrong, and roughly right, chairman and CEO of WD-40 company." Garry's introduction reminded me of what Hubert Joly, former Best Buy CEO, recounted in an interview with Adi Ignatius, editor-in-chief of *Harvard Business Review*: 'I think that a great leadership trend today is to be able to say, "My name is Hubert. I don't know. I'm going to need help. We're going to figure this out. We're going to experiment." The idea of the leader banging their fists on the table and saying that's the way it is? I don't think so.'[25] Hubert Joly was adamant that a sign of strong leadership is admitting you don't have all the answers: 'Top-down management simply doesn't work. As the CEO, I make very, very few decisions. And the key for me is to push them down as far as possible.'

Satya Nadella role models humility, recasting the Microsoft culture from a 'know-it-all' to a 'learn-it-all' company that learns from everyone around them. The game changer is overturning the idea of being the authority on every topic. Surround yourself with the best, absorb all they have to offer, and share that knowledge with your people. This shift to a learning culture has earned Nadella the title of 'most underrated CEO' by *Fortune* magazine for the sixth consecutive year. In *Fortune*'s estimation, 'While his predecessors supported hardball business tactics, Nadella took a different approach. He is known for his calm demeanour and applying positive feedback to reinforce good habits and motivate his team. As CEO of Microsoft, Nadella has overseen the company's increase in market cap from around USD 300 billion to more than 2 trillion.'[26] One need no longer be in doubt as to the ROK. Kindness impacts the bottom line.

With decision-making authority entrusted to teams, humility also enhances team synergy, germane to future work steadily transitioning out of hierarchical and centralized authority towards flatter organizational structures relying on networks of teams of a global, cross-functional, and fluid nature. While teamwork spurs a peer learning process, an unintended reality of teamwork is that team members often engage in *social comparison*, scrutinizing how certain aspects of ourselves stack up relative to our peers, creating tensions that discourage learning from occurring. Along with my research team, Dr Erica Xu, Professor Xu Huang, and Dr Man-Nok Wong, we examined how expressed humility might buffer the tendency of team members to avoid learning from higher performers on the team. In ongoing research, across two samples of a combined total of over 400 members in over 90 teams in the IT and manufacturing industries, we found that, in teams with higher performers who explicitly express humility, team members' proneness to disengage from learning from these better performing members (in terms of seeking advice, seeking feedback, and observational learning) was stifled. A slice of humble pie serves everyone well. Oh, and it's gluten free.

The Gift that Bach Gave

I was my own worst enemy when it came down to playing Bach just acceptable enough so as not to embarrass the master, or myself. Bill George's words 'The hardest person you will ever have to lead is yourself' are a difficult lesson to learn, and so many of us try valiantly but decide the inner work is too hard, or do not know the path to take to understand ourselves in a deeper way. Maybe it's thinking *This is just work—it doesn't matter*.

Except that it does. For your own sake and the sake of the people you lead. For your wellbeing and theirs. To honour the trust your organization has for you. To earn the trust of your people, who will only willingly follow, give their best effort, and sacrifice for a leader who they care about, which is most reliably determined by how much their leader cares for them. When leaders grant themselves permission to show up as their authentic self, flaws and all, they invite their people do the same. That's the authenticity piece. More than that. Self-awareness and the self-acceptance that follows is strong footing for emotional wellbeing and is the very pillar for developing strong interpersonal relationships and forging bonds of trust.[27] Leadership is about the relationship with your people.

The self-discovery voyage as a leader is never-ending, a process as exhausting as it is exhilarating, as raw as it is revealing. Leaders who pledge to doing the inner work lay a strong base for kindness. Little by little, leaders become enlightened and now, they can turn their full attention to their people.

Chapter Insights

- Companies pay people to do what they are great at, otherwise we would all be astronauts. Impact Drivers develop a mindset of abundance by growing the full capacity of their top talent, while relying on the collective strength of the team.
- Mindfulness is not squishy. Mindful awareness is an effective strategy for alleviating stress and anxiety, setting the stage for kindness. It also carries benefits on hardcore business outcomes.
- The best leaders are humble. This makes confident humility a simple way to amplify your leadership. You're a leader, not a superhero. No one expects you to know it all.

Chapter Exercise: Gratitude Reflection

The founder of Beyond Thank You, Dr Christopher Littlefield, wrote an article on gratitude for *Harvard Business Review*[28] which serves as the inspiration for this exercise. During trying leadership moments, such as when leading from anxiety, reflect on the following questions and how they relate to the cultivation of a grateful heart and the practice of gratitude:

1. What are three things I am grateful for right now?
2. What is a recent challenge I was able to overcome?
3. What am I better at today than I was a year ago?
4. What have I recently learned that helped me grow?
5. What specific gratitude can I express to my people today?

Part IV

RISE to Kind Leadership

Enlightened leaders can now RISE to kind leadership. In Part IV, I introduce and successively unpack the RISE framework. The RISE model can be applied to any team or organization. The RISE model can be applied in or out of sequence, in isolation or concurrently, depending on the dynamics of the situation, based on an assessment of the *kindness maturity* prevalent in the team or organization. Impact is strongest when leaders raise their people up through purposeful and cumulative application of all layers. When leaders rise to kind leadership, they both grow their leadership capability, while also exacting a positive influence on their people and the culture. Leaders are also never 'finished' rising to kindness. Kindness is not a destination. There is no finish line. There will always be new challenges, new opportunities, for leaders to rise to kindness.

RISE TO KIND LEADERSHIP

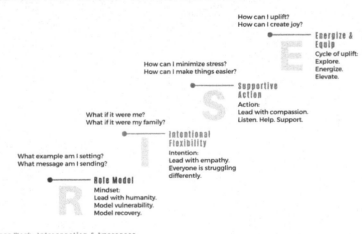

How can I uplift?
How can I create joy?

Energize & Equip
Cycle of uplift:
Explore.
Energize.
Elevate.

How can I minimize stress?
How can I make things easier?

Supportive Action
Action:
Lead with compassion.
Listen. Help. Support.

What if it were me?
What if it were my family?

Intentional Flexibility
Intention:
Lead with empathy.
Everyone is struggling differently.

What example am I setting?
What message am I sending?

Role Model
Mindset:
Lead with humanity.
Model vulnerability.
Model recovery.

Inner Work: Introspection & Awareness

Chapter 10

Be a Role Model for Kindness

The rise to kind leadership starts by modelling the change you want to see, with no limit to where you can take it.

Modelling Kindness Mirrors Kindness

Kindness is behaviour shaped by one's environment, making leading by example an effective leadership tool. More than that, role modelling is a strategic action leaders take to foster kind actions that build kind cultures. You can say the right words a hundred times, but if people don't see the right actions from you, nothing will change.

As a leader, what example are you setting for your team? Take your daily routine, for example; something which you may consider mundane or uneventful. Buyer beware: *people are watching.* Leaders don't often register, or pay attention to, the impact their everyday regimen has on their people. With good reason. *Gotta get through the bottomless to-do list.* A solid couple of days spent on strategic planning here, dedicated business travel there. Upon return, a full day is spent in the office, catching up on copious emails that have piled up. The rest of the week is at capacity with back-to-back meetings. Leaders may proclaim *My door is always open. My people know that!* People won't come if they don't feel safe or welcome. When was the last time genuine effort was exerted to get to know people on a human level? *That's impossible! There's hundreds of people in this company!* The daily behaviours and micro-habits of leaders, however seemingly irrelevant, become norms that inform and define the culture of the company. Culture is by design, or it becomes what it is, good or bad. Take your pick.

Leaders cannot expect the next layers down to lead with kindness if they are not behaving that way. For Lâle Kesebi, this is possible even when managing 4,000 people in forty countries, in her previous role as a senior executive at supply chain management company, Li & Fung. She would meet with her managers once a week and regularly had people over at her place, because, she says, 'How do you care about someone you don't know?' Lâle recalls: 'Of all the things that I accomplished as a leader at the company, this is the story that people tell about me: It was an unusually cold winter's day in Hong Kong. Our two receptionists were noticeably shivering. I asked our team to find a spare heater and sent it down to the lobby. I didn't think anything beyond it. By the end of the day the receptionists had told their colleagues and the story spread throughout the company. That's gratitude for life and real loyalty to leadership. Zero effort on my part. So, you can't tell me kindness doesn't have an impact.'

As the proxy for leadership, small acts of kindness give a human interface to, and carry lasting impressions of, the company overall: *Leadership cares.*

HKBN role models kindness by insisting on transparent, silo-free communication among their nearly 5,000 Talents through, among various socials, Chit-Chat Thursdays. They don't make excuses about the people to manager ratio. Accountability is evident through a Get Sh*t Done (GSD) report with follow-up actions generated by the leadership team and related departments in response to each constructive recommendation raised by their Talent during each session. Many punchy ideas that originated during these forums have been implemented to drive even greater influence, making HKBN stronger as a cohesive unit.

Leading by example is anchored on the self-awareness and self-reflection process, in which leaders come to an acceptance of who they are and what they stand for. Directed outwards, kindness is mirrored back in the kindness that takes off in the culture.

Flexing the Kindness Muscle

Kindness training is like weight training, and like any gym goer will tell you, without practice, the kindness muscle will weaken.

In my own research on kindness, I challenged sixty-five students in a Masters of Global Management program taking my course on workplace wellness to participate in a ten-day kindness challenge. So as not to bias the results, they were informed only of participating in a wellness challenge. Every morning during the first week, as a control condition, participants were asked to write about their daily tasks to ensure that any effects were not due to potential benefits of expressive writing. Every morning during the second week, they were asked to generate and commit to performing three specific kind actions that day. A few examples of the kindness goals they set for themselves:

- 'I plan to say thank you politely to everyone who has served me'
- 'For the group meeting, I want to give positive feedback and take up the tougher tasks'
- 'I plan to stay positive and listen to everyone's situation'

Every evening of the challenge, they reported on their wellbeing. On the days people participated in the kindness challenge, they perceived themselves to be kinder, which led to a host of benefits: social connectedness, thriving, wellbeing, and significantly lower levels of feeling anxious, depleted, and fatigued.

There was no way of knowing if they actually performed the kind acts they committed to. But it seems that simply committing to kindness—having a kind intention—was beneficial. Maybe these are good-hearted students who self-selected into my course. Well, yes they are. Fair point. To see if I could replicate these results with managers not enrolled in my course, I asked each student to recruit two to three full-time managers to participate in a separate ten-day kindness challenge. In a sample of approximately seventy managers, here are some kindness goals managers set for themselves each day:

- *'Today I will try to give my employees more chances to talk to me. I want to ensure we have a positive workplace. If I see someone who feels down, I will try to cheer them up.'*
- *'With several members of my team (or their immediate family) diagnosed with Covid, I need to be more in tune with their emotions and perhaps sub-optimal work efforts, and be more flexible.'*

The results for managers extend beyond the student sample, with implications for their leadership. On days managers participated in the kindness challenge, they perceived their leadership to be aligned with servant leadership, and they were more participative and empowering towards their people. This in turn led to an increase in self-benefits for managers' wellbeing and thriving. The results are encouraging, and feedback from my students suggests there is definitely hope for the future generation of leaders:

- *'I think being kind to yourself is the first step to being kind to others. So, I need to have self-compassion and care about my emotions first. When I don't deal with my negative emotions and fatigue, being kind to others will make me feel even more exhausted, and I won't have enough patience to be helpful. If I become a leader . . . I will first encourage people to pay attention to their physical and emotional changes, tell them don't be sorry for the negative state and don't be ashamed to ask for help. This will build a culture where people can express and talk about themselves.'*

- *'I noticed a change in my usual behaviour. I used to do whatever I wanted, but since I finished the [kindness challenge], I always unconsciously remind myself to be kind, and then do something to help others within my power.'*
- *'Kindness is crucial in building a culture of wellness, and fostering empathy, a positive environment, and an open and inclusive workplace. Before, I always thought the most important aspect of a leader is competence, which is still crucial, but now I think empathy is even more important. A leader should be an enabler, not a ruler. Furthermore, empathy builds trust. Without trust we cannot build meaningful relationships. Working with people we are in a good relationship with, makes the workplace much more fun, interactive, and collaborative. A leader that can create such an environment can ensure employees are more willing to admit mistakes and improve as a team.'*

This research aligns with other research findings[1] which suggests that being consistently kind over a period of ten days led to an increase in life satisfaction, as compared with those who did not perform kind acts. Kindness doesn't just affect short-lived spurts of happiness, it has the potential to affect our global perceptions. Looking for a simple and cost-effective way to be happier? Be kind.

The Vulnerability-Kindness Connection

Vulnerability builds connection on a human level. When guards are dropped, we feel empathy and compassion, and recognize the desire to be seen, heard, and valued. Leaders cannot expect their people to open up and share parts of themselves if they do not open up and share the deepest parts of themselves with their people, parts of which may be unpolished, unglamorous, even ugly. As Brené Brown states, 'there is no triumph without vulnerability.'[2] Vulnerability becomes sine qua non for leaders to leverage kindness as a change agent for establishing corporate wellness where mental health and wellbeing are prioritized.

That's not to say that leaders should concoct or embellish (tragic) stories in an unscrupulous attempt at connection. That's an authenticity foible. Not everyone has suffered personal trauma. So, where to start? Start by sharing your own personal development journey.[3] Your leadership journey. With humility and introspection, vulnerability as a leader means disclosing your fears, aha moments and lessons learned, experiences with imposter syndrome and leading through anxiety.

Next, role modelling vulnerability shows a willingness to ask for help and to learn from each other, building on collective strengths as the foundation for succeeding together.[4] Kindness as a leader is normalizing the words *I don't know* and *I made a mistake*. Rather than projecting weakness, this is a sign of a secure and credible leader. Surprise them and apologize.

Vulnerability signals approachability and organically brings leaders closer to their people. With vulnerability modelled, people start to peel back the layers, to speak frankly without restraint. Strong bonds of trust are formed, not just between you and your people, but networked bonds of trust are built across the organization. Your people feel invested in you and each other as human beings, just as you are invested in each of them as human beings. When people feel respected, they are inspired, and give the best of themselves to their work and to the company. Push that up and out, and you've now contributed to building a culture of loyalty.

If vulnerability was never in the leadership toolkit, the sudden shift will be uncomfortable. It's not easy. It's not meant to be easy. That's what makes it work. Research shows that when CEOs revealed critical feedback they received with their team, in comparison with those who did not self-disclose such information, their teams felt a greater degree of psychological safety. This effect was found even one year later.[5] In building a culture of kindness, take ownership for role modelling kindness.

Kind Models in Action

I was curious to learn why Francis Hyatt stayed with Liberty Mutual Insurance for three decades and counting. For Francis, it was a no brainer. He described a culture where every person commits to a common set of values—to put people first and treat one another with dignity and respect—that they live and breathe. That's individual accountability for collective action. Their values oblige them to be proactive in challenging convention, to act responsibly, and to do what's right with integrity.

I challenged Francis in observing, 'Most companies have nice sounding values displayed on their company walls or on their socials. It's another story whether people in the company act in a way that's aligned with these values.' Francis agreed wholeheartedly: 'With some companies, it's marketing speak. It's nothing but dots on a paper. At Liberty, it's driven from the C-suite down.' The leadership team demonstrates ownership by adopting company guidelines for behaviours that ground interpersonal interactions. This includes listening carefully to each other's perspective; not blaming, shaming, or attacking anyone, including yourself; being aware of the intent and impact of your words and actions; and practicing self-focus.

Francis recounts a specific example in 2021 during the pandemic when he was preparing for a series of consequential strategic meetings with the C-suite. The new team he formed was just six months old. As luck would have it, Francis fell ill with Covid-19. He felt exposed and anxious about not coming through on the initiatives he was trying to push out Then, he received a text from David Long, his CEO, that said: 'Hey, I hear you're down with Covid. I also know there are a number of things coming up that you're concerned about. I've got you. Don't worry about it. Unplug, stay at home and be safe.'

Francis described what he felt: 'That was the equivalent of him giving me a million dollars. Because I could breathe. I could exhale. The stress left. I knew that someone had my back. That, to me, is a practical example of how that trickles down in the organization. Through David's actions I have permission to do that with my team, which gives them permission to do that with their teams.' Kindness having been role modelled successfully, Francis and every other manager could now pay it back by paying it forward for their own people, mobilizing a positive cycle founded in abundance.

I asked Francis whether it was possible to scale something like this in a multinational enterprise such as Liberty Mutual Insurance, ranked 78 on the Fortune 100 list of largest corporations in the US, based on 2021 revenue.[6] Liberty Mutual Insurance takes a developmental approach to cultivating a growth mindset in their people, engaging its managers in immersive experiences where alignment is created around DEI through acquiring and practicing new skills. To make this concrete, people practice utilizing constructive language during conversations that are uncomfortable but necessary. Far from being Western-centric, the company adopts the perspective 'as global as necessary, as local as possible' because DEI work is multifaceted, and diversity carries different meaning around the world. The time and financial commitment invested to this ongoing endeavour for their approximately 4,000 managers is indicative of the company's resolve to build kind leaders.

Francis added another example. Let's suppose an important project goes sideways. Francis said, 'In some companies, that's the death knell. You now have a black mark on you. At Liberty, it's an arm around the shoulder, followed by 'Let's do some forensics here. What happened? What could we have done better? What did you learn, and what are we going to do differently to help you achieve success?' The bar has not been lowered. To the contrary, there are high expectations, accountability for delivering on your responsibilities, and even evaluation. The difference is in the support—tangible resource support to help you reach your goals and objectives.'

Francis was adamant that I do not take his word for it. He connected me with one of his direct reports, Rakhi Kumar, SVP Sustainability Solutions and Business Integration. Rakhi corroborates: 'In other companies, it's about what you produced. Here at Liberty, you also get credit for *how* you achieved the goal. If you miss a goal but approached it well, you still get credit for it. Leadership sets the tone that it's not just about getting the work done.' This balanced approach gives people the confidence to put their best into their work. It speaks volumes that Liberty Mutual Insurance integrates leadership behaviours into the performance evaluation process. Hitting targets and delivering business results through whatever means necessary won't cut it, because they emphasize process over outcomes.

Such is the effect of role modelling kindness. It's no wonder that 86 per cent of employees at Liberty Mutual Insurance say it is a great place to work compared to the average rating of 57 per cent of employees across US-based companies.[7]

Kindness Is Role Modelling Recovery

With kindness successfully role modelled, kindness becomes the reference point. When I first moved from Canada to Hong Kong, one of the top five overworked cities in the world,[8] I witnessed first-hand the infamous 996 work culture (9 a.m. to 9 p.m., 6 days a week), where overtime, as the norm, is worn almost like a badge of honour, as if that is what defined success. Suffice it to say that the global work-from-home experiment spurred by the pandemic caught many companies by surprise, so foreign was the concept of not being desk-bound. While some companies have leaned into a flexible work approach, others have gone in the opposite direction, turning the 996 into the 247. Cloudy, with zero chance of recovery.

To amplify kindness, role model recovery. In a Deloitte report surveying over 2,000 employees and C-suite executives across the US, UK, Canada, and Australia, 84 per cent agreed that when leaders are healthy, their people are also healthier. When leaders role model recovery, 72 per cent of their people reported above-average wellbeing. In contrast, only 57 per cent of people reported being well when leaders do not role model recovery.[9]

Recovering from work stress is a process of unwinding and restoring resources that are drained due to the demands of work.[10] Simply clocking off at the end of the workday doesn't presume recovery. This new world of work has blurred the boundaries between work and life, making *workplace telepressure*, or feeling obligated to immediately check and respond to work messages, a real issue.[11] Hearing a *ping* has conditioned us to automatically reach for our phones, like Pavlov's experimental subjects. Endless work limits recovery, and we trudge through this negative cycle of needing recovery but lacking respite. This *recovery paradox,* being unable to engage in recovery when we need it most, is a classic symptom of toxic workplaces.[12] In the same Deloitte report cited above, 63 per cent of employees and 73 per cent of C-suite leaders reported being unable to recover from work stress, in part due to work overload or feeling pressured to manage impressions of working hard, indicative of a dearth of leaders who role model recovery. Even C-suite leaders need a push, as 85 per cent indicated the desire to see other leaders taking care of their wellbeing. Peer role modelling. One fact is certain. A *lack* of a recovery period is correlated with increased health issues, which amounts to USD 62 billion in lost productivity, each year.[13]

The fine print. Wellbeing is an organizational issue. Putting that aside, self-care is essential. You are not invincible, even Superman has a weakness. Taking care of yourself yields capacity for caring for others in a kind and compassionate way. Role modelling recovery soft sells the health and wellbeing of your people. That's the *oxygen mask principle.* Standard pre-flight announcements instruct passengers to put on their own oxygen mask first before helping others in the event of an emergency. It is impossible to care for others when you are burned out yourself. An unwell you—chronically operating on lack of sleep and elevated stress—is irritable and unpleasant to be around. Not to mention, judgment and decision-making are negatively affected. Your people avoid you, or this evil twin of yours.

The basis for recovery from work stress is the principle of equilibrium.[14] Like our smartphones, we start the day at 100 per cent charged, batteries full. Our reserve of resources— attention, energy, patience—readies us to take on the challenges of the upcoming day. As the day unfolds, that tank steadily depletes. Some faster than others, depending on the events of the day or the people we encounter, and coffee notwithstanding.

Recovery balances the resources we expend and how much we can recoup. Input vs. Output. P vs. L. Recovery protects us from stress, anxiety, exhaustion, and burnout.

To paraphrase from my recent *Harvard Business Review* article titled 'How to Recover from Work Stress, According to Science' along with Alyson Meister, Nele Dael, and Franciska Krings, regardless of the activity that best helps you unwind and refuel, whether you prefer to join a workout class, try out a new restaurant, or simply Netflix and chill, a healthy dose of recovery *psychologically detaches* from thoughts of work.[15] Detachment is a key recovery experience underlying the recovery process, capturing the need to mentally switch off from thoughts of work, beyond physical separation from work. Just as the body demands rest when sick with the flu, your mind craves a clean break to recuperate. Detaching from thoughts of work has been linked to enhanced recovery, mood, and wellbeing, while a lack of detachment, particularly on days you need it most, has been linked to *rumination*, the inability to shut off your thoughts.[16]

You role model recovery for your people when they see you prioritize self-care. So, preach. Draw hard lines between life and work. Enable recovery for your people by implementing and enforcing policies that allow your people to enjoy full rest cycles. Evenings and weekends are not for work. That is protected time and space. Role model recovery by putting your phone away once the workday ends. On average, we check our phone 150x a day. To put this in perspective, if we assume that each distraction amounts to one minute, over the course of the day, we have wasted 2.5 hours.[17] Phone time is not conducive for recovery. I can hear the objections: *But my phone's on silent! I'm not even looking at it!* Well, research shows that simply having your phone lying around is distracting and lowers cognitive capacity.[18]

Bye bye brain cells. At minimum, put the phone away for a set chunk of time, go for a social media cleanse, and urge your people to do the same. Institute a *No Phone Challenge*. Incentivize it. Gamify it. Points awarded to those who go longer periods without phones.

Aside from recovering during non-work periods, role modelling recovery gains traction by promoting breaks *during* the workday. Our attention and energy cycles are estimated to be 90 to 120 minutes long (my students would tell you it's much shorter than that). Timing *micro-breaks* to these cycles is an act of self-kindness, and kindness for your people. Encourage people to regularly get up, stretch, drink some water. For real. Even mild dehydration contributes to fatigue, negative mood, and impairs cognitive function.[19] You're not grumpy, you're dehydrated. Or, take a (paid) nap at work. Despite the fact that sleep is one of the most natural ways our body recovers and heals, daytime naps have mostly been confined to the domain of, well, babies. They're on to something. In her book *The Sleep Revolution*, Arianna Huffington writes: 'We sacrifice sleep in the name of productivity, but ironically our loss of sleep, despite the extra hours we spend at work, adds up to 11 days of lost productivity per year per worker, or about USD 2280.'[20] Insufficient sleep has been estimated to cause economic injury—USD 411 billion each year in the United States alone.[21] The Centers for Disease Control and Prevention (CDC) has declared insufficient sleep a public health epidemic, after finding that approximately one-third of American adults are not getting enough consistent sleep.[22] Conundrum. Napping at work has always been frowned upon, an act of the lazy who are shunning their responsibilities. Seems snoozing no longer equates to losing, as companies such as Uber and Google are implementing naptime policies, investing in sleep pods or designated sleep rooms, to improve energy, concentration, productivity, and reduce anxiety and depression in their people.[23] As a public health issue with staggering wellbeing and economic implications, promoting healthy sleep practices become urgent.

If a siesta is not for you, try a daily dose of nature. On average, we spend 92 per cent of our lives indoors,[24] a figure that likely increased during the pandemic. Companies such as Samsung, Amazon, and Salesforce are incorporating biophilic work design to bring people closer to nature or natural elements in their workspaces during the day, whether thorough rooftop terraces, green or living walls, or recordings of nature sounds in open-plan environments. If you don't work in such a workspace, take a nature walk during lunch. Schedule walking meetings around the park. Our connection with nature for as little as ten minutes per day has been revealed to have benefits on our energy, mental health, and wellbeing.

If all else fails, on days you wake up and just think 'nope,' those meh days of languish, it's okay to take a day off. You are human. Not a machine. Giving yourself a day to reset, gives your people permission to do the same. That's role modelling recovery. That's taking responsibility for the wellbeing of your people. Make allowances for sad days and meh days, not just sick days.[25] Your out of office (OOO) message is an opportune time to send a clear message that role models recovery. Adjust the narrative—less about bandwidth and more about prioritizing your mental health and wellbeing: *Nobody works well under stress, so I'm taking the next few days to focus on my mental health! Don't forget to take care of yourself, and each other.*

Because wellbeing is a collective issue, leaders can role model recovery by incorporating a *relational pause*, a concept developed from social psychology, involving a brief team-level work break that addresses the high-level question of: 'How is our work affecting us as human beings?' Used effectively (*read:* not approaching this as a whining session), this purposeful exercise can be a meaningful exchange that creates safety, invites vulnerability through reflection, builds team resilience, and brings humanity back to work.[26] Use these relational pauses to bring to light how work is impacting your people by asking questions such as:

- What gives you energy?
- When do you feel engaged?
- What is creating anxiety or frustration?

During these relational pauses, your role as a leader is not to counsel or problem-solve. This is an occasion for members to build connections with one another on a human level. Your role is to serve as a sounding board. Reinforce expressions of vulnerability and compassion, listen, learn, and lead by example. Why not try this outdoors, to seize the healing power of nature?

Recovery Models in Action

I spoke with Dr Gary Gottlieb, former CEO of Partners in Health about role modelling recovery as an act of kindness. Gary was adamant that *accurate empathy,* a term defined by psychiatry, is the only element of leading with kindness that matters: 'Kindness is only effective if it is accurate, and only if it is empathic. Being able to listen to someone, to be able to understand, create, and reflect on the content in a way that is similar to the experience that the person has, or that affects that experience, is accurate empathy from a therapeutic perspective.' I asked Gary how these ideas about kindness and empathy, drawn from psychotherapy, might play out at work. For Gary: 'Understanding how a policy affects a middle-level manager vs. an entry-level worker vs. a senior-level executive in the whole of every transaction is what accurate empathy is about and is what good management is about, and relates directly to kindness. But it's kindness in service of a true return on investment.'

What might this look like? Well, a leader who sets meetings at 7 a.m. is explicitly not being empathic, because it makes things problematic for those who run households, which traditionally skew towards women and single parents. Role modelling recovery is a leader who says she can't start meetings before 9 a.m. before her kids start school, or a leader who proclaims that she needs to make time for running because that's non-negotiable for her wellbeing. A leader who role models recovery is someone who enforces boundaries around life-work integration. During the pandemic, when companies switched to a work-from-home model, Gordon Watson of AXA Asia and Africa recounts how, despite his own personal preference to work from the office during the pandemic, he worked from home so that his people would feel comfortable doing the same, and overcome the stigma, rampant in Asia, that if you're working from home, you're not working. Employee feedback he received indicated that his people appreciated how, despite work-from-home arrangements, he responded quickly and personally to everyone's queries.

As for company-wide initiatives, in February 2021, Spotify announced a new 'Work From Anywhere' policy, allowing its 6500 employees to work anywhere—in the world—they liked. One year later, Spotify reported lower turnover.[27] Online dating app Bumble has been taking active measures to reinforce the recovery of their people, with founder and CEO Whitney Wolfe Herd giving its 700 employees a paid week off for some R&R and *me time* in June 2021.[28] This is poles apart from recent moves, such as Elon Musk's decision to lay off approximately 80 per cent of Twitter's 7,500 workforce, scrap the company's work-from-home policy, and initiate a 'hardcore work' ultimatum which prompted an exodus of workers.

HKBN doesn't believe in work-life balance, rather, they run with a very clear LIFE-work priority, capitalization intended, based on a firm belief that personal wellbeing leads to happy and motivated Talent that achieve outstanding results. The company's policies follow through on this LIFE-work priority. No non-urgent emails are allowed on the weekends, period. Instead, many emails are set to 'delay' send at 6 a.m. Monday morning. HKBN Talents enjoy an impressive smorgasbord of flexibility, including versatile working hours, five days of paid marriage leave, one day of paid leave apiece to celebrate each Talent's work anniversary and each Talent's birthday month, option for a one-year sabbatical leave, and monthly half-day Fridays, just to name a few offerings.

Companies such as Netflix and BlackRock address life-work integration by adopting an unlimited vacation policy. Jury is still out on whether intended results have been realized—some early adopters have remarked that this is more of a marketing ploy to attract and recruit talent, and others allude to this policy as more of a test as companies tend to suggest minimum and maximum time frames for an 'acceptable' holiday. This has led to reservations in taking the preferred amount of time off, not to mention feeling pressured to be 'on' during vacation, thus precluding a process of recovery and defeating the purpose of such policies altogether.

Even so, these may be symptoms of growing pains, as seen by Netflix, who took years to get the policy right. It comes down to the leader's determination to see it through by role modelling and actively monitoring those behaviours, seeking feedback, and constantly fine-tuning their actions. Reed Hastings, co-founder, chairman, and co-CEO of Netflix, opines in his book, *No Rules Rules*: 'In the absence of a policy, the amount of vacation people take largely reflects what they see their boss and colleagues taking.'[29] Hastings himself aims for about six weeks of vacation each year, and unreservedly talks about them to role model recovery. Whether this will be a policy that more companies will adopt in the future or whether it will be quietly abandoned remains to be seen. In general, when done right, the 'Unlimited Vacation Policy' can attract talent and contribute to the wellbeing of the workforce.

Companies reap the benefits when their people are well-rested, recharged, and recovered. Leaders design for kind cultures by role modelling kindness, so long as these efforts are part of a comprehensive plan for promoting mental health and wellbeing, and not an end in and of itself. Giving people a week off to recharge when the remaining weeks of the year are spent in a toxic workplace is not going to suffice. It's the hard work within a kind culture that requires the leader to meet their people where they are. There is nothing ad hoc in this work.

Chapter Exercises

Ten-Day Kindness Challenge

- For a period of ten consecutive workdays, commit to performing three kind actions directed to your people each day. Every morning before starting work, take five minutes to reflect on, and write out three distinct kind behaviours you commit to carrying out that day. Log your entries in a journal.

- Post-challenge reflection:
  o What are your observations from the past ten days?
  o What surprised you about this challenge?
  o Was this challenge easier or harder than you thought it would be?
  o What reactions did you observe from others?

o   How does this exercise contribute to your leadership
    growth?
o   How can you build this Kindness Challenge out to
    your people?

Questions to Guide Role Modelling

1. What do my people need most from me at this time?
2. What is one action I can take today to model recovery for
    my people?
3. What is one policy I can institute or influence at the structural
    level to make recovery core?

Chapter 11

Kindness Is Being Intentionally Flexible

The workforce is exhausted. Lead, but make it kind. Be flexible. Flexibility, like those stretchy pants you wear to a buffet, is being versatile, accommodating. It is not an automatic response. Thoughtfulness and resolve are required. When practiced, it builds trust. Let's start there.

Trust Me, I'm the Leader

Trust is the glue that holds leaders and their people together. This is universal, and strikingly true during times of crisis.[1] The Edelman Trust Barometer, which measures public trust in companies, found, in 2020, that 71 per cent of those surveyed said they would permanently lose trust in a brand if it put profit over people.[2] The 2022 survey found that the financial services industry has been consistently ranked as the least trusted industry—for a decade. Moreover, 63 per cent of those surveyed are convinced that we are being purposely misled or lied to by business leaders, up 7 points from the previous year. This has made distrust in leadership the baseline, with 59 per cent defaulting towards distrust until seeing evidence to the contrary. The 2023 report indicates that globally, trust in CEOs has declined further, to 48 per cent.[3] Not trusted until proven trustworthy.

Research has documented that high-trust companies develop people personally and professionally by facilitating whole-person growth. People working in companies ranked as most trustworthy, reported 106 per cent more energy, experienced 76 per cent more work engagement, 74 per cent less stress, 40 per cent less burnout, and are 50 per cent more productive.[4]

If your people don't trust you, they won't deliver for you. Complication. Leaders cannot, upon inheriting a new team, simply say *hey you, trust me* and people will naively do so. No. Trust is a long game. In his *New York Times* best-seller *Leaders Eat Last*,[5] Simon Sinek traces trust back to caveman times, where anything outside of your immediate tribe represented danger: enemies, animals, another tribe plotting to steal your food. The safe space was inside, with your own people. The modern world is much the same, rife with outside dangers: competitors making a play for your customers, a global pandemic. Regardless of what form these threats take, we know they are constant, and outside of our control.

Threats are also present inside the organization. Layoffs, politics, competition for promotion. But these uncertainties are more controllable. It is the leader's responsibility to create a safety net around their people so that their time and energy can be devoted to uniting together to protect the organization from outside perils. If it's not safe inside, time and energy are wasted playing games (not fun ones) against each other, because leaders have modelled an environment that pushes cross-functional boundaries, friction of which, left untended, become toxic. Navigating office politics in these environments is much like manoeuvring a terrain filled with landmines.

How do you know if your working environment is a safe one? You'll know it when:

- people's voices are heard, respected, and celebrated
- people's contributions are appreciated and recognized
- people aren't pressured to self-edit or conceal their mistakes
- people mutually support and value their colleagues
- people are encouraged to collaborate and exchange information unreservedly
- people feel their leader is on their side

On this final point, HKBN invests in creating a strong culture of safety for its people. HKBN makes clear, in word and deed that it has a Talent obsession *first*, followed by a customer obsession. This, despite being a customer-facing company. NiQ Lai, Group CEO, describes:

> 'At HKBN, we prioritize our fellow Talents over Customers . . . Whilst all HKBNers must go out of our way to WOW our customers, when there is a dispute and the customer is clearly wrong, we will without hesitation back our Talent . . . In fact, if the customer is rude and abusive to our fellow HKBNers, I will personally blacklist the customer, irrespective of VIP status, to ensure they will not harm our colleagues again in the future.'

> The safety HKBN offers their Talent gives them the confidence to perform exceptional service to customers, knowing, in the event of a dispute, their leader will back them. That is kindness and toughness, served.

The Pyramid of Trust

According to Frances Frei and Anne Morriss, introduced in Chapter 3, trust is built on three drivers:

- **Authenticity:** People trust you when they think they are interacting with the real you
- **Empathy:** People trust you when they believe that you care about them
- **Logic:** People trust you when they are confident in your judgment and competence

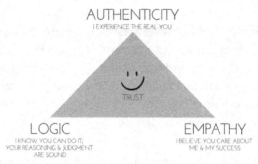

AUTHENTICITY
I EXPERIENCE THE REAL YOU

TRUST

LOGIC
I KNOW YOU CAN DO IT;
YOUR REASONING & JUDGMENT
ARE SOUND

EMPATHY
I BELIEVE YOU CARE ABOUT
ME & MY SUCCESS

ADAPTED AND REPRINTED WITH PERMISSION FROM "UNLEASHED" BY FRANCES X FREI, ANNE MORRIS.
© 2020 BY HARVARD BUSINESS PUBLISHING.

How often do you think about the way you carry yourself, about the image you project through your words and actions? Do you ever consider that your leadership may be undermining your own trustworthiness?

Trust does not start at net positive. Trust is earned. Just because you haven't crossed the line into bad leadership does not equate to having secured trust. Some leaders dismiss this as *not my problem. My people should be earning my trust, not the other way around!* This is unkind territory—the stuff of the Dictators or the Departed.

One difficulty in making headwinds with trust building can be attributed to intention. Without it, a lack of authenticity puts trust on the rocks. People have a radar for fakeness. *Will the real Slim Shady please stand up?* Inauthenticity hurts team collaboration and team performance. How draining is it to have suspicion as the default, with people second-guessing about motives. Leaders object: *I'm not hiding anything! If my people have a question, all they have to do is ask!* Authenticity does not imply oversharing. But it does nothing for trust if people don't know who you are as a person. Your true self creates impact for your people and makes room for others' authentic selves. It is in your life story that authentic leadership emerges, where the full narrative of your personal experiences inspires change and drives impact.

> Authenticity is about being present, not perfect. Authenticity is about being consistent, not contrived. Authenticity is about living your values with conviction. To be authentically you is to be human. Leaders make mistakes, as do their people. Approached with humility, authenticity is the conduit for kindness to perforate leadership.

If empathy is empty, conceivably your people feel you are self-serving. Consider people's *user experience* of you as leader. Pay close attention to micro-behaviours and micro-expressions when interacting with others, such as inconsiderate, even insulting behaviours—*ahem*, multitasking during meetings. Trust is built by moving the dialogue forward, even if it's not your meeting. Amplify the discussion with thought-provoking questions, engage others in the room, and contribute to making it a stimulating exchange for everyone. Meetings feed on energy, and a leader's energy carries greater weight in determining whether the conversation unfolds positively and productively. The time is already blocked. Commit to giving 100 per cent undivided attention to your people.

Trust figured prominently in my conversation on leadership and kindness with Gordon Watson. He considers it his responsibility as a leader to make people feel safe and comfortable speaking up during meetings, whether it's gently soliciting introverted individuals' insights or being sensitive to who's not talking, such as those who are more junior. This acute awareness, reading the situation and being attuned to non-verbals, stems from an intentionality towards kindness, something Gordon continually strives to work on to better himself as a leader.

During my conversation with author Ron Carucci, he noted: 'There is no currency in organizational life more valuable than trustworthiness.' It is a leader's duty to ensure that two questions are always off the table for their people. Leaders should never be the reason their people wonder 'Do I matter?' and 'Do I belong?' Any energy people devote to these questions is energy wasted. To communicate to people that they matter and that they belong, respect people's time. That's Trust, 101. Rarely observed, rarely practiced. Yet research indicates that *time* is what people most wanted from their boss as a symbol of respect.[6] When leaders show up on time, or, *gasp*, show up early, they hold their people's value in high regard. Time, our most valuable resource, is a simple gift and a basic action leaders can take to build trust.

Let's talk logic. If logic is the limiting factor, your people may have questioned your process or doubted your ability to execute. Hit it from two angles. First, ground your points in sound evidence—objective facts and data give legitimacy to your arguments. Speak on topics in which you are confident and have the humility to defer to experts. Second, a parade of facts delivered in a monotone will lose your audience. Conversely, too flowery and embellished comes across as salesy. Effective storytelling—the capacity to tell a compelling narrative—helps leaders inspire, persuade, and build credibility.[7] Beyond telling a cogent story, ask and invite questions to understand people's level of understanding and ensure everyone is on the same page.

It doesn't take long for people to know whether their leader supported them during tough times. Leaders who came through on promises and delivered on commitments. Leaders who care for their people's mental health and wellbeing. Trust—a leader's most valuable currency. Build it carefully, and with intention.

Trust Makes Tough, Kind

Impact Drivers prioritize people by building healthy relationships without sacrificing productivity and results. Once leaders establish, without equivocation, that kindness is immutable, leaders can be tough with their people. Kindness and toughness, then, are reciprocal elements in service of each other, grounded in trust. People appreciate that toughness in a kind leader makes the team successful. The alternative—one which the team will resent—is to live in the land of nice. Pushover territory where leaders feign having things under control, but somewhere down the line, things break down, or the business goes belly up.

This idea came through during my conversation with Dr Oliver Scott Curry of kindness.org, who shared: 'If you help someone, and don't expect or demand to be paid back, there is an expectation of a long-term relationship. We'll help each other. If I help you and expect something back today or tomorrow, what that says is, *I'm not expecting, nor do I want, this to be long-term.* That's two different relationships.' As depicted in the Kindness Matrix, a leader's behaviour, made up of varying degrees of kindness and toughness, is indicative of their investment in relational vs. transactional bonds. Impact Drivers forge durable, lasting relationships with their people, and cultivate a resolve of togetherness. Kindness is not transactional.

When leaders genuinely commit to helping their people succeed, leaders can have any number of difficult conversations with their people, because the intention is never in question. In our conversation about how trust makes tough, kind, Pierre Battah, author of *Humanity at Work*, states: 'If most of your conversations are positive, when you have a hard conversation, yes, your people might be angry with you, and yes, it may be difficult, awkward, and you might lose sleep and worry about it, but you also know you have a higher-order responsibility to intervene, because you care. But if you've created the right conditions to have this conversation, you can rest assured that your people know that this conversation was done in kindness, because they trust you and know that you have their back, and the advice and feedback you gave them was valuable.' Being kind in toughness creates an environment that enables all kinds of exchanges, where people can provide and receive feedback at will and disagree without being disagreeable.

Fact is, as you rise up the leadership ranks, you will naturally be perceived as being less kind, simply because you can't say yes to everything, lest you decide to wander into the Pushover arena. Leading with kindness is not a popularity contest. It is about challenging your people while providing the resources for them to succeed. It is about making tough decisions that benefit your people. Heavy is the head that wears the crown.

People may not see kind leadership for what it is if they don't like the outcome. Let's say Ssi didn't get that promotion. Certainly Ssi may be upset, but if she asked *Do I think my boss treated me with kindness during a difficult conversation?* She may answer in the affirmative if her boss articulated a clear and honest rationale as to why she was unsuccessful and offered a roadmap for her professional development.

Kind leadership should pre-empt such questions through regular check-ins that support structured progress. In cases where someone lacks the skills or resources to do their job well, training and mentorship are put in place to facilitate their development. In some instances, the person is likely unhappy with their role or where they're at. Then it becomes a series of kind conversations to understand the appropriate course of action, whether through job crafting, transferring to another role within the company, or, if there is a complete misalignment in fit, helping them find an external role that is better suited. In any case, it should not come as a surprise to anyone if they are denied a promotion or are let go.

As Lâle Kesebi observed: 'Imagine if it were you, and you never heard anything negative from your direct reports then, out of the blue, they tell you they want to leave. That's like waking up one day and your spouse tells you they want a divorce. It's kinder to be more than less predictable. But predictability is not the full formula. Kindness is knowing what you need to deliver. It is not kindness to keep low performers.'

Christine Ip of UOB describes the case of a poor performer who was not improving despite many developmental training opportunities. Christine first assessed their role and job fit, as likely this individual was dissatisfied with their current situation. Then Christine assessed their values, strengths, and weaknesses to determine whether they might be suitable for another role within the company. Leading with impact for Christine was the kindness shown in guiding them to the right opportunity in another industry, while being kind to the team and the company by not tolerating a low performer. If someone is miserable or disengaged in their work and consequently unable to achieve on their objectives, it is a form of kindness, for everyone involved, to recognize that this may be the wrong job for them. For Christine, impact comes from maintaining a fair and transparent process throughout. Otherwise, as she says, 'You don't deserve to be a leader.'

Transparency builds trust. This starts with purpose, mission, and values. It covers systems, policies, processes. It touches recruitment, promotion, and retention. It is a kindness to have clearly mapped objectives, linkages to performance, connections to reward structures. It is kind to give context and perspective for how this project and that task bridge company objectives. Lack of role clarity is one of the most frustrating sources of work stress for people, and so easily prevented with communication and clarity. This is where the toughness, in kindness, plays in service to providing direction to people.

On this topic, Pierre concludes: 'All leadership is situational, and leaders need enough tools to match the situation. The sublayer is this: Does everything I do as a leader come from a place of kindness, a human place that enables me to pull out the tools? Because if the answer is yes, it will be much easier for me to pull out a hammer, knowing it's not coming from a place of malice. It's not from ego. But it's with the knowledge that we're going to go through this challenge together, because I'm here for our mutual advancement. If you're going to repair an engine, don't you feel better equipped with twenty-seven tools than seven?'

When people trust that their leader has their best interests and advancement in mind, toughness becomes an act of kindness.

Trust Communicates Intentional Flexibility

With a kind intention in place, leaders can be flexible in finding resolutions to myriad situations they invariably face. What is unkind are rigid policies that force square pegs into round holes. What leaders find is that the bi-directionality of trust, both in earning people's trust and trusting people, contributes to more efficient processes and operations. During my conversation with Jeffery Tan of Jardine MINDSET Singapore, he emphasized the importance of empowering the middle layers of management to make the right decisions as a demonstrable feature of intentional flexibility. He shared an example from when he was a young lawyer: 'If we worked beyond a particular time, say 9 p.m., the firm would give you a taxi voucher, almost like a reward. If someone on your team finished at 8:50 p.m., would you, as a manager, say to this individual 'Oh, it's 8:50 p.m., sure you can go home, but you won't get the voucher!' Imagine that! People will stay for an extra 10 minutes to get the voucher, but they'll remember that you, a representative of this company, are a stickler, unable to see the bigger picture.' Sadly, this story, in various forms, is heard time and again. Companies that get caught up in bureaucracy and administrative processes, following extensive rule books outlining everything that one can and mostly cannot do to a T, with each rule being uniformly applied so as not to 'set a precedent'. Intentional flexibility is trusting your people to make kind decisions in the many shades of grey.

The Netflix culture earns recognition in part because Netflix decided to trust people over process. They refused to implement hard rules against the potential for bad seeds, which would punish the 99 per cent, whether in reference to their unlimited vacation policy or their expense policy, which consists of one sentence—to 'act in Netflix's best interests'. Netflix made an intentional choice to treat everyone as fully-formed adults and are unapologetic about this approach. Reed Hastings describes in his book *No Rules Rules*: 'Even if your employees spend a little more when you give them freedom, the cost is still less than having a workplace where they can't fly. If you limit their choices by making them check boxes and ask for permission, you won't just frustrate your people, you'll lose out on the speed and flexibility that comes from a low-rule environment.'[8] A mature culture of individuals committed to doing the inner homework, bring a shared understanding of what it means to treat each other with kindness in the context of an organization where people work industriously and responsibly to produce something meaningful, together. That's collective trust.

Leaders fear that being flexible somehow communicates that they have relaxed their standards. This is fear of change. They fear that flexibility will loosen their grip on control. Flexibility is not about lowering standards. It is about embracing new ways of working that might work better. It takes some getting used to, as was the case with PwC, who took over a decade to fully embrace a culture of flexibility. But what they learned was that throwing out the rule book paid dividends. PwC calls its approach 'everyday flexibility,' which allows teams to best determine what contributions are expected from each member in what time frame.[9] So long as people are delivering what they need to, when they need to, why does it matter where and when they do their work? What good does it do to force someone who works best at night, to be in the office at 8 a.m., when they're possibly at their worst? How does it benefit the company to deny a parent early leave to attend to a family matter, when that may well spiral into a series of hassles that affect the whole family? What productivity can you still expect from that individual? The same degree of flexibility, applied to everyone, recognizes and appreciates each individual's unique situation. If you believed enough in someone to hire them, you should trust them enough to get their work done. The ROK associated with intentional flexibility is that people reciprocate the care and concern showed to them by being more engaged and devoting more effort to their work. By adapting to the changing needs of a diverse workforce, people are happier, more committed, and more productive.

When Flexibility Bends and Breaks

Leadership is often fraught with missteps, playing out as a rehearsal, not the main act. The irony of leadership is that, despite the best of intentions, leaders at times accidentally stress their people out even more. Here are two ways leaders inadvertently do this: [10]

1. **Being overly negative:** The use of words or phrases such as *that's a problem*, *that's unacceptable*, or *that's stupid*,

along with micro-expressions such as a disinterested sneer, live in The Dictator territory. Not only do these behaviours inhibit trust, people internalize negativity, triggering anxiety. Being overly negative, even pessimistic, is demotivating, and people disengage as they start feeling like, *Why bother? Nothing I do ever pleases you.*

2. **Neglecting people's emotions:** In times of crisis and change, people are justifiably worried about their future with the company. Leaders need to be extra empathetic, extra compassionate. A lot of leaders aren't comfortable with this: *I haven't had training!* Leaders aren't therapists and people don't expect them to be. But leaders have to listen, acknowledge, and support. *I hear you. What can I do?*

Coincidentally, as I write this, I received an email from NiQ Lai, in which he shared a message sent to all HKBN Talents on a day when Hong Kong was experiencing heavy rainstorms:

> Dear All Fellow HKBN Elite Sports Teammates,
> When there is bad weather that impacts traffic, let's exercise HKBN flexibility to care for our fellow teammates . . . please coordinate amongst our team members to be as flexible as needed . . . We are 1-HKBN, but we consist of vastly different regions and vastly different job functions, hence we cannot have one-rule-fits-all . . . Most legacy companies force-fit their operations . . . with one-rule-fits-all policies. This often means setting rules for the worst case, i.e. assuming staff will cheat the system, which then means rules on rules and results in very thick staff policy handbooks. At HKBN, we assume the far majority of Talents will do the right thing, and for the exceptional few who abuse our trust, we exit them, rather than penalizing the far majority of good Talents with excessive micro-management resulting in bureaucracy.

It's understandable when people have a bad day, or something unavoidable comes up. We are human and life happens. Life is messy. There will always be intense periods of challenges and unforeseen setbacks. Kind leadership is being malleable, agile, adapting to the situation and helping as and where needed. During periods of uncertainty and chaos, your people need less inspirational speeches and more practical actions that support them through a difficult time. Initial research is indicative of mental health and wellbeing benefits stemming from flexible work arrangements.[11] Because mental health and wellbeing are fluid and ever-changing, it is impossible to have hard edges on the support provided to people. Intentional flexibility indicates leaders' willingness to accommodate their people's needs while meeting work goals and company objectives.

Kind leaders self-reflect on a regular basis: *What might my people be feeling right now?* Kind leaders ask their people: *How can I help?* Intentional flexibility acknowledges that people's needs are diverse and may occasion different forms of help at different times. Flexibility is not one-size-fits-all. Where Xin might prefer frequent check-ins, this same behaviour might be perceived as overcrowding or micromanagement for Anya. Be the trusted stretchy pants. Give some wiggle room. So long as work quality is not affected, leaving a meaningful mark in your people's home life, mental health, and wellbeing is an invaluable kindness.

While leadership missteps—being overly negative or neglecting people's emotions—are blatantly stressful when on the receiving end, other commonly adopted leadership behaviours may be well-intentioned, but may have an accidentally diminishing impact:[12]

3. **Being an idea machine:** This is clearly well-intentioned. No one can accuse you of being a Pushover

or a Departed! You have so many ideas, you're waking up in the middle of the night to jot them down, excited to tell your team about all of them. But this can be overwhelming and confusing to your people. *Do I keep working on the idea you were excited about yesterday? Or do I drop everything and pick up this new idea you're excited about today? Worse, am I expected to work on all of them?* Too many ideas sacrifices strategic direction. Before sharing an idea, think through what the expectations are for your people. Instead of sharing your ideas, create space for others to share theirs.

4. **Playing hero:** This is well-meaning because leaders are lending a helping hand through problem-solving. For all intents and purposes, this is beneficial, so long as leaders are mindful of giving fish vs. teaching how to fish. As Liz Wiseman says, swooping in too soon or too often contributes to people who are dependent. Complacent. Putting out fires deprives people of the learning that comes from making mistakes. Next time a team member flags a problem, ask them for the solve, and a recommended plan for moving forward. Empowering people confers trust, and expecting complete solutions builds accountability, all while stretching people to their full potential.

Leaders need to strike the right balance between intentional flexibility and over-intentioned support. Overdoing flexibility cripples intent.

To Flex, Press Pause

Kind leadership is about helping people rise. But leadership is hard. People make mistakes that put you in the red. People miss deadlines that affect your own deliverables. People don't do things the way you would have done them, or the way you would have liked. Frustration is only natural. At times, leaders may lash out because they're leading from anxiety. Resist the urge to react in haste, as responding in the heat of the moment can only shatter trust so carefully built with your people.[13]

Instead, activate mindful intention. Initiating the *art of the pause* allows leaders to recognize that they have been operating from an alter ego, their evil twin that is impulsive, reactive, and quick to blame. Experiencing negativity—anxiety, frustration, annoyance—is the tip-off that the evil twin is preparing for a takedown. This is exactly the time to pause. Corresponding to the first R, rest, in the 3Rs described in Chapter 5, the art of the pause prevents leaders from uttering impetuous words that embarrass or demean. The pause allows leaders to shift back to their deliberative and rational self, making a planful response based on kind intentionality.

Sigal Atzmon of Medix Global sees pausing as a state of mind where leaders can disconnect and re-centre. A leadership hack that allows her to check her own ego and perspective as a leader and be fully in the moment with her people. Taking the time to pause and ponder a person's situation is a seemingly trivial gesture but is what, for Sigal, establishes strong bonds of trust with her people.

For Christine Ip of UOB, accumulated experience in difficult situations has taught her to excuse herself or pause a meeting during heated discussion so that both parties can cool off and return to the table, continuing the conversation as adults. Christine considers pausing to be timely moments for self-reflection, such a critical part of her leadership that she starts each day humbly reflecting on the previous day's activities and interactions with her people. To develop herself as a leader, she reflects on whether any of her communications, verbal and non-verbal, may have been unintentionally diminishing, and takes corrective action that day.

Recognizing when to press pause is a kindness leaders give to themselves and their people. As leaders, what intentional flexibility boils down to, and indeed the only guiding principle for a leader to follow, is to *be kind by being flexible. You never know what someone is going through.*

Chapter Exercises

Trust Reflection

Frances Frei and Anne Morriss' book *Unleashed: The Unapologetic Leader's Guide to Empowering Everyone Around You* inspired this exercise. Reflect on a few recent instances when you were not trusted as much as you wanted to be.

- Which of the three trust pillars (authenticity, empathy, logic) went shaky on you?
- Which of the three trust pillars held strong?
- Identify patterns across examples. Was the same pillar shaky, the same pillar holding tight? What does this tell you?
- Do a trust analysis. Identify trust triggers—people, situations, stressful periods, where the same pillar becomes shaky.
- What actions can you take to build more trust with those around you?

Cue the Pause

Following from the Trust Reflection exercise above, once you have identified your trust triggers, you are well-placed to develop a cue to link to that trigger. It could be as simple as repeating the phrase *press pause* slowly 5x in your mind. Following a conditioning principle, this cue becomes linked to your trigger, serving as a gentle reminder for you to 'cue the pause'. Step back, even if it means taking a short physical break from a meeting, to regroup in your personal bubble of safety. Activate the 3Rs: Rest, Reflect, Reframe.

Questions to Guide Intentional Flexibility

1. What is one way I might have been letting my own anxiety diminish my people?
2. What is one way I might have been overdoing flexibility?
3. What is one action I can take today to course correct and demonstrate intentional flexibility for my people?

Chapter 12

Support 'em with Kindness

Being intentionally flexible segues into providing supportive action that helps your people rise. Leaders are accustomed to acting decisively, reacting swiftly, and defending their position, however uninformed a decision may be. Business schools push for skills that demand, even reward, combative debate and negotiation that articulates a defence. The corporate set-up doesn't help. Position and title often override the one supportive practice that can benefit all leaders, which is to listen.

When leaders chart a new course that elevates their people by learning from them, they gain better insight into people and process. Those on the front lines hold the workarounds to cumbersome operational mechanisms and are best placed to offer suggestions to make the work, and by extension, the company, better. Connecting with your people is the only way to understand the pulse of the business and how to support them. Garry Ridge briefed me about speaking to his tribe members every minute of every day, because: 'How do you know what's going on if you don't talk to your people?'

Like it or not, conversation is happening in your company. You can either foster inclusive communication for greater alignment and a sense of working purposefully together or learn to tolerate uninspired results from people who do not feel a sense of belonging, inclusion, or loyalty to the company.

Kind Leaders Listen

Expectation: Leaders are confident in having clearly communicated a message.
Reality: People deem an overall lack of communication from their leaders that further confuses.

Leaders generally and generously overestimate their communication skills. In practice, *mis*communication represents a glaring leadership bottleneck. When a leader is called out for poor communication, they tend to berate the listener for *not getting it.* This insulates leaders from the voice of the people and from what is really going on in the company. As playwright George Bernard Shaw stated: 'The single biggest problem in communication is the illusion that it has taken place.' Good communication, like a tango, takes two. It also takes two to quarrel, and two to know, as Pink Floyd sang. Throw in the power dynamics, and it quickly becomes apparent that, while effective communication takes two, people are not going to be as forthcoming with raising concerns or challenging a leader's views if the context has not been properly set. In a world where most leaders are talking and asserting their authority, such a context, rooted in kindness, adopts listening. After all, the tango is a tangled dance.

Listening is a discipline. In a conversation, there is a window of between twenty and forty seconds after which our conversation partner starts to lose interest.[1] For newer generations growing up watching fifteen-second TikTok videos, this window is probably narrower.

For all the data supporting listening as a critical skill of effective leaders,[2] and despite what leaders may implicitly know to be true, listening, like kindness, is uncommon in leaders due to the forces permeating toxic cultures and the rise of bad bosses. Feeling the pressure to know it all, leaders don't listen to understand; rather, they listen to respond. Listening itself is an art—just ask any spouse (many of whom learned the hard way). This spouse would tell you that listening is *not* being a silent recipient of information with the occasional nod or 'mmm-hmm,' indicative of half-hearted or distracted listening. Just the opposite. Listening is an active process that transmits genuine interest in the other person's thinking, feeling, opinion, and experience.

What's your listening style? Experts outline four styles of listening:[3]

- **Analytical listening:** Aims to analyze problems
- **Relational listening:** Aims to build connections and understand underlying emotions
- **Critical listening:** Aims to judge conversation content and speaker
- **Task-focused listening:** Aims to efficiently transfer information

Identifying our listening default and learning to adapt and switch styles according to what the speaker needs can improve the impact and value we bring to a conversation. In addition, every conversation would benefit from incorporating six levels of listening:[4]

- **Level 1 listener:** Creates a safe space for difficult conversations
- **Level 2 listener:** Places attention squarely on the other party (*read:* put the phone away!)
- **Level 3 listener:** Seeks to understand the substance of what is being said through active listening

- **Level 4 listener:** Observes non-verbal cues and body language for a deeper understanding
- **Level 5 listener:** Strives to empathize and validate the other person's emotions
- **Level 6 listener:** Asks thoughtful questions to clarify assumptions and intended meaning to check understanding and reframes issues to add new insights

While not every conversation reaches a Level 6, each level builds one from the next, offering prescriptive guidance for leaders to sharpen their listening skills. Done well, being an active and empathetic listener cultivates trust, respect, and psychologically safe environments.

Kind Leaders Ask Good Questions

Listening is one part of a kind conversation. Impact Drivers create a feeling of inclusivity for their people. Research has revealed that when people interact with leaders who made them feel included, not only did they feel valued and feel a sense of belonging, 80 per cent of participants also felt *confident* about their capabilities.[5]

Kind leadership is being an involved exchange partner. As important as linear listening is for a leader, Impact Drivers strike an appropriate balance between two types of communication behaviours. *Advocacy* is evident when leaders dominate the conversation. Leaders projecting advocacy enforce their viewpoint. This is the common stance of the bad Dictator bosses who relish in making decisions and influencing others. They don't ask, they tell. *Inquiry* maps on to listening mode, asking questions, seeking others' perspectives. Leaders adopting inquiry don't assert, they aspire to learn.[6,7]

Kindness is reflected in a balance of advocacy and inquiry, where conversation is collaborative and mutual learning takes place. Constructive debate is stimulated in a back-and-forth exchange: *What are your thoughts on my reasoning? Is there anything I am unaware of, or may have overlooked? Is there additional information we should be considering here?*

Imbalance from an advocacy perspective is evidenced in scenarios where leaders don't share the floor, where people feel exasperated and diminished as leaders impose their views. Imbalance from an inquiry perspective plays off more like an interview, which translates to being perceived as an indecisive leader. Lacking both advocacy and inquiry is defeating for your people, and are hallmark behaviours of the Departed, where people might as well talk to a brick wall.

Beyond balancing the quantity or ratio of advocacy to inquiry during conversation, the quality of conversation behaviours matter. Advocacy can be effective when leaders engage in transparent communication, walking people through assumptions made, facts considered, and evidence brought to bear on judgments. On the inquiry side, asking closed questions (*yes or no*) precludes generation of rich information; asking pointed questions puts people on the spot; and asking rhetorical or leading questions is just advocacy in disguise. Open-ended questions that probe, or high-level questions that inspire people to think bigger, are more fruitful: *What are the emerging mental health and wellbeing needs of our people that we need to meet?*

Leading with Kindness Is Feedback-Forward

If listening is hard, giving and receiving feedback can seem like a Herculean challenge. Who actually enjoys receiving feedback? It is difficult not to take feedback personally. Our brain processes the words 'opportunities for improvement' as a personal attack, no matter how constructively it is framed. Moreover, any feedback that triggers a personal insecurity detonates like an unsolicited truth bomb. As a result, people end up rebuffing or repressing feedback because avoidance is easier.

Seeing as most leaders have not had training in conveying effective feedback, the entire process runs the gamut from unhelpful, arcane, to straight up savage! This affects self-esteem, confidence, and even the relationship.[8]

Leaders tend to give people a feedback sandwich: stuff the unappetizing chunk in between two pieces of palatable carbs. This is considered a balanced approach that softens the blow of criticism while ending on a more positive note. Recent research shows that feedback sandwiches are unhealthy. Gluten is bad. It's confusing to people to properly pick out relevant pieces and know what to do with it, undermining leaders' feedback, and their authority overall.[9]

This shouldn't be taken to mean avoid carbs altogether (positive feedback). Carbs are delicious, and everyone loves them, much to the chagrin of the gluten free. When leaders understand gaffes in delivering feedback, and appreciate people's feedback anxiety, they can hold tough conversations in kindness.

Kind leaders aim to provide transparent and impactful feedback, which requires the approach of a coach, or a mentor.[10] With a foundation of trust laid, people are more prone to view kind leaders as advocating for their success, a beacon that lights a path forward. Immediately, this removes any pretext from a distressing appraisal and repositions to one of mutual support and learning.

Rather than an annual feedback relay, kind leaders engage their people in ongoing conversation, allowing feedback to be provided in real-time. This allows leaders to work collaboratively with their team to understand the issues and their perception of the issues; to identify vulnerabilities and barriers to success; to consult on potential structural factors that may have contributed to misunderstandings; to explore strategies for circumventing the issues; to plan next steps, and to consider support and resources that can be put in place to help each person succeed.

Kind leaders, as a guiding light, refrain from providing solutions and opt for curiosity questions aimed at exploration that facilitate learning. These can be partitioned into defining the problem and lighting a path forward:[11]

Diagnose

- What is your perception of what is happening?
- What outcomes are you trying to achieve?
- What have you tried so far?
- How have you handled similar challenges in the past?
- Have you tried to resolve this challenge?
- Can you walk me through the process?

Overcome

- What are different ways of addressing this issue?
- What would happen if you tried this?
- How can I support you in your progress?

Impact Drivers are also mindful of unconscious biases influencing the feedback process. Research shows that women tend to receive vague feedback ('You had a great year'), as compared with specific feedback men receive that is directly tied to outcomes ('Once you deepen your domain knowledge here, you will be able to contribute to design decisions'). This feedback obfuscates developmental progress and is a disadvantage for women's progression, so difficult it is to make a case for advancement with throwaway broad strokes comments.

To protect against these potential biases, kind leaders take intentional action that systematizes the feedback process, described by Stanford professor Shelley Correll's team:[12]

- outline specific criteria
- define behaviours that indicate mastery for each criteria

- use the same criteria for everyone at the same level
- set a goal of discussing three specific business outcomes with everyone
- make feedback specific and tied to business outcomes. Instead of 'People like working with you', try 'You are effective at building team outcomes. You successfully resolved the divide between the engineering and product teams on which features to prioritize in our last sprint, leading us to ship the product on time.'
- focus on development and make it actionable
- set targets and accompanying timelines
- incorporate 360-degree feedback to ensure each person receives insight from multiple relevant sources[13]

Approached with kind intention, feedback is less Herculean and can even produce joy.[14]

Create Communication Circles

Despite having access to all channels of communication, the missed opportunity for leaders is trapping themselves in an inner circle promoting confirmation bias. Kind leaders construct designated listening and feedback channels to protect against blind spots. To do so:

- **Reward bad news:** People need to be convinced that being the bearer of bad news is a commendable act. As it should be. Discovering problems after the fact is a waste of resources. Incentivize contrasting opinions. In their *Harvard Business Review* article[15], Adam Bryant, managing director of Merryck & Co, and Kevin W. Sharer, former CEO and chairman of Amgen, describe how Penny Pritzker, who served as the US secretary of commerce from 2013 to 2017, told candidates that the one way to get fired is to keep problems to themselves. This level of empowerment is needed to persuade people to disagree as a safeguard from groupthink. Assemble a dedicated team to identify potential risks and play devil's advocate, the result of which is securing a greater pool of information that leads to more informed decisions.

- **Collect leadership feedback:** Aside from giving feedback, kind leaders proactively seek upward and 360-degree feedback, earnestly looking to grow their leadership to better serve their people's needs. These are important opportunities that build trust. The challenge is making people feel safe doing so and needs to be continually encouraged. Get people into the habit of offering this feedback. Soft call on your people by giving them a heads-up with ample time to prepare. Make it an agenda item on your next one-on-one, and caution against sandwiches! Use the traffic light system: What should I *start* doing? What should I *stop* doing? What should I *continue* doing? Or, try asking for advice, not feedback. Research shows that, when people are asked to provide advice, more critical and actionable areas of improvement are identified, as compared with asking people to provide feedback, which tends to result in vague positive comments. Whereas feedback triggers evaluation, advice triggers improvement.[15]

On the receiving end, the next time you receive feedback, press pause, assume positive intent, reflect on the underlying message, commit to making changes to strengthen your leadership, and express gratitude, because it is not easy to deliver feedback to the boss. Make *Thank you for the feedback!* a habit.

Impact Drivers adopt a communication approach that is ongoing, personal, direct, and interactive, an intimate dance that balances listening, dialogue, giving, and receiving feedback. Active and empathic listening cuts barriers and gets to the heart of people issues that foster human connection. Listening is an undervalued supportive action for leaders. You listen well in service to others.

Chapter Exercises

Kind Conversation Reflection

In this exercise, provide an honest self-reflection on your typical communication patterns.

- Listening assessment:
  o What is my listening style?
  o What level of listener (Level 1 to 6) am I?
  o What is my advocacy to inquiry (talking to listening) ratio?
  o What is the quality of my advocacy and inquiry behaviours?
  o How can I implement active and empathic listening to make my people feel safe, included, and confident?
  o How can I make better use of big picture questions to support my people?

- Feedback assessment:
  o What is my feedback approach, in terms of process, timing, delivery, and response?
  o How might I have been unintentionally providing biased feedback to different people? What can I do to course correct?
  o How can I incorporate feedback-forward strategies to deliver impactful feedback?

Questions to Guide Kind Conversation

1. How can I create a communication network, through rewarding bad news?
2. Who will I invite to provide upward and 360-degree feedback on my leadership?

Chapter 13

Servant Leadership Needs a New PR Manager

While the concept of kind leadership may be new, the idea of leader as servant has been around since ancient Chinese philosophy. Chinese philosopher Lao Tzu has been attributed with words to the effect of: 'As for the best leader, the people do not notice their existence. When the best leader's work is done, the people say, we did it ourselves.' This captures a sense of thanklessness in being a leader. And that's kind of the point. Servant leaders aren't in it for glory. Robert Greenleaf, founder of the modern servant leadership movement and the Greenleaf Center for Servant Leadership, stated that being a servant leader 'begins with the natural feeling that one wants to serve, to serve first. Then conscious choice brings one to aspire to lead.'[1] Servant leadership is about supportive actions that benefit your people. To serve your people's best interest. In 2015, Howard Schultz, who built Starbucks into an international brand, wrote an op-ed for *The New York Times*, declaring that we are in 'desperate need of servant leaders.' According to Schultz, 'the values of servant leadership—putting others first and leading from the heart—need to emerge from every corner of American life, including the business community.'[2]

Dan Cable, author of *Alive at Work*, and Professor at London Business School, has written extensively about servant leadership: 'When you're a leader—no matter how long you've been in your role or how hard the journey was to get there—you are merely overhead unless you're bringing out the best in your employees. Unfortunately, many leaders lose sight of this. The way to change this is with humility as a servant leader.'[3] There has been a recent push for values-based leadership—empathetic leadership, authentic leadership, even ESG leadership. These leadership approaches are suggestive that one is either a servant leader or one is not. You are an empathetic leader or you are not. This is the wrong message. These approaches are rooted in the nexus of action—in behaviours that are kind and that serve people. When you unpack the mindset and behaviours that make up servant leadership, you have kindness as the foundation.

Do Your Actions Serve You or Your People?

The centrepiece of servant leadership is about people, first. The *motive* of servant leadership stems from an external desire to be a steward of the organization rather than an internal desire to be a leader. The *mode* of servant leadership calls for one-on-one interactions that build deep and genuine connections with your people; prioritizing their needs, interests, and goals above those of your own; and recognizing and appreciating that each member of your team has different needs, interests, goals, strengths, and limitations, which change over time. The *mindset* of servant leaders is that of a trustee. Empowerment and development are deliberate actions provided to those entrusted to your care, with an overarching concern towards the wellbeing of the larger community.[4] Servant leadership identifies with creating shared value through promoting the interests of multiple stakeholders. The ideology of servant leaders is that of stakeholder-centric management, where putting the needs of the people first does not come at a cost to the business.

Researchers have identified seven elements of servant leadership that are connected with behaviours that kind leaders adopt to support their people:[5]

- **Emotional healing:** Sensitivity to your people's personal concerns
- **Community value:** Genuine interest for helping the community
- **Empowerment:** Entrusting people with autonomy and decision-making authority
- **People first:** Prioritizing your people through words and actions
- **Helping people grow and succeed:** Advancing your people's personal and professional growth
- **Ethical:** Interacting fairly, honestly, and with integrity
- **Conceptual skills:** Knowledge of tasks, opportunities, and constraints of the organization to effectively assist your people

The servant approach engages people in numerous dimensions, including relational, emotional, ethical, and even spiritual. Contrary to its labelling, a kind, servant leader, is not a pushover. These leaders do not blindly give in to their people's demands. They are competent, sharp, effective business leaders, while providing autonomy and responsibility to their people. They are flexible, but unyielding when the situation demands. They treat people with respect, dignity, empathy, and kindness. As partners. Branding-wise, servant leaders need a little PR refresh.

Cumulative research on servant leadership overwhelmingly demonstrates the benefits of servant leadership for employees and organizations. People are not only more engaged, satisfied, and committed under a servant leader, but in addition collaboration and innovation improve; the climate of the team and organization change for the better; and employee, team, and organization performance increase, as do wellbeing and work-life balance.[6,7]

The Unicorns of Business

A survey of over 1500 working adults from the American Psychological Association's *Work and Wellbeing Survey* shows that, in those with a supportive leader:[8]

- 91 per cent feel motivated to do their best
- 91 per cent experience job satisfaction
- 91 per cent have a positive relationship with their leader
- 93 per cent have a positive relationship with their colleagues
- 89 per cent are more likely to recommend their company as a great place to work

This all seems pretty convincing. So, why don't we see more servant leaders out there? For the same reasons we don't see more kind leaders. Servant leadership gets a bad rep because it is beneath those leaders who operate from ego, to serve. *Servant Leader—Kind Leader*—doesn't have as satisfying a ring to it the way *BOSS* does.[9] Therein lies the problem. In modern society, people suffer from a sense of entitlement led by self-interest— the 'me disease.' Kindness and empathy are overlooked by leaders, so incompatible it is with their self-aggrandizing nature. The skillset that landed them the position was about *me me me*. Their new role as a leader is about *the people*. Not even close, and now they are hopelessly unqualified for this new responsibility. While being a great privilege, leadership demands great sacrifice. When things go right, leaders have to give away all the credit. When things go wrong, leaders have to step up and take responsibility. Such is the burden of leadership.

Serving Others Serves You Too

One of the challenges facing those who are on the fence about servant leadership is that servant leadership is taxing, especially if you have a large team or company. Think about it. Constantly prioritizing your people, putting their needs and interests ahead of your own, the self-sacrifice involved in succession planning. Sounds exhausting! In fact, recent research suggests that servant leadership is potentially depleting for leaders.[10] Well, great. That can't be it.

I wanted to affirm whether self-benefits exist for leaders who practice servant leadership. If we are to convince leaders to adopt these behaviours, it seemed logical to demonstrate the advantages afforded by servant leadership to leaders themselves, beyond gains to other stakeholders. During the pandemic, in 2020, arguably when we needed servant leaders the most, along with my DBA student at the time, now Dr Cecilia Leung, former senior executive of Cathay Pacific Group, Hong Kong's flagship carrier, we developed a servant leadership program and trained over 100 senior executives from a wide range of industries, from finance to healthcare, to adopt servant leadership on a daily basis. If servant leadership is manifested in behaviours, we reasoned that we could train leaders to adopt these behaviours day-to-day with a simple prompt at the start of their workday. Drawing from research demonstrating the benefits of self-reflection, expressive writing, and self-management,[11,12] we asked each leader to reflect, write, and commit to three behaviours exemplifying stewardship directed towards their people each day. Some examples of self-generated behaviours:

- *'P's family are struggling just now due to a loss in the family. I could speak to them today to see if there are any ways we can be more flexible with work to allow them some extra time to help their family.'* (Laboratory Manager, environmental industry)
- *'K needs support with impressing on his team the need for culture change in the organisation to improve. . . safety and quality performance. I will help him by demonstrating my support for the project at a steering committee meeting later this morning. J is rather overwhelmed by the number of projects and tasks she has on hand. While she is capable of delivering on them, she needs to be encouraged to prioritise and make sure she reserves enough personal time for herself and her family. I will coach her on this when I speak to her over the next couple of days.'* (Group Director, aerospace industry)

We conducted this training across ten consecutive workdays. During the first week, leaders were assigned to a control condition, where they were asked to write about neutral experiences, such as a description of their surrounding work environment. During the second week, leaders received the servant leadership training prompt each morning.

We found that, on days leaders engaged in the servant leadership training, there were statistically significant improvements in their management and leadership functions as compared with the week they did not participate in the training (the control week). Participating in the training enabled leaders to be better managers and leaders, in terms of providing more structure and inspiring their people through uplifting interactions that build people up. Beyond these benefits to their people, on days leaders were prompted to exhibit these behaviours, their wellbeing was enhanced. They perceived higher levels of thriving and a sense that their work is meaningful, as compared with the control week.

We also considered what explains these benefits. We found that on days leaders participated in the training, leaders perceived greater prosocial impact to their people; that is, they were more likely to observe the positive meaning their actions were having on their people. This, in turn, motivated leaders to continue along the lines of 'being a good leader' that day, to engage in supportive behaviours for their people. Servant leadership contributes to a self-reinforcing cycle of benefits for leaders themselves. Servant leadership is also energizing and builds positivity.

The best part of this is that it can be implemented by anyone. This training was provided to busy executives during the height of Covid-19. A small nudge inviting leaders to reflect, develop, and exemplify three servant leadership behaviours each day helped leaders perceive the impact their behaviours were having on their people, resulting in positive change, for their people, and for their own wellbeing. Unsolicited feedback from these senior leaders post-training was overwhelmingly positive. We did not realize the extent of the impact this training had, until many reached out to express their commitment to continue developing these behaviours into habits:

- *'I can see and feel the benefits of practicing servant leadership. Never knew I can be a servant leader!'* (Managing Director, multinational finance company)
- *'Only after the* [training] *I realized it is possible to put subordinates' individual priority above my own and, most*

importantly, that makes me feel great and can accomplish more at work. I am not paying lip service to corporate jargon 'people come first,' but really doing it.' (Manager, multinational transportation company)

I Feel You. I Support You.

Leave it to Oprah Winfrey, a woman who has dedicated her decades long career to connecting with people, to conclude after forty years that leadership is about empathy, for the purpose of inspiring and empowering lives. That's something worthy of note when considering how to help people rise through demonstrations of supportive behaviour.

When leaders fall short on empathy, or feign the appearance of empathy, the damage is costly for the leader and the company, in terms of reputation and financial repercussions. On April 9, 2017, four United Airlines employees needed to get on a fully booked plane leaving from Chicago's O'Hare airport. Passengers, already boarded, were not about to give up their seat in exchange for a travel voucher. The airline picked individuals to bump off the plane, including Dr David Dao. Dr Dao refused to leave, and the airline called in security officers. The world watched incredulously as videos turned up on the internet of Dr Dao being forcibly dragged off the plane, eyeglasses hanging off his bloodied face.

It took United's (now former) CEO, Oscar Munoz, several attempts before his public response showed any empathy. His initial statement came a day later and apologized for having to re-accommodate customers, missing the mark entirely. He issued another statement blaming Dr Dao for being defiant and belligerent, despite videos and passenger testimony to the contrary. Only a few days later did he follow-up with an apology, promising to do better. Whether this was tied to the sharp drop in United's stock price following this debacle is debatable, but examples abound of significant business cost when leaders display a lack of empathy.

By contrast, Bob Iger, former (now current) CEO of The Walt Disney Company, describes in his book *The Ride of a Lifetime*[13] an incident in June 2016, when he was in China for the opening of Shanghai Disney, a project that took eighteen years and a USD 6 billion investment. The day before, as he was about to lead a VIP tour of the new park, he was informed that a two-year-old boy was killed in an alligator attack at Disney World Florida. A Disney crisis team was already on the scene. Bob issued a public statement offering the company's deepest sympathies, but felt compelled to call the boy's parents, against his legal team's advice due to potential liability. He spoke to the parents from his hotel room, telling them that, as a father, he couldn't fathom what they must be going through. In his book, he describes how he sat, shaking on the edge of his bed: 'I'd been crying so hard that both my contact lenses had come out.' It doesn't bring the boy back, no, but it does reveal the humanity in leadership during a heart-wrenching situation.

Former prime minister of New Zealand, Jacinda Ardern, proves that bold leadership is empathetic *and* strong. In interviews, she notes how kindness, driven by empathy, is the most important quality that has underpinned her leadership. She describes how her leadership has been criticized for not being assertive enough, how her kindness has insinuated weakness. Ardern rebels against this notion: 'I refuse to believe that you cannot be both compassionate and strong. It takes strength to be an empathetic leader.'[14] How refreshing to witness a political leader who recognizes that empathy is the quality that is most needed from leaders who are confronting global challenges. Ardern states: 'We need our leaders to be able to empathize with . . . the next generation that we're making decisions on behalf of. And if we focus only on being seen to be the strongest, most powerful person in the room, then I think we lose what we're meant to be here for. So I'm proudly focused on empathy, because you can be both empathetic and strong.'[15] As we can see from the results she has continually delivered during her term, it's effective.

Thankfully, empathy is something that can be trained. Developed. Psychologist Daniel Goleman, the pioneer of emotional and social intelligence, outlined three types of empathy leaders can express:[16]

- **Cognitive empathy:** Putting yourself in someone else's shoes and seeing their perspective. Understanding how another person thinks and feels.
- **Emotional empathy:** Connecting with the feelings of another person, to feel what they feel. Bob Iger displayed emotional empathy when he spoke with the father of the young child who died.
- **Compassion:** Sharing in the experience of another person. Compassion drives action. It is a motivated behaviour.

Leaders support their people when they take the perspective of their people. Fundamentally, we all know what kindness looks like, because we know how we want to be treated. Role reversal, asking *What if it were me?* allows leaders to act with consideration and support. When leaders can put themselves in their people's situation, the empathy and compassion comes through. Asking *What if it were my family?* prevents leaders from losing sight of their peoples' struggle, as leaders often take on so much, they have developed a tough exterior. Then, *How can I make this person's day better? What is one thing I can do today to minimize the stress of this person?* This is the action piece that opens up a world of possibilities, so limitless are the moments available to leaders to create magic for their people.[17]

As with any skill, it takes consistency to develop empathy into a habit. There are glimpses of empathy entering the business world, as exemplified by leaders such as Satya Nadella and Jacinda Ardern. During Apple CEO Tim Cook's 2017 MIT commencement address, he warned graduates that 'people will try to convince you that you should keep empathy out of your career. Don't accept this false premise.'[18] At the time he made this statement, about 20 per cent of US employers offered empathy training for managers.[19,20] As of 2019, a survey of 150 CEOs revealed that over 80 per cent recognized empathy as a key to success.[21] That's an enormous performance gap, and kindness remains a nice thought unless united with action. And that leads us to the apex of RISE—how leaders energize and equip their team by lifting people up and building a culture of kindness that brings us full circle to a healthy, dynamic, and happy workplace.

Chapter Exercises

Ten-day Servant Leadership Challenge

- For a period of ten consecutive workdays, commit to performing three specific actions directed to your people that exemplify servant leadership that day. Each morning before starting work, take five minutes to reflect on, and write out three distinct behaviours reflecting servant leadership that you intend to carry out that day. The more specific you can be, the better. Please refer to the seven elements of servant leadership. Log your entries in a journal.

- Post-challenge reflection:
  o What are your observations from the past ten days?
  o What surprised you about this challenge?
  o Was this challenge easier or harder than you thought it would be? Why?
  o What reactions did you observe from others?
  o How does this exercise contribute to your leadership growth?
  o How can you build this Servant Leadership Challenge out to your leadership team, your middle managers, your team leads?

Questions to Guide Supportive Action

1. Where do I stand on each of the seven elements of servant leadership?
2. How can I exhibit cognitive empathy, emotional empathy, and compassion towards my people?
3. How can I dial up these elements of empathy to provide supportive action to my people?
4. What is one action I can take today to support my people?

Chapter 14

Supercharge Your Kindness

What if I were to tell you that energy is the greatest predictor of success for leaders, outstripping charisma, influence, or power.[1] You'd ask: Why energy? Because energy is a dynamic motivational force with a bias towards action. We channel energy into our people. Our work. Our community. People 'read the room' by picking up on others' energy. A leader's energy force field is capable of lifting people up when positive or dragging them down when negative.[2] *What energy do you give off?*

Our energy, as a finite personal resource, is limited. Physical energy can be replenished when we prioritize nutrition, exercise, and adequate rest. Emotional energy can be refreshed through relaxation, recovery, and connection to others. Mindful energy can be renewed through meditation and doing away with distractions. Spiritual energy can be accessed when we devote time to meaningful activities, set goals and learn something new, and practice gratitude.[3,4] A major source of energy—*relational energy*—is brought about from the social interactions we have at work. As much as we protect our energy by surrounding ourselves with people who energize us, and avoiding those who de-energize us, leaders need to *give* positive energy to others and protect their people from those who destabilize or diminish energy. The Dictators. The Departed. The Pushovers. Impact Drivers emit a contagious positive energy.

During social interaction, people make judgments about relational and emotional energy. *Is this person energizing me, or sapping me of my energy?* Because energy is reinforcing, people seek to extend and replicate situations that boost energy, while avoiding people that drain energy.[5] Despite what this may imply, leaders don't have to have outsized personalities to energize their people. Research shows that *positive energizers* are people who are virtuous, meaning kind, compassionate, humble, and generous.[6] Energy signals reliance and trustworthiness, and it is kind leaders who cultivate and nurture quality connections that build social cohesion and enhance emotional and relational energy for their people.[7]

Our energy is so valuable, research by Tiziana Casciaro, Professor at the Rotman School of Management, University of Toronto, indicates that people will actually forfeit the acquisition of information if it means protecting their energy.[8] People are determining that it's not worth expending their energy to interact with certain individuals even if they hold instrumental value, as they appraise affective value laden in energy as more critical. People want to be around those that make them feel good. *Positive vibes only.* Sounds logical in everyday situations, but Professor Casciaro's research finds that, even at work, when faced with convoluted challenges, people still preferred likeability over ability, choosing to work with 'lovable fools' over 'competent jerks.'[9] As psychologist Robert Cialdini's thirty-plus years of research on influence has revealed,[10] being well-liked is the strongest predictor of influence, or, more plainly, the best way to influence people is to win friends, as author of the bestselling classic Dale Carnegie[11] would say. Behaviours that are energy depleting comes at a heavy cost, to leaders, their people, and the culture.

Netflix has a clear policy designed to protect their carefully curated energy: 'No Assholes Allowed.' Yes, even if they're a high performer, because that does not give them license to be unkind.[12] How many workplaces tolerate jerks because leadership has made it clear that the compromise is worth making—that competence or know-how is more valuable than being a kind person? The toll of tolerating a toxic person is the rest of the team. The soul-sucker is not worth your energy.

Beyond the fact that our networks help us build resilience, our networks also represent levers of energy that help us recharge. People feel energized when they interact with those who increase their basic human needs. They experience a sense of autonomy, competence, or relatedness.[13] As leaders, issuing a directive (*do this*) does nothing by way of helping people fulfil these needs to the same extent as putting forward a collective goal that distributes power. This promotes a perception of autonomy (*You can decide how to do this*), a sense of competence (*I trust in your ability to do this*), and a sense of belonging (*We're in this together*).

I spoke about the importance of energy during my discussion with Cathryn Gunther of Mars, Incorporated. Cathryn is a staunch believer in human energy as an outcome of holistic health. Mars advances the wellbeing of their Associates intentionally through energy-management training programs, something not many companies do, that help their Associates build effective energy management practices by assessing and encouraging small behaviour changes across the domains of physical, emotional, mental, and spiritual (purpose) health. Program evaluations show that Associates who report having sufficient energy are more likely to be engaged at work, and are up to 3x as likely to stay with Mars. The data also show that energized leaders have more engaged teams, with people who care about each other, who hold conversations that extend beyond the work, and who work together effectively, enhancing performance. Currently, about 25 per cent of the Mars workforce in Australia and New Zealand participate in energy management programs. It's one of the many ways Mars values Associates and helps them bring their best energy to do what matters most—at work and at home.

When leaders transform the work culture to one that is kindness-forward, they get more out of people by investing energy *into* them rather than demanding productivity *out of* them.

Kind Is Happy

To energize your people, bring happiness to the foreground. There is a positive correlation between kindness and happiness. In a meta-analysis of twenty-seven studies investigating whether being kind makes you happier, researchers from the University of Oxford found a clear positive effect.[14] Happiness is boosted by approximately 1 whole point on a 10-point scale owing to being kind, helping others, and creating happiness for others. Yet another ROK.

I spoke at length with Garry Ridge about how happiness spreads through the application of kindness: 'Imagine a place where you go to work every day, make a contribution to something bigger than yourself, you learn something new, you're protected and set free by a compelling set of values, and you go home happy. Happy people create happy families. Happy families create happy communities. And happy communities create a happy world, and we need a happy world. I believe that businesses that send people home happy, are a force for good in the world today.'

Cathryn Gunther agrees with this perspective: 'Anyone who has responsibility for leading or managing people has an opportunity to bring humanity and joy into the workplace. The moments you do that can be fleeting, but there are plenty of them. And to do that really requires an understanding of kindness. Managers are incredibly influential to those who report to them. Leaders with a servant mindset, which is all about focusing on others rather than yourself, do that particularly well.'

We spend, on average, 90,000 hours of our lives at work. That is, to be clear, one-third of our lifespan. It behooves leaders to make workplaces kinder and happier. A place where people, yourself included, *want*, even *choose*, to go.

Chickens, Eggs, and Happiness

It is not new news that happier people are more productive. The management literature is replete with research telling us that happier people are more productive. They are more satisfied with their work, voluntarily work harder, and that translates into more effective performance. Happy people are, on average, 31 per cent more productive. Happy people also make 37 per cent more sales and are 3x more creative than unhappy people.[15]

The chicken and egg of happiness is that people think success will bring them happiness, so end up on a wild goose chase of status, money, and a collection of shiny objects. With each new promotion, rank, and material possession acquired, the happiness target shifts, always just out of reach. Inverting the equation, however, shows that a pursuit of happiness stems from—shocker—within! A positive mindset. In what author Shawn Achor calls the *happiness advantage*, happiness leads to success.[16] Meta-analytic work of 225 studies found a causal effect between happiness and business success, including performance, as well as success across multiple life domains.[17]

Due in part to this convincing body of work and notions of 'happy people are productive people,' and possibly as a response to the push for corporate wellness, companies have been delegating the *job* of happiness to roles such as Chief Happiness Officer.

However laudable, companies need to be cognizant of aggressively shoving happiness down people's throats. Toxic positivity aside, sometimes, people just want to live in their feels. It is impractical, and exhausting, to force feelings of happiness at all times. Research shows that when happiness becomes a chore, people feel *less* happy—a happiness backfire.[18,19] Surface acting, or appearing happy when one is not, as we know, impacts wellbeing.[20] Yet service with a smile is obligated of many customer-facing professions. The looming issue is, as with all solutions that are narrow or limited in scope, happiness on account of free pizza is not going to fix a broken culture. Happiness does not magically appear because you require people to be. The groundwork for a kind culture must first be laid.

Admonition in mind, be a source of joy for your people. Doing purposeful work with a trusted team has been shown to produce oxytocin, the happiness drug.[21] Support people in achieving small wins. Research analyzing 12,000 daily employee diary entries reveals that, on the days people felt the most joy at work, progress, no matter how small the step forward, occurred in 76 per cent of those days.[22] Using thoughtful humour, such as by sharing amusing personal stories of disarray during the pandemic creates light-hearted moments while building safe and trustworthy spaces.[23] Boosting genuine happiness involves kindness. At work, one of the best ways to do this is by supporting and helping each other. Shawn Achor's research with Harvard psychology professor Phil Stone and lecturer Tal Ben-Shahr of 1648 students found a 0.71 correlation between happiness and social support. As a reference point, they cite the correlation between smoking and cancer as 0.37.[24]

Kindness is contagious. Research has found that those on the receiving end of kindness were a whopping 278 per cent more kind to others.[25,26] Not only do people imitate kind acts received, but the scale of generosity expands. Picture a culture of generosity where people pay it back, pay it forward, and pay it sideways. The more kindness is present in organizations, the more collaborative people are, sparking innovation.[27] Performance is higher, and people are less likely to leave. Those who help others are 10x more likely to be engaged at work than those who do not help others. Check this out—they are also 40 per cent more likely to get a promotion.[28] Kindness wins again.

The science behind kindness—*upstream reciprocity theory*—suggests that when people encounter kind acts, they experience a feeling of warmth that makes them more likely to help others. Do good to feel good. Even unkind people in a work setting, for whatever reason—maybe due to too many years working in a toxic culture—are kind in other contexts, with their family and friends. The self-reflection process is what allows the Dictator, the Departed, the Pushover, to face up to their unkind past and re-design a new future. It is up to leaders to create energizing, uplifting, and strong contexts that become norms. Kindness goes up dramatically by being around kind people.

There are also benefits simply by *observing* kindness! An experience of *elevation*—a positive emotion associated with a feeling of uplift, has been distinctly linked to observing kindness. Elevation inspires people to be better versions of themselves and spread kindness. This contagion effect is so strong that Stanford psychology professor Jamil Zaki has found that simply believing that others are kind and empathetic towards others is a motivating force to be prosocial and kind themselves. Believe in good to do good. As much as bad influences and negative peer pressure propagates, there are opportunities to be a positive force for good—*positive conformity*. In his work, Zaki finds, not only is kindness contagious, but, like a virus, it mutates and takes on new forms.[29] A little less coronavirus, a little more kindnessvirus, please.

Not only is kindness contagious, kindness is addictive. Kindness can change your brain. Being kind produces the feel-good chemicals in your brain. Kindness boosts oxytocin, the 'love' hormone that makes you feel connected and close to others. It boosts serotonin, the 'regulator' of our moods and emotions, which explains how kindness helps us feel less anxious, less depressed, and lifts our spirits. It also boosts dopamine, the 'addiction' hormone linked with reward regions in our brain.

Adam Grant's research demonstrates that kind people who give (*givers*) are ones who thrive, even in competitive business environments, beyond those who look out for their own interests (*takers*), and people who maintain reciprocal relationships based on quid pro quo arrangements (*matchers*).[30] There is balance to be had in giving. If you're constantly giving of your time and resources to others to the detriment of your own tasks and responsibilities, that will affect your own productivity. No surprise there. Being too kind lands you in Pushover territory. Research found that a good strategy is to 'bundle' giving. People who do five random acts of kindness at one time were found to be significantly happier than those who performed five random acts of kindness at random times across a week's timeframe.[31] It may be that doing a bunch of nice things in cumulative fashion compounds benefits and meaning for yourself and the receivers.

Reframe the work culture to think about success as contribution, building cultures that support kindness—*givers*—as valuable assets. Kindness should be unrestrained, talked about widely. It is something that needs to be celebrated, weaved into the very fabric of the organization. Positive emotions broaden and builds linkages between thought and action.[32] For example, experiencing joy prompts us to think outside the box and be creative, to play. This enlarges our cognitive capacity to take on more, be engaged in our role, and derive meaning in our work. People who see meaning in their work are more likely to view their work as a calling, rather than simply a job or a career.[33]

Does it really matter how we view our work? *Work is work*. It seems so. Recent work[34] by my colleague Dr Yuna Cho found that people who perceive their work to be a calling have objectively better career success—earning a higher income—over those who perceive their work to be a job, because their bosses *misperceive* these individuals as better performers, who are more committed to the company. There is an inherent joy that comes from being a kind leader in service to your people. Kind leaders energize and create happiness for their people, growing kindness into an unstoppable movement.

Chapter Exercises

Twelve-hour Acts of Kindness Challenge

- This is a snack-size version of the ten-day kindness challenge. Within a period of twelve hours, commit to performing three to five acts of kindness. Engage your team to participate. At the start of the twelve-hour period, note the acts of kindness you intend on carrying out. Log your entries in a journal.

- Post-challenge reflection:
  o What surprised you about this challenge?
  o Was this challenge easier or harder than you thought it would be? Why?
  o What reactions did you observe from others?

o   How does this exercise contribute to your
    leadership growth?
o   How did your team members fare with the challenge?
    What are their takeaways?

Questions to Guide Energizing Your People

1. What energy do I give off at work?
2. How can I generate contagious positive energy for my people?
3. How can I increase a sense of autonomy, competence, and
    relatedness during my interactions with my people?
4. How can I capitalize on energy as an enabler of wellbeing for
    my people?
5. How can I harness collaborative networks as sources of
    relational energy?
6. How can I create joy for my people, both through accessible
    means, and through meatier structural initiatives I can
    put in place?
7. If kindness is contagious, what are some ways I can initiate a
    kindness waterfall?

Chapter 15

Energize through a Cycle of Uplift

Kindness, as an intentional action, contributes to happy and healthy people in happy and healthy organizations. To create impact, leaders who role model, demonstrate flexibility, and support their people are in a prime position to launch a kindness pipeline, setting in motion a Cycle of Uplift that energizes a whole culture.

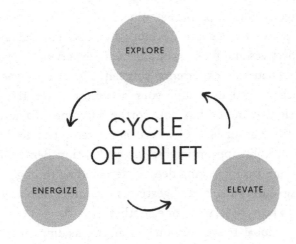

Cycle of Uplift: Explore

Kind leaders lift their people up through an *exploratory* process. Exploration involves 3As:

- **Attentiveness:** Being in tune with your people
- **Acknowledgement:** Understanding what your people are going through
- **Anticipation:** Proactively addressing the needs of your people

For certain individuals, building bridges impels a deeper level of care. People often suffer silently for weeks, months, even years before having the courage to speak up, so strong is the stigma of mental health. The purpose of exploration is to provide a safe space for the person in front of you to share their story, their concerns, to unload what's bothering them. Exploration takes patience and understanding, doubling back to role modelling vulnerability and creating safe spaces. These actions build trust. Even then, voicing may come in many different shades of ambiguity. Use empathic listening.

As we saw in Chapter 13, empathy is about understanding the perspectives and feelings of a person's experience despite never having had this experience yourself. Empathy is *not* creating a false narrative around your assumptions of this person's experiences. Subtle but noteworthy difference. To avoid falling into the trap of leaders who over-relate and under-listen, the Cycle of Uplift appropriately seeks exploration. Being curious and open-minded in seeking deep understanding through listening, asking questions, and digesting new information, harkening back to how we relate to one another.

As global teams become the norm, leading with kindness leans into cultural flexibility. The best course of action for leaders when unsure about how to approach an individual or situation is to simply reach out, lean in, and listen empathetically. This action communicates a genuine desire to learn and understand. It is a principled investment in your people's wellbeing.

It is also scalable at the organizational level. We saw from Francis, Dawn, and Melanie's individual accounts how David Long, Chairman and CEO of Liberty Mutual Insurance, imparts kindness in his leadership through frequent and meaningful employee communication, investing his time holding fireside chats and informal discussion to hear the voices of various employee groups. He listened attentively and sought to understand the reality of African-Americans following the death of George Floyd, Asian-Americans following hate crimes on AAPI individuals, and challenges faced by LGBTQIA+ communities to gain better perspective.

Jean Guan, SVP and General Manager, Global Retail Market US Operations, Liberty Mutual Insurance, shared how, amidst attacks on Asian Americans in the US during the pandemic, David personally called her to check in and ask how she was doing, worried she might fear for her safety in public. David encourages everyone in the company to share stories of unconscious bias, a relational process that develops shared understanding, stronger bonds, and the creation of positive inclusive environments. When I asked Jean about exploring the diversity of people as a part of kind leadership, she was reflective and thoughtful in her observation: 'Leading with kindness expands. It helps all kinds of people to be successful. It challenges traditional thinking of white male as leader. The impact is that leading with kindness in itself creates diverse workforces to foster innovation.' Kindness is what gives leaders a competitive business advantage. Jean continues: 'The world is so dynamic. No one will have the answer alone. You have to have teams that are diverse, to build relationships and trust. You have to have open spaces to figure out the best answer together. It's a given now. You have to do it. You need to mimic the customer base you serve. That's how you understand them and know what products to offer.'

Create support groups and employee assistance programs to back various communities, with a commitment from senior leadership to advocate and advance their positions within the company. Kindness gives leaders the space to go above and beyond for their people. Even if kindness can't change the situation, it provides an easier transition and a softer landing. The ROK pays dividends in the culture, where people feel the workplace is more than a collection of processes and is an inclusive place of belonging.

Exploration takes into consideration several components:

- **WHO—Check-in on:**
  o Those who are reticent, or who exhibit changing moods or energy levels
  o Those who may feel pressure to present an image of strength, or who always posture happiness and for whom everything appears 'fine'
  o Those who recently experienced trauma, suffering, or a major life shift
  o Those who recently joined the team, with whom you have not yet formed strong bonds
- **WHAT—Appraise the situation:**
  o What might this person be going through?
  o What might this person be feeling right now?
  o What might be the reason this person is downplaying their situation?
  o What is the intended meaning behind what they have shared with me?

- **WHERE—Assess cultural considerations:**
  - o Where is this person located regionally, nationally, culturally?
  - o Where is this person's family located?
  - o Where is this person's main support network located?
  - o Where might there be points of (dis)connection that may enrich or limit my understanding of this person's experience?

Cycle of Uplift: Energize

Relating to your people through exploration puts leaders in an enlightened position to *energize*. Understanding another person's perspective is inconsequential without action. Leaders enable. Kindness gets you there. This rendering of kindness through action was at the forefront during my discussion with Professor Tettey at the University of Toronto, who asserts: 'Transformation comes from little acts of kindness that can impact people. If you cannot draw inspiration from that, then you're not worth a leader. Because it is not about you. It is always about the people. There is a sense of fulfilment that comes from being able to positively impact somebody else. If you're a leader who is not moved to helping others, lifting others up, then you're just an individual who just happens to be in a role that does stuff. But if you're truly a leader, then you should be impacting others. And that should be your focus.'

During my conversation with Dr Gary Gottlieb, he noted that leadership is about asking yourself: 'What's hard for them that you can make easier? What's fun for them that you can make more fun? What in their life is challenging their ability to be able to produce towards that mission, and how can you facilitate it or accelerate it? And how can you make all of those folks part of a whole in such a way that they share that sense of understanding one another's perspective, being able to act on that understanding, and being mission committed, which makes the individuals who are the parts, so much more overall as a whole?'

HKBN is an organization that energizes through purposeful action that creates impact, when and where it matters. As all strategic decisions are guided by their purpose to 'Make Our Home a Better Place to Live', during the pandemic, the company offered one-month free broadband service to underserved, poverty-stricken communities, a decision which cost them 20 per cent of their profits that year. *Why would a company do such a thing?* Because their leadership team felt compelled to kindness. Says NiQ Lai, Group CEO: 'Can you imagine living in a lockdown without broadband? Sure, it hurt us in the short term. But in the long term, it was the right thing to do. We say our priority is profit and purpose. But when there's a conflict, purpose takes precedence.'

To put forth an energized response, consider:

- **HOW—Create impact through action:**
    o How can I provide tangible resources to assist my people during this period?
    o How can I provide intangible resources to assist my people during this period?
    o How can I reinforce my commitment to my people?
    o How can I go above and beyond for my people?

Cycle of Uplift: Elevate

The third driver of the Cycle of Uplift is *elevating* leadership through deliberate reflection on purpose alignment. This feedback mechanism connects leaders straight back to the exploration phase in a virtuous cycle. It also melds back to the introspective phase embedded in self-leadership.

Professor Tettey described the gratification that comes from an other-focused leadership: 'The fulfilment that you get from serving others is what should motivate you to take on leadership. If it's something other than that, then your drivers are very different. Look at the opportunities that the privilege of leadership gives you to be able to impact others in very positive ways. It's a very unique opportunity to be able to help transform and to make better.'

Kind leaders create a legacy, though David Long would be the first to gently remonstrate being kind for this purpose. David announced his retirement at the end of 2022. Immediately, comments flooded the company's internal social site with examples of the impact his kind leadership had, on building a kind culture that allowed people to bring their full self to work.

Continuous reflection enables a cyclical and synthesized process of learning, shaping leadership development. To elevate your leadership, provide honest answers to the following questions:

Assessment on impact:

- What impact did my actions have on those involved?
- What could I have done differently or better?
- What did I learn from this experience?
- How did this experience shape me as a person—as a leader?

Forward-looking reflection:

- What processes can I initiate to make things easier for my people?
- What processes can I discontinue to make things easier for my people?

- What actions can I take now to make things easier for my people?
- How can I equip my people with the support they need during this time?

With kindness as the base, the Cycle of Uplift creates the conditions to relate to individuals as human beings through exploration, prompting energized action and elevated reflection. When leaders appraise and approach every situation with kindness, the result is a workplace that wins together. This makes the Cycle of Uplift a cohesive and iterative process, much like a high-performance engine with all parts operating in sync to drive excellence, procuring performance improvements for leaders and their teams.

Chapter Exercise

Questions to Guide Activating a Cycle of Uplift

1. What context do I need to set to initiate and promote a Cycle of Uplift?
2. What is one action I can take today to uplift through exploration?
3. What is one action I can take today to uplift through energy?
4. What is one action I can take today to uplift through elevation?
5. How can I continue to iterate the Cycle of Uplift to make greater impact?

Chapter 16

Architect a Culture of Kindness

Companies with leaders who adopt kind values as their raison d'être, build strong cultures guided by these values. Research has found that employees who rated their workplace as excellent also reported the highest percentage of their workplace rewarding acts of kindness.[1] They weather the storm much better and retain people longer. This starts with purpose—knowing with conviction why you exist as a company and what you're in business to do.

Make Kindness Your Purpose

Contrary to popular belief, profit is not your purpose. Simon Sinek has made this clear through one simple directive: Start with why.[2] Profit is the consequence of a company's objectives and goals, separate from the 'why.'

This point was illustrated by Hubert Joly, former CEO of Best Buy: 'If I had joined the company and said, "The key thing we're going to do in the new few years is double the share price or the earning per shares," who would've cared at the company? This is not motivating. And so what we did a few years into the journey was to redefine who we were. And we said, "We are not actually a consumer electronics retailer. We're a company that's in the business of enriching lives through technology by addressing key human needs."'[3]

Kind cultures are felt, when it's there in spades, and when a culture is devoid of it. Recall my conversation with Garry Ridge, who proudly shared WD-40 Company's purpose with me: 'We're in the memories business. And we create positive lasting memories by solving problems in factories, homes, and workshops, all around the world. We solve problems, and we create opportunities.' What a tremendous way of creating meaning by bringing people together. Everyone in the WD-40 Company tribe, regardless of the 176 countries where their products are sold, values creating positive lasting memories in each relationship they build. Not only with end users, but anybody who has a stake in the business. Their purpose is all encompassing, affecting the very formulation of their product that respects the environment, in the spirit of creating positive lasting memories. This purpose also guides decision-making throughout the company. Says Garry: 'When decisions are made in line with the values of the company, values that are clearly defined, even though people may not always agree with you, they will support you, and that's important.'

The Great Pivot: Changing Unkind Cultures

When I talk to my MBA students about culture, without fail I spot someone sitting in contemplative silence. When asked to express their thoughts, they say something to the effect of: 'The company cultures we discuss in class sound like a utopia. The company I'm in doesn't even *have* a culture.' They proceed to describe a monotonous environment reminiscent of that depicted in the cult classic, *Office Space.*

You see, there *is* a culture in these companies. Culture builds from what leaders' role model. Culture grows from a collective feeling of being in the organization. Culture is how people treat each other, apparent even when you walk the virtual halls. If there is no norm for saying good morning to people at work, no norm for knowledge sharing, no norm for spontaneous and collaborative work, no norm for celebrating each other's successes, that *is* the culture. The only difference lies in whether culture is intentionally designed or left to chance, where it takes on a form of its own. Whether it's a culture you're proud of.

Well, we're just a [insert industry] company. What sort of culture do you expect us to have? The same could be said of WD-40. They're 'just' a company that sells oil in a can! No. They're a company dedicated to creating lasting positive memories. HKBN is 'just' a telecommunications company. But wait. They're a company whose purpose it is to make Hong Kong a better place to live.

Maybe you're stuck in *Office Space*—long established, uninspired cultures where things don't change because *this is how we've always done things around here*. Can cultures be changed? Short answer, yes. Changing a culture requires a movement.[4] Here's a four-step process for leading the Great Pivot towards kindness:

Step 1: Generate energy through a values refresh

Leaders designing for kind cultures must frame change within the context of purpose. Build on the sense of dissatisfaction with the status quo and amplify the Cycle of Uplift. Stir up and rouse people's emotion to propel momentum driving change. Make it so spirited it is positively electrifying. People buy-in and act when they feel passionate about an issue. Make them see this is not a corporate wellness one-off. It cannot feel like another task, another item on the to-do list.

Create a sense of togetherness as the company embarks on a journey to kindness. Involve all stakeholders in a values refresh to optimize energy and gain momentum. For a movement to find traction, people need *to be* part of the change, need *to feel* part of the change. Value words are abstract, can be misinterpreted, and are all around meaningless if they are not framed in behaviours. Ritz Carlton did this through their three steps of service that everyone follows through on to exemplify kindness—(1) A warm and sincere personalized greeting; (2) Anticipating and fulfilling each guest's needs; (3) A fond and personalized farewell. Make values concrete. Kindness is an action. Hold collective discussions addressing the following questions:

- How do we define kindness?
- What does kindness look like and feel like?
- What does *un*kindness look like and feel like?
- What are our guidelines for kind behaviour?
- What are our guidelines for calling out *un*kind behaviours?
- What are the grey areas, and how do we work through them?

Foster appropriate and acceptable behaviours, while curtailing inappropriate or unacceptable behaviours through ongoing discussions, workshops, experiential learning and role play exercises designed to develop shared speech and guidance on approaching various scenarios from kindness.

Demonstrate strong top-down commitment with a clear call to action, because nothing halts change faster than confusion. Stating a message once is not enough. Sending an email is not enough. When you start to sound like a broken record, only then, is your message starting to break through. People rarely complain about over-communication. Then act on the commitment.

A kind company is vested in supportive leadership. Leading with kindness leaves no grey area here. At the board and governance level, it's resetting the table to the extent of working out how to align fiduciary duties, the duty to care, to bring kindness forward. If organizational policies are not providing the support people need, the policies need to change. Behaviours must then be consistently role modelled by leadership for changes to roll in. Show people how everyday kindness is the visible expression of foundational values. It's the everyday pieces that matter, because the cleaning staff member on the receiving end of kindness becomes your ambassador who articulates your impact, your mission.

With an eye on the prize, leaders punctuate the pivot through consistent value workshops and sentiment surveys so that it remains top of mind for everyone. Simplification of the overall company vision is an effective strategy to accentuate what matters.

Step 2: Accelerate kindness through small wins

To sustain change, your people need to experience a few successive, quick wins. This is the thrust of establishing change, dating back to John Kotter's change model.[5] You have now created awareness and perhaps even a kindness imperative, but kindness as a behaviour needs to form the basis of every interaction on a daily basis. Leaders tap in to the power of the collective, spreading kindness one person, one interaction, at a time. Otherwise, momentum will wax and wane, especially as priorities keep shifting in a dynamic environment. Momentum fades as people go through the motions of yet another exercise in futility, remaining their same unchanged selves. Each new win builds the energy towards the next small step forward. Gradually, the kindness movement builds.

Research shows that feeling a sense of progress is what motivates people day to day.[6] This *progress principle* can be applied to chartering kind cultures. Quantum leaps are few and far between, so focus on incremental progress. However small, forward is forward. Start a kindness campaign. Make some headway, captured through multiple touchpoints, celebrate engagement, and make them public. Then build out a series of wins until it begins to take shape and inform a culture shift towards kindness.

Step 3: Equip champions of change

Building a culture of kindness needs to be wholly and fully owned by leaders. Leaders can't be let off the hook. Shirking responsibility of caring for your people's mental health and wellbeing is akin to palming off the responsibility for employee engagement to HR or other managers.

That said, designing for kindness involves the entire ecosystem. This starts with adopting a code of kindness in the boardroom and putting pressure on leaders to do the same. Then, identify change agents at all levels of the company, because kindness must be distributed to create a movement. Find the influencers. The informal leaders with a wide reach. The energetic change makers with a strong network. Mobilize the troops to grow the kindness movement. This is also, coincidentally, a great exercise in building bridges that cross silos and unite groups that might have been fractured or disjointed.

For maximum impact, align leadership and management. Middle management is a critical piece of the kindness movement. Middle managers are the connectors, vital sources of information that collect and distribute messaging. They are the first point of contact for enquiries; they elaborate on the *whys* and the *hows* of the kindness mission. They enforce and reward. They regulate the energy. The middle layers need to feel empowered or execution will stall and change won't stick. To achieve this, engage middle managers in ongoing and frequent conversation, incorporating their feedback. As kind allies spread infectious positive energy, people embrace new beliefs and adopt new behaviours, and a new culture of kindness is reinforced.

Step 4: Protect the energy

As the new culture of kindness starts to stick, it is at this stage that new behaviours and practices must be safeguarded, to enable continuous movement forward. Take the temperature of the organization through frequent conversation and pulse surveys, rather than waiting for an annual engagement survey.

Hold each other accountable for kindness. For mental health and wellbeing. For inclusivity and DEI.[7] As the new culture sets, people will have a watchful eye for what behaviours are accepted and condoned. A kindness accountability system develops a *collective accountability for kindness*, where every level of the company structure is committed to kindness.

Restructure the evaluation process so that kindness is built into performance metrics, ensuring that leaders are not only accountable for delivering business results, but *how* they get there. Set leadership objectives geared towards kindness, with self-assessments, check-ins, stakeholder observations and feedback, calibrated to gauge progress. The tighter the linkage between kindness objectives and key results (OKRs), the greater the impact and the healthier the outcomes for the company, in terms of the wellbeing of the people and financial performance.[8] This entails working through:

- What are our high-level, collective goals for kindness?

- What are the anticipated outcomes and measurable results?
- How will we track progress and create alignment?

Give people permission to call out unkind behaviours, regardless of position. Develop shared language around it and make people feel safe doing so. A culture where people are accountable for one another is one that holds a proneness to action. We saw how Liberty Mutual Insurance role models this process through experiential role plays. Rakhi Kumar says it's about *how* people push culture, noting that she has personally observed other senior leaders respectfully being called out by their peers if they feel the leader spoke to someone in a derisive tone. These behaviours activate a culture of kindness, as people have solid examples of what is acceptable, and the consequences of unacceptable behaviours.

Make it clear that unkind behaviours will not be tolerated, and act on it if necessary. Hiring and firing must be concomitant with protecting the culture. Says Jacqueline Carter: 'There are things that's core to the company that you hire for, fire for, promote for. Compassion should absolutely be one of those things! It enables psychological safety, wellbeing, and innovation. It's hard to find companies that say they don't want a compassionate culture. There are certainly ruthless companies out there, but let's see how long they last.' Where will you draw the line with unkind behaviours?

With a process for kindness in place, something spectacular happens in the organization. Behaviours change. People are uplifted. Elevated. A culture of kindness is born. The potential unleashed is extraordinary.

The Kindness Sandbox

Leading with kindness commits leaders to intentional actions in service of, and for the betterment of, the people. As leaders re-design culture, use kindness as a catalyst for embedding learning into every aspect of the company. Driving impact in this regard makes upskilling and reskilling a top priority for kind companies in attracting and retaining talent and developing a healthy talent pipeline.

Learning and development are baked into the sustenance of a healthy and happy culture. Unfortunately, many companies focus on the wrong things when it comes to learning.[9] For one thing, leaders are driven by efficiency over exploration. Exploration is considered aimless (*code for not working*), and therefore, a second strike against exploration is that it is costly.

Rather than providing arbitrary offerings—a lunch-and-learn here, a workshop there—a company's learning and development portfolio must be part of an integrated approach, accounting for talent development, succession planning, and promotion systems. Within this purview, on-the-job training, experiential learning, education and awareness campaigns, and management trainee and leadership programs need to be crafted to strategically align with a clearly articulated long-range agenda. Transitioning to learning cultures rests on meticulous development of key learning objectives, an appraisal of relevant capabilities required of talent to achieve these goals, identification of talent skill gaps, and a corresponding assessment of current learning practices and resources. Successful companies that nourish their people's growth and development are ones that build out a durable and robust talent pipeline.

For example, aligning learning and development with employee wellbeing as an integrated strategic imperative produces clear targets for action. At minimum, this would start with a values refresh to establish a baseline for learning and education on kindness. It would focus on promoting understanding and awareness of mental health at all levels of the corporate hierarchy, normalizing its occurrence and eliminating stigma on mental health. It would incorporate forums and workshops facilitating dialogue on DEI, with leadership at the helm. It would be data-driven by design, with a consistent process for monitoring the wellbeing life cycle in the organization, starting from people's entry to the organization, using a variety of metrics to triangulate effectiveness. This allows for greater learning to supplement targeted interventions when stress is spiking, before escalating to dangerous levels.

Companies adopting learning cultures have a distinct advantage. Learning cultivates resilience, agility, and adaptability, engines of growth in a complicated business environment. When leaders encourage learning and provide a context supporting curiosity and experimentation, people feel psychologically safe and speak up with new ideas to improve organizational effectiveness.[10] They raise more constructive suggestions for pressing organizational problems, facilitating communication among team members and enhancing performance.

Curating curiosity begins with role modelling curiosity. Building on the processes described throughout this book, kind leaders embrace curiosity components, the confident humility of knowing what you don't know, relying on your team, presenting high-level guiding questions, listening to understand, balancing advocacy with inquiry, asking open and inquisitive questions, focusing on process over outcome, and inviting sessions dedicated to exploration.

Growth cultures are forged when people learn through failures. Kind leaders foster learning moments in legitimizing mistakes through role modelling failure. NiQ Lai has been very open and honest with his people on this front, unreservedly sharing: 'I have failed more than average: I was an immigrant to Australia and C grade student who couldn't find a job in Perth, Australia, so had come to Hong Kong to look for work in 1990. I still have a stack of job rejections which I keep as a reminder. I was almost personally bankrupt twice, once in 1997 and then again 2008. In 1998 when I got married, I had to max out my credit cards and had to borrow from my brother and sister-in-law.'

These experiences shaped his leadership and the culture of learning he builds at HKBN. NiQ continues: 'Failures allow us to find our limits so that we can blow past them, rather than be suffocated by them. HKBN proudly makes far more mistakes than other companies, and we intend to make even more going forward. We are not smarter than others, but we learn faster via making mistakes. The key is to make affordable mistakes, so as to find the successes, and then scale the success. In short, to thrive rather than survive, chase and embrace your failures, so as to break your comfort zone limitations.'

When kind leaders nurture a learning environment, people feel safe to own up to mistakes. A learning culture is one where people share failures, mistakes are celebrated, and learning reflections benefit the whole team. Netflix is a company that boldly whisper wins and shout mistakes. Reed Hastings describes in his book *No Rules Rules* feeling insecure about admitting to mistakes during his early days as a leader. He soon realized that not only did he feel relief when he openly admitted screwing up, but as a leader he started noticing that his people seemed to trust him more after he did so: 'Since then, every time I feel I've made a mistake, I talk about it fully, publicly, and frequently. I quickly came to see the biggest advantage of sunshining a leader's errors is to encourage everyone to think of making mistakes as normal. This in turn encourages employees to take risks when success is uncertain . . . which leads to great innovation across the company. Self-disclosure builds trust, seeking help boosts learning, admitting mistakes fosters forgiveness, and broadcasting failures encourages your people to act courageously.'[11]

Garry Ridge points to the advantage of building a culture of learning moments—not 'failures'—to tackle the pressure of perfectionism, because they acknowledge and accept that people aren't going to be perfect. How does WD-40 Company define learning moments? 'A learning moment is a positive or negative outcome of any situation that is openly and freely shared to the benefit of all people.' How freeing—these moments of caring based on candour, accountability, and responsibility, all of which reduce fear and any need for perfectionistic strivings.

Growth cultures guided by exploration applaud mistakes, so long as there's a dissection and reflection process about what went wrong and what the learning is. This is the very basis for innovation, for staying ahead in competitive markets. To facilitate a growth culture, incorporate ongoing opportunities for people to learn, unlearn, and relearn. Here are two ways to do this, capitalizing on the strength of the collective network:[12]

- **Curiosity coffees:** We spend most of our day with our colleagues, but how often do we learn from our peers? Set a target of having one curiosity coffee with a different colleague each month. Those with a generational gap can serve as a reverse mentor. Those with a tenure gap can bring valuable new insight. Those from different cultural or ethnic backgrounds bring new opportunities for understanding, appreciation, and awareness. Those from different functional roles enable interdisciplinary collaborations. Seek new understanding by asking exploratory questions: 'How would you approach this challenge?' or 'What has been your experience?'

- **Learning labs:** Everyone has something to learn and to teach. Set up a regular learning sandbox, with a different topic each time. Experiment with new tools or adapt new ways of doing the same task. Swap skills. Prompt new ways of thinking. Offer creative problem-solving or decision-making strategies. Trial-and-error new ideas, where mistakes are encouraged. Post-mortems reflect on the learning, whether the experimentation was successful or not. Make it a fun last Friday of the month event.

Progressive, kind, cultures value learning through experimentation, play, exploration, and curiosity. Curiosity didn't kill the cat; it learned to become a lion.

A Collective Accountability for Kindness

Because a culture of kindness must be protected at all costs, one of the most pivotal decisions affecting the culture concerns who is put into leadership positions. As Hubert Joly said: 'For many years I put most of my emphasis on experience and expertise. I wanted the best e-commerce person, the best marketing person, the best supply chain person. Now I place much more emphasis on, "Who is this person? What kind of a leader is this? What drives the individual? What kind of impact do they want to live? How do they want to be remembered?" That's what I focus on.'[13]

As leaders embark on a kindness reset, the long-term challenge of sustaining kind leadership represents a collective responsibility for kindness. The cost of a toxic leader could be the whole culture. During my conversation with Alain Li, Richemont Asia Pacific, he noted that the cultural behaviours enacted to reach organizational goals must be grounded in a culture of mutual respect and help, because it transcends beyond one person. Kindness is a team effort: 'When you create an environment in which everyone looks out for one another, a collective kindness, that is something that will make people want to come to work and want to achieve the goals a leader sets, because it feels good—it goes beyond professional development—it's personal growth.'

Following from my discussion with Dr Gary Gottlieb on accurate empathy as the substantiation of kindness, we rounded out our conversation by landing on setting strategic imperatives for kindness: 'Impact is greatest on organizational success, and direct effects on mental health and wellbeing are a reflection of how the workplace culture evolves from that overall vision of kindness. Kindness, from an institutional perspective, represents a deep and passionate commitment to mission; and from a management perspective and a behavioural perspective is a true understanding of the position of the people working in the organization and what optimizes that position.'

In the face of toxic bosses, toxic workplaces, and the number of people joining the Great Escape, not to mention challenges surrounding recruitment and retention, kind leadership that places a premium on employee mental health and wellbeing is a sure way, the only way, to future-proof your company. And when the mission is right, the bottom line will follow.

Kind leaders serve as a beacon when they energize and equip their people, when they align strategy with culture. Once kindness is embedded in the culture, it becomes a sustainable competitive edge. There is such a massive scale of positive effects that dominos when leaders care for the mental health and wellbeing of the people. To create this paradigm shift, leaders need to recalibrate and rise to kindness. And because not all heroes wear capes, leadership is required from all of us. We need to take individual responsibility and ownership to build a collective ambition for kindness. We are stronger, together.

The Future of Leadership Is Kind

Daniel Pink, *New York Times* best-selling author, revealed in his World Regret Survey with over 15,000 participating from 105 countries, that one of the biggest regrets people lamented was not being kinder. He shares one regret from a forty-one year-old man in the UK: 'I regret not being kinder to people. I was too often concerned with being right, instead of being kind.'[14] How powerful it is to know that, upon looking back on one's life, it was kindness, or the lack of it, that stood out to people.

Kindness, far from being an oversimplified schematic, is a concrete, foundational approach for leaders to address the complex challenges faced by companies today. The practical roadmap to drive impact, create shared value, and help your people rise is laid bare. The way you choose to lead matters, not only for the people under your care, the company, the community, and the society you operate in, it matters for yourself. It defines your reputation and the legacy you leave behind. It is the only business decision that really matters.

The top priority for leaders is to stop living in generations past, to rewrite the leadership playbook grounded in kindness. It is a leader's imperative to role model kindness, to expect kindness, to promote kindness, to advocate for kindness, to defend kindness, to live and breathe kindness, across all aspects of work.

The revolution has already begun. Globally, there are movements towards kindness. For example, October 10 is World Mental Health Day. November 13 is World Kindness Day. World Wellbeing week is in June. The month of May is Mental Health Awareness month.

Admirable initiatives that raise awareness, but kindness is not an annual event. Each new day brings fresh opportunities to take a step forward. Consistent small steps change the world. Let kindness guide your every action. Commit to being just 1 per cent kinder each day. The future of leadership is kindness. The future of work is (still) human. Rise up.

The time is now.

The choice is yours.

Chapter Exercise

Questions to Guide Architecting a Culture of Kindness

Use the four-step process outlined in this chapter as a driver of culture change. Along with your team, discuss the directives of each step in considerable detail, with accountabilities and timelines:

Step 1: Generate energy through a values refresh
Step 2: Accelerate kindness through small wins
Step 3: Equip champions of change
Step 4: Protect the energy

Acknowledgements

There is no limit to the *Return on Kindness*, and I have been so fortunate to be on the receiving end from so many. This book would not have been possible without the support of incredible people who believed in the core message of kind leadership from day one. Thank you to my remarkable team at Penguin Random House for your trust and care. I am grateful to my fellow Canadian Pierre Battah, who led me to my editor, Don Loney. Don, thanks to your calm and gentle nature, many moments of sheer panic were (nearly) averted. Thank you to Adam Grant for your confidence in me as an author and for helping me navigate the world of book publishing. I am indebted to all the senior executives—all kind leaders—around the world who selflessly contributed their time sharing their personal narratives around kindness. Your lived experiences and collective wisdom were foundational to shaping my thinking around kind leadership and brought the pages of this book to life. I can only hope I've done our exchanges justice. I send my heartfelt appreciation to Daryl Tol, Gordon Watson, and Kathy Pike for going above and beyond connecting me with kind leaders on a global scale. I sincerely thank those whose research informed my exploration. I thank all my students who inspire and teach me something new every day. I have more knowledge of TikTok and K-pop than I know what to do with. To my family, loved ones, mentors, collaborators, and dear friends near and far. my gratitude runs deep. Each of you have shown me a kindness I can never repay, except by paying it forward. Thank you.

Notes

Chapter 1: The Case for Kindness

1. Hubert Joly and Adi Ignatius, 'Former Best Buy CEO Hubert Joly: Empowering Workers to Create Magic', *Harvard Business Review* (December 2, 2021).

2. Jean-Jacques Hublin, 'The Prehistory of Compassion', *Proceedings of the National Academy of Sciences* 106, no. 16 (2009): 6429–6430.

3. Pierre Battah, *Humanity at Work: Leading for Better Relationships and Results* (Los Angeles: Wonderwell, 2020).

4. Aaron De Smet et al., 'Gone for Now or Gone for Good? How to Play the New Talent Game and Win Back Workers,' McKinsey and Company (March 9, 2022).

5. Aaron De Smet et al., 'The Great Attrition Is Making Hiring Harder,' McKinsey and Company (July 13, 2022).

6. Jack Kelly, 'The Great Realization Has Inspired People to Seek Happiness in Their Jobs and Careers,' *Forbes* (September 9, 2021).

7. Garry Ridge, 'The Great Resignation or Great Escape? Create the Culture that Invites Great Talent to Run to You,' LinkedIn (May 31, 2022).

8. Frederick Herzberg, 'The motivation-hygiene concept and problems of manpower' *Personnel Administration* 27, no. 1 (1964): 3–7.

9. Aaron De Smet et al., '"Great Attrition" or "Great Attraction"? The Choice Is Yours', McKinsey and Company (September 8, 2021).

10. Mary Abbajay, 'What to Do When You have a Bad Boss,' *Harvard Business Review* (September 7, 2018).

11. Refer to Note 7.

12. Anna Nyberg et al., 'Managerial Leadership and Ischaemic Heart Disease among Employees: The Swedish WOLF Study,' *Occupational and Environmental Medicine* 66, no. 1 (2009): 51–55.

13. Daniel Bortz, 'What Makes a Good Manager and Are You Ready to Take the Leap?' Monster.

14. World Health Organization and International Labour Organization, 'Long working hours increasing deaths from heart disease and stroke.' Joint news release, Geneva (May 17, 2021).

15. UK Government, 'Maximum weekly working hours'.

16. Tom Nolan and Jane Smith, 'The No. 1 Employee Benefit that No One's Talking About', Gallup (October 12, 2017).

17. Ryan M. Vogel and Mark C. Bolino, 'Recurring Nightmares and Silver Linings: Understanding How Past Abusive Supervision May Lead to Posttraumatic Stress and Posttraumatic Growth', *Academy of Management Review* 45, no. 3 (2020): 549–569.

18. Steve Hatfield et al., 'The C-suite's Role in Well-being,' Deloitte Insights (June 22, 2022).

19. Michael Dufner et al., 'Self-enhancement and Psychological Adjustment: A Meta-analytic Review,' *Personality and Social Psychology Review* 23, no. 1 (2019): 48–72.

20. 'When It Comes to Driving, Most People Think Their Skills Are Above Average,' Association for Psychological Science (August 28, 2014).

21. Mind Share Partners, *2021 Mental Health at Work Report.*

22. John P. Kotter, 'Management Is Still Not Leadership,' *Harvard Business Review* (January 9, 2013).

23. Chris Westfall, 'Leadership Development Is a $366 Billion Industry: Here's Why Most Programs Don't Work,' *Forbes* (June 20, 2019).

24. David A. Garvin, 'How Google Sold Its Engineers on Management,' *Harvard Business Review* (December 1, 2013).

25. Robert L. Katz, *Skills of an Effective Administrator* (Cambridge, MA: Harvard Business Review Press, 2009).

26. John Helliwell et al. (Ed.), *World Happiness Report 2022* (New York: Sustainable Development Solutions Network).

27. World Economic Forum, *The Future of Jobs Report 2020.*

28. Heather Boushey and Sarah Jane Glynn, 'There Are Significant Business Costs to Replacing Employees,' Center for American Progress (November 16, 2012).

29. Roberta Matuson, 'The True Cost of Employee Turnover: It's Way More than You Think,' LinkedIn (August 30, 2021).

Chapter 2: The Anatomy of Kindness

1. Jacqueline Carter and Rasmus Hougaard, *Compassionate Leadership: How to Do Hard Things in a Human Way* (Cambridge, MA: Harvard Business Review Press, 2022).

2. Adam Grant, *Give and Take: Why Helping Others Drives Our Success* (New York: Penguin, 2013).

3. Rasmus Hougaard and Jacqueline Carter, 'Ego Is the Enemy of Good Leadership,' *Harvard Business Review* (November 2018).

4. Sussex Centre for Research on Kindness, *The Kindness Test*.

5. Susan Cain, *Quiet: The Power of Introverts in a World that Can't Stop Talking* (New York: Crown, 2012).

6. Jason Aten, 'Microsoft CEO Satya Nadella Says This 1 Trait Is More Important than Talent or Experience,' *Inc.* Magazine (November 2021).

7. Tracy Brower, 'Empathy Is the Most Important Leadership Skill According to Research,' *Forbes* (September 19, 2021).

8. Aliza Knox, 'The New Meaning of CEO: Chief Empathy Officer. 4 Reasons Leaders Need Empathy Now,' *Forbes* (September 28, 2021).

9. State of Workplace Empathy Study, Businesssolver (2018; 2019).

10. Jardine MINDSET Singapore is a registered charity of the Jardine Matheson Group, begun in 2011, which focuses on mental health initiatives in the Singapore area. Jardine Matheson Holdings Limited is a Hong Kong-based Bermuda-domiciled British multinational conglomerate, with listings on the London Stock Exchange, Singapore Exchange and Bermuda Stock Exchange.

11. Alain Cohn et al., 'Civic Honesty Around the Globe,' *Science* (June 20, 2019).

12. Robert E. McGrath, 'Character Strengths in 75 Nations: An Update,' *The Journal of Positive Psychology* 10, no. 1 (2019): 41–52.

Chapter 3: Leading with Impact = Kindness + Toughness

1. Frances Frei and Anne Morriss, *Unleashed: The Unapologetic Leader's Guide to Empowering Everyone Around You* (Harvard Business Review Press, 2020).
2. Robert R. Blake et al., *Managerial Grid,* Advanced Management - Office Executive 1, no. 9 (1962): 12–15.
3. Jim Collins, 'Genius of the AND'.
4. Ella Miron-Spektor et al., 'Microfoundations of Organizational Paradox: The Problem Is How We Think about the Problem,' *Academy of Management Journal* 61, no. 1 (2018): 26–45.
5. Thomas Fischer et al., 'Abusive supervision: A systematic review and fundamental rethink,' *The Leadership Quarterly* 32, no. 6, (2021): 101540.
6. Stuart D. Sidle, 'Workplace Incivility: How Should Employees and Managers Respond?', *Academy of Management Perspectives* 23, no. 4 (November 2009): 88–89.
7. Anders Skogstad et al., 'The Destructiveness of Laissez-faire Leadership Behavior,' *Journal of Occupational Health Psychology* 12, no. 1 (2007): 80–92.
8. Kelli Harding, *The Rabbit Effect: Live Longer, Happier, and Healthier with the Groundbreaking Science of Kindness* (New York: Atria Books, 2019).
9. Mark Mortensen and Heidi Gardner, 'Leaders Don't Have to Choose between Compassion and Performance,' *Harvard Business Review* (February 16, 2022).

Chapter 4: Kind Leadership Is Genderless

1. 'The gender gap in employment: What's holding women back?' International Labour Organization (2017, 2022).
2. Tiffany Burns et al., 'Women in the Workplace 2021,' McKinsey and Company (September 27, 2021).
3. Peter Beinart, 'Fear of a Female President,' *The Atlantic* (October 15, 2016).
4. Jennifer Jones, 'Hillary Clinton talks more like a man than she used to,' *The Washington Post* (August 19, 2016).

5. 'Facts and figures: Women's leadership and political participation,' UN Women (March 7, 2023).

6. Timothy A. Judge et al., 'Do Nice Guys—and Gals—Really Finish Last? The Joint Effects of Sex and Agreeableness on Income,' *Journal of Personality and Social Psychology* 102, no. 2 (2012): 390–407.

7. Simon Little, "'I've Been There at the Abyss": UBC President Shares Personal Mental Health Journey,' *Global News* (August 28, 2019).

8. Pauline Rose Clance and Suzanne Ament Imes, 'The Imposter Phenomenon in High-Achieving Women: Dynamics and Therapeutic Intervention,' *Psychotherapy* 15, no. 3 (1978).

9. Kess Eruteya, 'You're Not an Imposter. You're Actually Pretty Amazing,' *Harvard Business Review* (January 3, 2022).

10. Alice H. Eagly et al., 'Gender and the Evaluation of Leaders: A Meta-analysis,' *Psychological Bulletin* 111, no. 1 (1992): 3–22.

11. Harry T. Reis et al., 'What Is Smiling Is Beautiful and Good,' *European Journal of Social Psychology* 20, no. 3 (May-June 1990): 259–267.

12. Supriya Garikipati and Uma Kambhampati, 'Leading the Fight Against the Pandemic: Does Gender Really Matter?', *Feminist Economics* 27, no. 1–2 (2021): 401–418.

13. Ruchika Tulshyan and Jodi-Ann Bury, 'Stop Telling Women They Have Imposter Syndrome,' *Harvard Business Review* (February 11, 2021).

14. David G. Smith et al., 'The Different Words We Use to Describe Male and Female Leaders,' *Harvard Business Review* (May 25, 2018).

15. Marco Dondi et al., 'Defining the Skills Citizens Will Need in the Future World of Work,' McKinsey and Company (June 25, 2021).

16. Crystal I. C. Farh et al., 'Token Female Voice Enactment in Traditionally Male-dominated Teams: Facilitating Conditions and Consequences for Performance,' *Academy of Management Journal* 63, no. 3 (2020): 832–856.

17. Vishal K. Gupta et al., 'CFO Gender and Financial Statement Irregularities,' *Academy of Management Journal* 63, no. 3 (2020): 802–831.

18. Tsedale M. Melaku and Christoph Winkler, 'How Women Can Identify Male Allies in the Workplace,' *Harvard Business Review* (May 4, 2022).

19. W. Brad Johnson and David G. Smith, 'Men, Stop Calling Yourselves Allies. Act Like One,' *Harvard Business Review* (August 5, 2022).

Chapter 5: The Return on Kindness

1. Larry Fink, 'Larry Fink's 2022 Letter to CEOs: The Power of Capitalism,' (2022).
2. Mark R. Kramer and Marc W. Pfitzer, 'The Ecosystem of Shared Value,' *Harvard Business Review* (October 2016).
3. Mark Conway, 'The Key Performance Indicator – Keep People Inspired,' Oak Consult (June 14, 2012).
4. Ron A. Carucci, *To Be Honest: Lead with the Power of Truth, Justice and Purpose* (New York: Kogan Page, 2021).
5. PR Newswire, 'Global Corporate Wellness Market Report 2022: Markets to Reach $90.4 Billion by 2026. AI Emerges as the Wellness Expert in the Corporate Space,' (2022).
6. Elizabeth Hampson et al., 'Mental Health and Employees: The Case for Investment—Pandemic and Beyond', Deloitte (March 2022).
7. PWC, *Creating a Mentally Healthy Workplace: Return on Investment Analysis*, PricewaterhouseCoopers (March 2014).
8. Sarah Chapman et al., 'The ROI in Workplace Mental Health Programs: Good for People; Good for Business', Deloitte (2019).
9. Gallup, *State of the Global Workplace: 2022 Report*.
10. Jack Zenger and Joseph Folkman, 'Quiet Quitting Is about Bad Bosses, Not Bad Employees,' *Harvard Business Review* (August 31, 2022).
11. James K. Harter et al., *Gallup Q$^{12®}$ Meta-Analysis,* Gallup (2020).
12. Roy F. Baumeister et al., 'Bad Is Stronger Than God,' *Review of General Psychology* 5, no. 4 (2001): 323–370.
13. Tiffany A. Ito et al., 'Negative Information Weighs More Heavily on the Brain: The Negativity Bias in Evaluative Categorizations,' *Journal of Personality and Social Psychology* 75, no. 4 (1998): 887–900.
14. Michael Timms, 'Blame Culture Is Toxic: Here's How to Stop It,' *Harvard Business Review* (February 9, 2022).
15. Andrew G. Miner et al., 'Experience Sampling Mood and Its Correlates at Work,' *Journal of Occupational and Organizational Psychology* 78, no. 2 (2005): 171–193.
16. Signature Consultants. *Humankindex Executive Summary* (July 2022).

Chapter 6: Kindness as the Basis for Corporate Wellness

1. Gallup, *State of the Global Workplace: 2022 Report.*
2. World Health Organization, 'COVID-19 pandemic triggers 25% increase in prevalence of anxiety and depression worldwide' (March 2, 2022).
3. World Health Organization, 'Mental Health and Substance Use' (2022).
4. Vanessa Candeias and Arnaud Bernaert, '7 Steps to Build a Mentally Healthy Workplace,' World Economic Forum (April 7, 2017).
5. Gretchen Berlin at al., 'Around the World, Nurses Say Meaningful Work Keeps Them Going,' McKinsey and Company (May 12, 2022).
6. Kelly Greenwood and Julia Anas, 'It's a New Era for Mental Health at Work,' *Harvard Business Review* (October 4, 2021).
7. American Psychological Association, 'Workplace Well-being Linked to Senior Leadership Support, New Study Finds' (2016).
8. Mind Share Partners' *2021 Mental Health at Work Report.*
9. World Health Organization, 'Mental Health: Strengthening Our Response' (June 17, 2022).
10. Adam Grant, 'There's a Name for the Blah You're Feeling: It's Called Languishing,' *The New York Times* (April 19, 2021 and December 3, 2021).
11. Corey L. M. Keyes, 'The Mental Health Continuum: From Languishing to Flourishing in Life,' *Journal of Health and Social Behavior* 43, no. 2 (2002): 207–222.
12. Don Mordecai, 'Mental Health in the Workplace — and the Cost of Staying Silent,' (November 23, 2022).
13. Elizabeth Hampson et al., 'Mental Health and Employers: The Case for Investment', Deloitte (October 2017).
14. Centers for Disease Control and Prevention, Workplace Health Strategies—Depression. 'Depression Evaluation Measures.' (April 2016).

See also Walter F. Stewart et al., 'Cost of Lost Productive Time among US Workers with Depression,' *Journal of the American Medical Association* 289, no. 23 (June 18, 2003): 3135–3144.

15. Steve Hatfield et al., 'The C-suite's Role in Well-being,' Deloitte Insights (June 22, 2022).

16. Michelle A. Barton et al., 'Stop Framing Wellness Programs Around Self-care,' *Harvard Business Review* (April 4, 2022).

17. Lara B. Aknin and Ashley V. Whillans, 'Helping and Happiness: A Review and Guide for Public Policy', *Social Issues and Policy Review* 15, no. 1 (2021): 3–34.

18. Oliver Scott Curry et al., 'Happy to help? A systematic review and meta-analysis of the effects of performing acts of kindness on the well-being of the actor', *Journal of Experimental Social Psychology*, 76 (2018): 320–329.

19. Lee Rowland and Oliver Scott Curry, 'A Range of Kindness Activities Boost Happiness,' *Journal of Social Psychology* 159, no. 3 (2019): 340–343.

20. S Katherine Nelson et al., 'Do Unto Others or Treat Yourself? The Effects of Prosocial and Self-focused Behavior on Psychological Flourishing,' *Emotion* 16, no. 6 (September 2016): 850–861.

21. Refer to Note 19.

22. Refer to Note 19.

23. Eric S. Kim et al., 'Volunteering and Subsequent Health and Well-being in Older Adults: An Outcome-Wide Longitudinal Approach,' *American Journal of Preventive Medicine* 59, no. 2 (August 2020): 176–186.

24. Refer to Note 23.

25. S. Katherine Nelson-Coffey et al., 'Kindness in the blood: A randomized controlled trial of the gene regulatory impact of prosocial behavior,' *Psychoneuroendocrinology* 81 (March 2017): 8–13.

26. Elizabeth B. Raposa et al., 'Prosocial Behavior Mitigates the Negative Effects of Stress in Everyday Life,' *Clinical Psychological Science* 4, no. 4 (July 2016): 691–698.

27. Jennifer L. Trew and Lynn E. Alden, 'Kindness Reduces Avoidance Goals in Socially Anxious Individuals,' *Motivation and Emotion* (July 1, 2015): 892–907.

28. Sarah D. Pressman et al., 'It's Good to Do good and Receive Good: The Impact of a 'Pay-It-Forward' Style Kindness Intervention on Giver and Receiver Well-being,' *The Journal of Positive Psychology* 10, no. 4 (October 17, 2014): 293–302.

29. Alexis Solanes et al., 'Can we increase the subjective well-being of the general population? An umbrella review of the evidence,' *Revista de Psiquiatría y Salud Mental* 14, no. 1 (2021): 50–64.

30. Stephanie L. Brown et al., 'Providing Social Support May Be More Beneficial Than Receiving It: Results from a Prospective Study on Mortality,' *Psychological Science* 14, no. 4 (August 2003): 320–327.

31. Stephanie L. Brown et al., 'Caregiving Behavior Is Associated with Decreased Mortality Risk,' *Psychological Science* 20, no. 4 (April 2009): 488–494.

32. David A. Fryburg, 'Kindness as a Stress Reduction-Health Promotion Intervention: A Review of the Psychobiology of Caring,' *American Journal of Lifestyle Medicine* 16, no. 1 (January 29, 2021): 89–100.

Chapter 7: Kindness and the Mental Health Revolution

1. Shefali Armilli et al., 'Designing An Effective Workplace Mental Wellbeing Strategy,' Neurum Health (2020).

2. Vasundhara Sawhney, 'It's Okay Not to Be Okay,' *Harvard Business Review* (November 10, 2020).

3. Alicia A. Grandey, 'When 'The Show Must Go On': Surface Acting and Deep Acting as Determinants of Emotional Exhaustion and Peer-Rated Service Delivery,' *Academy of Management Journal* 46, no. 1 (November 30, 2017): 86–96.

4. Ute R. Hülsheger and Anna F. Schewe, 'On the Costs and Benefits of Emotional Labor: A Meta-Analysis of Three Decades of Research,' *Journal of Occupational Health Psychology* 16, no. 3 (2011): 361–389.

5. Morra Aarons-Mele, 'Leading through Anxiety: Inspiring Others When You're Struggling Yourself,' *Harvard Business Review* (May 11, 2020).

6. Sabina Nawaz, 'How Anxiety Traps Us, and How We Can Break Free.' *Harvard Business Review* (January 2, 2020).

7. Marian Joëls and Tallie Z Baram, 'The neuro-symphony of stress', *Nature Reviews Neuroscience*, 10 (2009): 459–466.

8. Cathy Cassata, 'Michael Phelps: 'My Depression and Anxiety Is Never Going to Just Disappear.' Healthline (May 17, 2022).

9. Simon Spichak, 'The Backlash Against Naomi Osaka Proves Many People Don't Care about Mental Health,' *Medium* (June 01, 2021).

10. Jacqueline Brassey et al., 'Addressing Employee Burnout: Are You Solving the Right Problem?' McKinsey Health Institute (May 27, 2022).

11. Christina Maslach et al., Maslach Burnout Inventory™ (MBI), Mind Garden.

12. World Health Organization, 'Burn-out an 'Occupational Phenomenon': International Classification of Diseases' (May 28, 2019).

13. Kira Schabram and Yu Tse Heng, 'How Other- and Self-compassion Reduce Burnout through Resource Replenishment,' *Academy of Management Journal* 65, no. 2 (2022): 453–478.

14. Ben Wigert, 'Employee Burnout: The Biggest Myth', Gallup (March 13, 2020).

15. Refer to Note 10.

16. Michelle A. Barton et al., 'Stop Framing Wellness Programs Around Self-care,' *Harvard Business Review* (April 4, 2022).

17. Jennifer Moss, *The Burnout Epidemic: The Rise of Chronic Stress and How We Can Fix It* (Cambridge, MA: Harvard Business Review Press, 2019).

18. Shawn Achor, 'Growth after Disaster: Going Beyond Resilience,' *Harvard Business Review* (March 15, 2011).

19. Shawn Achor, *The Happiness Advantage: How a Positive Brain Fuels Success in Work and Life* (New York: Crown, 2018).

20. ADP Research Institute, *Global Workplace Study 2020*.

21. Refer to Note 18.

22. Rob Cross et al., 'The Secret to Building Resilience,' *Harvard Business Review* (January 29, 2021).

23. Refer to Note 16.

24. Keith Ferrazzi et al., '7 Strategies to Build a More Resilient Team' *Harvard Business Review* (January 21, 2021).

25. Roderick I. Swaab et al., 'The Too-Much-Talent Effect: Team Interdependence Determines When More Talent is Too Much or Not Enough,' *Psychological Science* 25, no. 8 (2014): 1581–1591.
26. Refer to Note 10.
27. Amy C. Edmondson and Zhike Lei, 'Psychological safety: The history, renaissance, and future of an interpersonal construct,' *Annual Review of Organizational Psychology and Organizational Behavior*, 1(2014): 23–43.

Chapter 8: Kindness Is an Inside Job

1. Bill George, *Discover Your True North: Becoming an Authentic Leader* (New York: Wiley, 2015).
2. Amy Blaschka, 'The Two Essential (Yet Underrated) Leadership Traits You Need to Master,' *Forbes* (January 29, 2022).
3. Chris Westfall, 'Leadership Development Is a $366 Billion Dollar Industry: Here's Why Most Programs Don't Work,' *Forbes* (June 20, 2019).
4. Dan Rust, '+$50 Billion Wasted Annually on Leadership Development. Why?' LinkedIn (August 31, 2021).
5. Research and Data, 'Top 5 Business Challenges Faced by Executives,' *Forbes* (October 15, 2018).
6. Tasha Eurich, 'What Self-Awareness Really Is (and How to Cultivate It),' *Harvard Business Review* (January 4, 2018).
7. Rob Goffee and Gareth Jones, *Why Should Anyone Be Led by You? What It Takes to Be an Authentic Leader* (Cambridge, MA: Harvard Business Review Press, 2006).
8. Alain Morin, 'Possible Links between Self-awareness and Inner Speech Theoretical Background, Underlying Mechanisms, and Empirical Evidence,' *Journal of Consciousness Studies* 12, no. 4–5 (2005): 115–134.
9. Christopher L. Heavey and Russell T. Hurlburt, 'The Phenomena of Inner Experience,' *Consciousness and Cognition* 17, no. 3 (2003): 798–810.
10. Russell T. Hurlburt, *Investigating Pristine Inner Experience: Moments of Truth* (Cambridge, MA: Cambridge University Press, 2011).
11. Refer to Note 6.

12. R. E. Jennings et al., 'Self-compassion at work: A self-regulation perspective on its beneficial effects for work performance and wellbeing,' *Personnel Psychology* 76, no. 1 (2022): 279–309.

13. Klodiana Lanaj et al., 'When Leader Self-care Begets Other Care: Leader Role Self-compassion and Helping at Work,' *Journal of Applied Psychology* 107, no. 9 (2022): 1543–1560.

14. Bill Boulding, 'For Leaders, Decency Is Just as Important as Intelligence,' *Harvard Business Review* (July 16, 2019).

15. Ron Carucci, 'Build Your Reputation as a Trustworthy Leader,' *Harvard Business Review* (June 11, 2021).

Chapter 9: Get Your Mind Right

1. Malcolm Gladwell, *Outliers: The Story of Success* (New York: Little, Brown and Company, 2008).

2. Brooke N. Macnamara and Megha Maitra, 'The Role of Deliberate Practice in Expert Performance: Revisiting Ericsson, Krampe & Tesch-Römer,' *Royal Society Open Science* 6, no. 8 (August 21, 2019): 190327.

3. Brooke N. Macnamara et al., 'The Relationship Between Deliberate Practice and Performance in Sports: A Meta-Analysis,' *Perspectives on Psychological Science* 11, no. 3 (May 22, 2016): 333–350.

4. Gallup Strengthsfinder.

5. Denise Quinlan et al., 'Character Strengths Interventions: Building on What We Know for Improved Outcomes,' *Journal of Happiness Studies* 13, no. 6 (2012): 1145–1163.

6. Patty McCord, 'How Netflix Reinvented HR,' *Harvard Business Review* (January–February 2014).

7. Ron Carucci, 'How to Actually Encourage Employee Accountability,' *Harvard Business Review* (November 23, 2020).

8. Larissa Bartlett et al., 'A systematic review and meta-analysis of workplace mindfulness training randomized controlled trials', *Journal of Occupational Health Psychology* 24, no. 1 (2019): 108–126.

9. Jenny Gu et al., 'How do mindfulness-based cognitive therapy and mindfulness-based stress reduction improve mental health and wellbeing? A systematic review and meta-analysis of mediation studies', *Clinical Psychology Review* 37 (April 2015): 1–12.

10. Theresa M. Glomb et al., 'Mindfulness at Work,' *Research in Personnel and Human Resource Management* 30 (2012): 115–157.

11. Rich Fernandez, '5 Ways to Boost Your Resilience at Work,' *Harvard Business Review* (June 27, 2016).

12. Rinske A. Gotink et al., '8-week Mindfulness Based Stress Reduction Induces Brain Changes Similar to Traditional Long-term Meditation Practice: A Systematic Review,' *Brain and Cognition* 108 (October 2016): 32–41.

13. Annika Nübold et al., 'Be(com)ing Real: A Multi-source and an Intervention Study on Mindfulness and Authentic Leadership,' *Journal of Business and Psychology* 35, no. 4 (2020): 469–488.

14. Thomas I. Vaughan-Johnston et al., 'Mind-body Practices and Self-enhancement: Direct Replications of Gebauer et al.'s (2018) Experiments 1 and 2,' *Psychological Science* 32, no. 9 (2021): 1510–1521.

15. David DeSteno, 'How to Cultivate Gratitude, Compassion, and Pride on Your Team,' *Harvard Business Review* (February 20, 2018).

16. Christopher Littlefield, 'Use Gratitude to Counter Stress and Uncertainty,' *Harvard Business Review* (October 20, 2020).

17. Joyce E. Bono et al., 'Building Positive Resources: Effects of Positive Events and Positive Reflection on Work Stress and Health,' *Academy of Management Journal* 56, no. 6 (2013): 1601–1627.

18. Ovul Sezer et al., 'Don't Underestimate the Power of Kindness at Work,' *Harvard Business Review* (May 7, 2021).

19. Kristie Rogers and Beth Shinoff, 'Disrespected Employees Are Quitting: What Can Managers Do Differently?' *MIT Sloan Management Review* (July 28, 2022).

20. Guy Winch, *Emotional First Aid: Healing Rejection, Guilt, Failure, and Other Everyday Hurts* (New York: Penguin, 2013).

21. Jim Collins, *Good to Great: Why Some Companies make the Leap . . . and Others Don't* (New York: HarperCollins, 2001).

22. Bradley P. Owens et al., 'Expressed Humility in Organizations: Implications for Performance, Teams, and Leadership,' *Organization Science* 24, no. 5 (2013): 1517–1538.

23. Adam Grant, *Think Again: The Power of Knowing What You Don't Know* (New York: Penguin, 2021).

24. John Hagel, 'Good Leadership Is About Asking Good Questions,' *Harvard Business Review* (January 8, 2021).

25. Hubert Joly and Adi Ignatius, 'Former Best Buy CEO Hubert Joly: Empowering Workers to Create 'Magic',' *Harvard Business Review* (December 2, 2021).

26. Carmela Chirinos, 'How Microsoft's Satya Nadella Rejected a 'Know-It-All' Mentality and Earned the Title of 'Most Underrated CEO',' *Fortune* (February 4, 2022).

27. Refer to Note 10.

28. Refer to Note 16.

Chapter 10: Be a Role Model for Kindness

1. Kathryn E. Buchanan and Anat Bardi, 'Acts of Kindness and Acts of Novelty Affect Life Satisfaction,' *The Journal of Social Psychology* 150, no. 3 (2010): 235–237.

2. Brené Brown, *Daring Greatly: How the Courage to Be Vulnerable Transforms the Way We Live, Love, Parent, and Lead* (New York: Penguin, 2015).

3. Dan Cable, 'How to Build Confidence About Showing Vulnerability,' *Harvard Business Review* (July 14, 2022).

4. Amy C. Edmondson and Tomas Chamorro-Premuzic, 'Today's Leaders Need Vulnerability, Not Bravado,' *Harvard Business Review* (October 19, 2020).

5. Constantinos G.V. Coutifaris and Adam Grant, 'Taking Your Team Behind the Curtain: The Effects of Leader Feedback-Sharing and Feedback-Seeking on Team Psychological Safety,' *Organization Science* 33, no. 4 (August 17, 2021): 1574–1598.

6. Fortune, 'Brand Rankings: Fortune U.S. 500(100)'.

7. Liberty Mutual Insurance, 'Great Place to Work Certified' (July 2022–July 2023).

8. Jo Constantz, 'These Are the Best—and Worst—Cities for Work-Life Balance,' *Bloomberg* (May 25, 2022).

9. Steve Hatfield et al., 'The C-suite's Role in Wellbeing,' Deloitte Insights (June 22, 2022).

10. Sabine Sonnentag et al., 'Recovery from Work: Advancing the Field toward the Future', *Annual Review of Organizational Psychology and Organizational Behavior* 9, no. 1 (2022): 33–60.

11. Larissa K. Barber and Alecia M. Santuzzi, 'Please Respond ASAP: Workplace Telepressure and Employee Recovery,' *Journal of Occupational Health Psychology* 20, no. 2 (2015): 172–189.

12. Sabine Sonnentag, 'The Recovery Paradox: Portraying the Complex Interplay between Job Stressors, Lack of Recovery, and Poor Well-being,' *Research in Organizational Behavior* 38 (2018): 169–185.

13. Shawn Achor and Michelle Giellan, 'Resilience Is about How You Recharge, Not How You Endure,' *Harvard Business Review* (June 24, 2016).

14. Refer to Note 13.

15. Refer to Note 10.

16. Refer to Note 10.

17. Amy Blankson, *The Future of Happiness: 5 Modern Strategies for Balancing Productivity and Well-being in the Digital Era* (Dallas, TX: Benbella Books, 2017).

18. Bill Thornton et al., 'The Mere Presence of a Cell Phone May Be Distracting: Implications for Attention and Task Performance,' *Social Psychology* 45, no. 6 (January 1, 2014): 479–488.

19. Hydration for Health, 'Hydration, Mood State, and Cognitive Function'.

20. Arianna Huffington, *The Sleep Revolution: Transforming Your Life, One Night at a Time* (New York: Harmony/Rodale, 2017).

21. Marco Hafner et al., 'Why Sleep Matters: The Economic Costs of Insufficient Sleep,' Rand Corporation (November 30, 2016).

22. Vijay Kumar Chattu et al., 'The Global Problem of Insufficient Sleep and Its Serious Health Implications,' *Healthcare (Basel)* 7, no. 1 (December 20, 2018): 1.

23. Zoë Henry, '6 Companies (Including Uber) Where It's Okay to Nap,' *Inc.* Magazine (September 4, 2015).

24. Anthony C. Klotz, 'Creating Jobs and Workspaces that Energize People.' *MIT Sloan Management Review* (May 4, 2020).

25. 'We should allow sad days, not just sick days,' *Worklife Podcast with Adam Grant*.

26. Michelle A. Barton et al., 'Stop Framing Wellness Programs Around Self-care,' *Harvard Business Review* (April 4, 2022).

27. Aman Kidwai, 'Spotify Allowed Its 6,500 Employees to Work from Anywhere in the World. Its Turnover Rate Dropped,' *Fortune* (August 2, 2022).

28. Lora Jones, 'Bumble Closes to Give 'Burnt-Out' Staff a Week's Break,' *BBC News* (June 22, 2021).

29. Reed Hastings and Erin Myers, *No Rules Rules: Netflix and the Culture of Reinvention* (New York: Penguin, 2020).

Chapter 11: Kindness Is Being Intentionally Flexible

1. Jeffrey M. Jones, 'Confidence in U.S. Institutions Down; Average at New Low,' Gallup (July 5, 2022).

2. Edelman Trust Barometer Special Report: *Brand Trust and the Coronavirus Pandemic* (March 30, 2020).

3. Refer to Note 2.

4. Paul Zak, 'The Neuroscience of Trust,' *Harvard Business Review* (January 1, 2017).

5. Simon Sinek, *Leaders Eat Last: Why Some Teams Pull Together and Others Don't* (New York: Penguin, 2017).

6. Kristie Rogers and Beth Schinoff, 'Disrespected Employees Are Quitting. What Can Managers Do Differently?', *MIT Sloan Management Review* (July 28, 2022).

7. Jeff Gothelf, 'Storytelling Can Make or Break Your Leadership,' *Harvard Business Review* (October 19, 2020).

8. Reed Hastings and Erin Myers, *No Rules Rules: Netflix and the Culture of Reinvention* (New York: Penguin, 2020).

9. Anne Donovan, 'What PwC Learned from Its Policy of Flexible Work for Everyone,' *Harvard Business Review* (January 28, 2019).

10. Tomas Chamorro-Premuzic, '5 Ways Leaders Accidentally Stress Out Their Employees,' *Harvard Business Review* (May 11, 2020).

11. Tarani Chandola et al., 'Are Flexible Work Arrangements Associated with Lower Levels of Chronic Stress-Related Biomarkers? A Study of 6025 Employees in the UK Household Longitudinal Study', *Sociology* 53, no. 4 (2019): 779–799.

12. Liz Wiseman, *Multipliers: How the Best Leaders Make Everyone Smarter* (New York: HarperCollins, 2010).

13. Emma Seppälä, 'Why Compassion Is a Better Managerial Tactic than Toughness,' *Harvard Business Review* (May 7, 2015).

Chapter 12: Support 'em with Kindness

1. Mark Goulston, 'How to Know If You Talk Too Much,' *Harvard Business Review* (June 3, 2015).
2. Avraham N. Kluger and Guy Itzchakov, 'The Power of Listening at Work,' *Annual Review of Organizational Psychology and Organizational Behavior*, 9 (January 2022): 121–146.
3. Rebecca D. Minehart et al., 'What's Your listening Style?' *Harvard Business Review* (May 31, 2022).
4. Jack Zenger and Joseph Folkman, 'What Great Listeners Actually Do,' *Harvard Business Review* (July 14, 2016).
5. Bejoy Philip and Dana Kaminstein, 'Boost Employee Confidence and Inclusion by Creating Voice Space,' *MIT Sloan Management Review* (August 25, 2022).
6. David A. Garvin and Michael Roberto, 'What You Don't Know about Making Decisions,' *Harvard Business Review* (September 2001).
7. Chris Argyris and Donald A. Schön (1996). *Organizational Learning II: Theory, Method and Practice* (Boston, MA: Addison-Wesley).
8. Douglas Stone and Sheila Heenan, 'Difficult Conversations 2.0: Thanks for the Feedback!,' *Rotman Management Magazine* (April 1, 2014).
9. Roger Schwarz, 'The 'Sandwich Approach' Undermines Your Feedback,' *Harvard Business Review* (April 19, 2013).
10. Peter Bregman and Howie Jacobson, 'Feedback Isn't Enough to Help Your People Grow,' *Harvard Business Review* (December 10, 2021).
11. Joe Hirsch, 'Good Feedback Is a Two-Way Conversation,' *Harvard Business Review* (June 1, 2020).
12. Shelley J. Correll and Caroline Simard, 'Research: Vague Feedback Is Holding Women Back,' *Harvard Business Review* (April 29, 2016).
13. Craig Chappelow and Cindy McCauly, 'What Good Feedback Really Looks Like,' *Harvard Business Review* (May 13, 2019).
14. Joe Hirsch, 'The Joy of Getting Feedback,' TEDxTarrytown.
15. Adam Bryant and Kevin W. Sharer, 'Are You Really Listening?', *Harvard Business Review* (March 1, 2021).
16. Jaewon Yoon et al., 'Why Asking for Advice Is More Effective Than Asking for Feedback,' *Harvard Business Review* (September 20, 2019).

Chapter 13: Servant Leadership Needs a New PR Manager

1. Robert K. Greenleaf, *Servant Leadership: A Journey into the Nature of Legitimate Power and Greatness* (New York: Paulist Press, 1977).

2. Howard Schultz, 'America Deserves a Servant Leader,' *The New York Times* (August 6, 2015).

3. Dan Cable, 'How Humble Leadership Really Works,' *Harvard Business Review* (April 23, 2018).

4. Nathan Eva et al., 'Servant Leadership: A Systematic Review and Call for Future Research,' *The Leadership Quarterly* 30, no. 1 (February 2019): 111–132.

5. Robert C. Liden et al., 'Servant leadership: Validation of a short form of the SL-28,' *The Leadership Quarterly* 26, no. 2 (April 2015): 254–269.

6. Refer to Note 4.

7. Robert C. Liden et al., 'Servant Leadership: Development of a Multidimensional Measure and Multi-level Assessment,' *The Leadership Quarterly* 19, no. 2 (April 2008): 161–177.

8. American Psychological Association, 'Workplace Well-being Linked to Senior Leadership Support, New Survey Finds,' APA 2016 Work and Well-being Survey.

9. Carol A. Walker, 'New Managers Need a Philosophy about How They'll Lead,' *Harvard Business Review* (September 15, 2015).

10. Chenwei Liao et al., 'Serving You Depletes Me? A Leader-Centric Examination of Servant Leadership Behaviors,' *Journal of Management* 47, no. 5 (March 3, 2020): 1185–1218.

11. Klodiana Lanaj et al., 'Energizing Leaders via Self-reflection: A Within-person Field Experiment,' *Journal of Applied Psychology* 104, no. 1 (2019): 1–18.

12. James W. Pennebaker, *Opening Up: The Healing Power of Expressing Emotions* (New York: Guilford Press, 1997).

13. Robert Iger, *The Ride of a Lifetime: Lessons Learned from 15 Years as the CEO of the Walt Disney Company* (New York: Random House, 2019).

14. BBC News, 'Jacinda Ardern: It Takes Strength to be an Empathetic Leader', (November 14, 2018).

15. Geoff Blackwell, 'Jacinda Ardern: 'Political Leaders Can Be Both Empathetic and Strong,' *The Guardian* (May 30, 2020).
16. Daniel Goleman, *The Emotionally Intelligent Leader* (Boston, Massachusetts: Harvard Business Review Press, 2019).
17. Hubert Joly and Adi Ignatius, 'Former Best Buy CEO Hubert Joly Empowering Workers to Create 'Magic',' *Harvard Business Review* (December 2, 2021).
18. Tim Cook, 'Tim Cook's MIT Commencement Address 2017,' Massachusetts Institute of Technology (MIT). Streamed on June 9, 2017, YouTube video, 15:33.
19. Joann S. Lublin, 'Companies Try a New Strategy: Empathy Training,' *The Wall Street Journal* (June 21, 2016).
20. Jamil Zaki, 'Making Empathy Central to Your Company Culture,' *Harvard Business Review* (May 30, 2019).
21. Businesssolver, *2022 State of Workplace Empathy*.

Chapter 14: Supercharge Your Kindness

1. Emma Seppälä and Kim Cameron, 'The Best Leaders Have a Contagious Positive Energy,' *Harvard Business Review* (April 18, 2022).
2. Randy Shattuck, 'How a Leader's Energy Field Impacts Team Productivity,' *Forbes* (June 1, 2022).
3. Wayne E. Baker, 'Emotional Energy, Relational Energy, and Organizational Energy: Toward a Multilevel Model,' *Annual Review of Organizational Psychology and Organizational Behavior* 6, no. 1 (2019): 373–395.
4. Tony Schwartz and Catherine McCarthy, 'Manage Your Energy, Not Your Time,' *Harvard Business Review* (October 2007).
5. Randall Collins, 'Emotional Energy as the Common Denominator of Rational Action,' *Rationality and Society* 5, no. 2 (1993): 203–230.
6. Refer to Note 1.
7. Abraham Carmeli and Gretchen M. Spreitzer, 'Trust, Connectivity, and Thriving: Implications for Innovative Behaviors at Work,' *Journal of Creative Behavior* 43 (December 22, 2011): 169–191.
8. Tiziana Casciaro and Miguel Sousa Lobo, 'Affective Primacy in Intraorganizational Task Networks,' *Organization Science* 26, no. 2 (2015): 373–389.

9. Tiziana Casciaro and Miguel Sousa Lobo, 'Competent Jerks, Lovable Fools, and the Formation of Social Networks,' *Harvard Business Review* (June 2005).

10. Robert B. Cialdini, 'Harnessing the Science of Persuasion,' *Harvard Business Review* (October 2001).

11. Dale Carnegie et al., *How to Win Friends & Influence People* (New York: Gallery Books, 1998).

12. Reed Hastings and Erin Meyer, *No Rules Rules: Netflix and the Culture of Reinvention* (New York: Penguin, 2020).

13. Richard M. Ryan and Edward L. Deci, 'Self-determination Theory and the Facilitation of Intrinsic Motivation, Social Development, and Well-being,' *American Psychologist* 55, no. 1 (2000): 68–78.

14. Oliver Scott Curry et al., 'Happy to Help? A Systematic Review and Meta-analysis of the Effects of Performing Acts of Kindness on the Well-being of the Actor,' *Journal of Experimental Social Psychology* 76 (2018): 320–329.

15. Shawn Achor, 'Positive Intelligence,' *Harvard Business Review* (January-February 2012).

16. Shawn Achor, *The Happiness Advantage: How a Positive Brain Fuels Success in Work and Life* (New York: Crown, 2018).

17. Sonja Lyubomirsky et al., 'The Benefits of Frequent Positive Affect: Does Happiness Lead to Success?' *Psychological Bulletin* 131, no. 6 (2005): 803–855.

18. André Spicer and Carl Cederström, 'The Research We've Ignored about Happiness at Work,' *Harvard Business Review* (July 21, 2015).

19. Iris B. Mauss et al., 'Can seeking happiness make people unhappy? Paradoxical effects of valuing happiness', *Emotion* 11, no. 4 (August 2011): 807–815.

20. Ute R. Hülsheger and Anna F. Schewe, 'On the Costs and Benefits of Emotional Labor: A Meta-analysis of Three Decades of Research,' *Journal of Occupational Health Psychology* 16, no. 3 (2011): 361–389.

21. Paul Zak, 'The Neuroscience of Trust,' *Harvard Business Review* (January 1, 2017).

22. Teresa M. Amabile and Steven J. Kramer, 'The Power of Small Wins,' *Harvard Business Review* (May 1, 2011).

23. Ron Carucci, 'How to Lead Your Team Through the Transition Back to the Office,' *Harvard Business Review* (June 16, 2021).

24. Refer to Note 15.

25. Joseph Chancellor et al., 'Everyday Prosociality in the Workplace: The Reinforcing Benefits of Giving, Getting, and Glimpsing,' *Emotion* 18, no. 4 (2018): 507–517.

26. Erik C. Nook et al., 'Prosocial Conformity: Prosocial Norms Generalize Across Behavior and Empathy,' *Personality and Social Psychology Bulletin* 42, no. 8 (2016): 1045–1062.

27. Ovul Sezer et al., 'Don't Underestimate the Power of Kindness at Work,' *Harvard Business Review* (May 7, 2021).

28. Refer to Note 15.

29. Jamil Zaki, 'Kindness Contagion: Witnessing Kindness Inspires Kindness, Causing It to Spread Like a Virus,' *Scientific American* (July 26, 2016).

30. Adam Grant, *Give and Take: A Revolutionary Approach to Success* (New York: Penguin, 2013).

31. Sonja Lyubomirsky et al., 'Pursuing Happiness: The Architecture of Sustainable Change,' *Review of General Psychology* 9, no. 2 (June 1, 2005): 111–131.

32. Barbara L. Fredrickson, 'The Role of Positive Emotions in Positive Psychology: The Broaden-and-Build Theory of Positive Emotions,' *American Psychologist* 56, no. 3 (2001): 218–226.

33. Amy Wrzesniewski et al., 'Jobs, Careers, and Callings: People's Relations to Their Work,' *Journal of Research in Personality* 31, no. 1 (1997): 21–33.

34. Yuna Cho and Winnie Y. Jiang, 'If You Do What You Love, Will the Money Follow? How Work Orientation Impacts Objective Career Outcomes via Managerial (Mis)perceptions,' *Academy of Management Journal* (2021).

Chapter 16: Architect a Culture of Kindness

1. US Chamber of Commerce, *Business of Kindness Survey Results* (November 2016).

2. Simon Sinek, *Start with Why: How Great Leaders Inspire Everyone to Take Action* (London: Penguin, 2011).

3. Hubert Joly and Adi Ignatius, 'Former Best Buy CEO Hubert Joly: Empowering Workers to Create 'Magic',' *Harvard Business Review* (December 2, 2021).

4. Bryan Walker and Sarah A. Soule, 'Changing Company Culture Requires a Movement, Not a Mandate,' *Harvard Business Review* (June 20, 2017).

5. John P. Kotter, *Leading Change* (Cambridge, MA: Harvard Business Review Press, 2012).

6. Teresa M. Amabile and Steven J. Kramer, 'The Power of Small Wins,' *Harvard Business Review* (May 2011).

7. Grace Lordan and Teresa Almeida, 'How Empathy and Competence Promote a Diverse Leadership Culture,' *MIT Sloan Management Review* (June 14, 2022).

8. Jeff Gothelf, 'Use OKRs to Set Goals for Teams, Not Individuals,' *Harvard Business Review* (December 17, 2020).

9. Shlomo Ben-Hur et al., 'Aligning Corporate Learning with Strategy,' *MIT Sloan Management Review* (September 15, 2015).

10. Phillip S. Thompson and Anthony C. Klotz, 'Led by curiosity and responding with voice: The influence of leader displays of curiosity and leader gender on follower reactions of psychological safety and voice', *Organizational Behavior and Human Decision Processes*, 172 (2022): 104170.

11. Reed Hastings and Erin Myers, *No Rules Rules: Netflix and the Culture of Reinvention* (New York: Penguin, 2020).

12. Helen Tupper and Sarah Ellis, 'Make Learning a Part of Your Daily Routine,' *Harvard Business Review* (November 4, 2021).

13. Refer to Note 3.

14. Daniel H. Pink, *The Power of Regret: How Looking Backward Moves Us Forward* (New York: Riverhead Books, 2022).

Index